Irene – Bon Voyage!

Dec. 2014

mustsees
France

Église du Dôme, Hôtel National des Invalides / © Y. Kanazawa/Michelin

W9-CBE-492

mustsees **France**

Editorial Director	Cynthia Clayton Ochterbeck
Produced by	Jonathan Gilbert, Azalay Media
Principal Writer	Mike Pedley
Production Manager	Natasha G. George
Cartography	Peter Wrenn
Photo Editor	Sean Sachon
Layout	Jonathan Gilbert, Natasha G. George
Cover & Interior Design	Chris Bell
Cover Design & Layout	Natasha G. George
Contact Us	Michelin Travel and Lifestyle North America
	One Parkway South
	Greenville, SC 29615, USA
	travel.lifestyle@us.michelin.com
	www.michelintravel.com
	Michelin Travel Partner
	Hannay House
	39 Clarendon Road
	Watford, Herts WD17 1JA, UK
	www.ViaMichelin.com
	travelpubsales@uk.michelin.com
Special Sales	For information regarding bulk sales, customized editions and premium sales, please contact us at:
	travel.lifestyle@us.michelin.com
	www.michelintravel.com

Michelin Travel Partner

Société par actions simplifiées au capital de 11 629 590 EUR
27 cours de l'Ile Seguin - 92100 Boulogne Billancourt (France)
R.C.S. Nanterre 433 677 721

© 2013 Michelin Travel Partner
ISBN 978-2-067182-01-1
Printed: October 2012
Printed and bound in Italy

MIX
Paper from
responsible sources
FSC® C015829

Note to the reader:
While every effort is made to ensure that all information printed in this guide is correct
and up-to-date, Michelin Travel Partner accepts no liability for any direct, indirect or
consequential losses howsoever caused so far as such can be excluded by law. Admission
prices listed for sights in this guide are for a single adult, unless otherwise specified.

Welcome to France

Château d'Azay-le-Rideau

TABLE OF CONTENTS

p 117

TABLE OF CONTENTS

★★★ATTRACTIONS

Unmissable attractions awarded three stars in this guide include:

Turrets of Château de Chambord, Blois p 74

Mer de Glace and the Montenvers Railway p 105

Château d'Angers p 69

MUST KNOW

© World Illustrated/Photoshot

Adoration of the Shepherds (c. 1644) by Georges de la Tour,
Musée du Louvre p 36

© R. Mattès/MICHELIN

Côte Sauvage at Presqu'île de Quiberon   p 66

© Tibor Bognár/agefotostock

Place de la Liberté at night, Sarlat-la-Canéda   p 123

★★★ ATTRACTIONS

Unmissable sights in and around France
For more than 75 years people have used the Michelin stars to take the guesswork out of travel. Our star-rating system helps you make the best decision on where to go, what to do, and what to see.

★★★	Absolutely Must See
★★	Really Must See
★	Must See
No Star	See

Galerie des Glaces, Château de Versailles **p 44**

© Bertrand Rieger/hemis.fr

STAR ATTRACTIONS

ACTIVITIES

Unmissable events, shows, restaurants and more in France.
We recommend every activity in this guide, but our top picks are highlighted with the Michelin Man logo. *Look-out for the Michelin Man throughout the guide for the top activities.*

Events

Musical fountains at Versailles *p 12*
Cannes Film Festival *p 12*
Arts at the Avignon Festival *p 145*
Fireworks, music theatre and dance in Carcassonne *p 14*
Water jousting and fireworks in Sète *p 14, 129*
Strasbourg Christmas market *p 15*

For Kids

Inspiration at Paris' Cité des Sciences and Palais de la Découverte *p 43,*
Main Street Electrical Parade – Disneyland Paris *p 46*
Go underground at Aven-Armand *p 130*
Walk inside a Glacier at the Mer de Glace *p 105*
Surf's up in Biarritz *p 121*

Hotels

Arles, 15C charm in Hôtel d'Arlatan *p 212*
St Tropez, pretty Lou Cagnard *p 215*
Biarritz, Atlantic views at Hôtel Atalaye *p 209*
Carcassonne, stay inside the walls at Le Donjon *p 211*
Paris, stylish splurge at 7Eiffel *p 199*

Restaurants

Paris, classic brasseries Bofinger & La Coupole *p 178*
Lille, Estaminet du Rijsel *p 180*
Alsatian Winstub – le Pigeon, or Chez Yvonne *p 184, 185*
Lyonnais bouchon, Brunet or Le Mercière *p 189*
Cassoulet in Carcassonne – Dame Carcas *p 193*
Bouillabaisse in le Miramar *p 194*

Bars / Clubs

St Tropez – join the jet set at Sénéquier *p 166*
La Rochelle – belle époque Café de la Paix *p 190*
Cannes – piano bar chic at L'Amiral *p 166*
Nice – le Relais, Hotel Negresco's piano bar *p 165*
Arles – starry nights at Cafe Van Gogh *p 163*

Outdoor action

Cycling in Alsace, along the Vosges Scenic Road *p 89*
Exploring the Camargue *p 141*
Canoe the Gorges du Tarn *p 130*
High-altitude thrills in Chamonix *p 105*
Hike in the Grand Canyon du Verdon *p 109*

On the water

Cruise the Canal du Midi *p 132*
See the *calanque* coast from Marseille *p 139*
Rhône cruising in Avignon *p 177*
Take a boat around Colmar's ' Little Venice' *p 87*
Sail out to Brittany's Belle-Ile *p 66*

Wine tours

Taste Champagne in Reims *p 90*
Tour Burgundy's legendary vineyards *p 95*

On the road

24 heures du Mans *p 12, 13, 69*
Riviera cruising – drive the Corniches *p 148*

MUST KNOW

Carcassonne, stay inside the walls at Le Donjon   p 211

Hike in the Grand Canyon du Verdon   p 109

Sail out to Brittany's Belle-Ile p 66

Canoe the Gorges du Tarn   p 130

STAR ATTRACTIONS

CALENDAR OF EVENTS

The following selection of events is far from comprehensive; almost every village has a festival at some time during the year. Book accommodation well in advance at festival times, even out of season.

January

Clermont-Ferrand International Short-Film Festival, 04 73 91 65 73 www.clermont.filmfest.com
Angoulême Comic Strip Festival, www.bdangouleme.com.

February

Chalon-sur-Saône Carnival and fur fairs 03 85 48 08 39
Limoux Traditional carnival *Blanquette* parties. 04 68 31 11 82, www.limoux.fr
Menton Lemon Festival. 04 92 41 76 76 www.fete-du-citron.com
Nice Carnival. 0892 70 74 07 www.nicecarnaval.com
Paris International Agricultural Show www.salon-agriculture.com
Prats-de-Mollo, St-Laurent-de Cerdans, Arles-sur-Tech Carnival, 04 68 39 70 83, www.pratsdemollolapreste.com
Toulouse Fête de la Violette (violet festival). 05 62 16 31 31 www.toulouse-tourisme.com
Le Touquet Motorbike race along the beach. 03 21 06 72 00

March

Clermont-Ferrand *Vidéoformes*: Multimedia festival , 04 73 17 02 17, www.videoformes.com
Clermont-Ferrand Poetry week 04 73 31 72 87. www.auvergne. iufm.fr/poesie.htm
Lyon International Fair. 04 72 22 33 37. www.foiredelyon.com

Mid-March–mid-July

Lille Music, art and theatre. 03 28 52 30 00

Late March–Late October

Versailles Fountain display (*Les Grandes Eaux Musicales*) 01 30 83 78 98

April

Bourges Music Festival 02 48 27 28 29
Chartres Students' Pilgrimage 02 37 21 51 91 www.chartres-tourisme.com
Chartres Music festival 02 22 06 87 87 www.chartres-tourisme.com
Cournon-d'Auvergne Festival for young people: theatre, puppets, dance, music. 04 73 69 90 40
Gérardmer Flower Festival 03 29 27 27 27
Le Mans 24-hour motorcycle race. 02 43 40 24 24 www.lemans.org

April–October

Parc national des Cévennes Nature festival: themed walks, exhibitions, shows, markets 04 66 49 53 01 www.cevennes-parcnational.fr
Chaumont-sur-Loire International Garden Festival 02 54 20 99 22

May

Aubrac *Fête de la transhumance*: seasonal shepherd's festival held on the weekend nearest to May 25. 05 65 44 21 15, www.traditionsenaubrac.com
Cannes International Film Festival. 01 53 59 61 00.

www.festival-cannes.com
Évian Classical music
04 50 26 85 00
Maguelone Festival of ancient and Baroque music (1st two weeks). 04 67 60 69 92
Montauban Music festival
05 63 63 66 77
Orléans Joan of Arc Festival
02 38 24 05 05
www.tourisme-orleans.fr
Orange Music and opera
02 40 14 58 60
Rouen Joan of Arc Festival
02 35 08 32 40
Les Saintes-Maries-de-la-Mer
Gypsy Pilgrimage
04 90 97 82 55
Touraine The Day of the Loire to celebrate the Loire and its countryside. 02 47 31 42 88
www.jourdeloire.com

May–October
Vichy *Une Saison en Eté*: theatre, classical music, opera, variety shows at the Vichy Opera House
04 70 30 50 30
www.ville-vichy.fr

June
Bellac Drama, music.
05 55 60 87 61
Clermont-Ferrand Medieval Festival in Montferrand. 04 73 23 19 29, www.montferrand medieval.org
Le Mans 24-hour car race.
03 43 40 24 24. www.lemans.org
Montpellier International Festival of Dance. 0 800 600 740, www.montpellierdanse.com
Perpignan Saint-Jean Festa Major (with mid-summer bonfires around June 21). 04 68 66 30 30, www.perpignantourisme.com
La Rochelle International Regatta. 05 46 41 14 68

Toulouse Rio Loco Festival. 05 61 32 77 28 www.rio-loco.org
Tours *Florilège Vocal*: Choral Festival. 02 47 21 65 26
www.florilegevocal.com
Vic-le-Comte Celtrad: Celtic music festival. 04 73 69 02 12
Villefranche-sur-Saône
Midsummer Night: bonfires, singers, illuminations
04 74 65 04 48

Mid-June–Mid-July
Pau Theatre, music and dance
05 59 27 27 08

Mid-June–mid-October
Anjou Anjou Festival in the historical sites of Maine-et-Loire
02 41 88 14 14
www.festivaldanjou.com
Chaumont-sur-Loire
International Garden Festival
02 54 20 99 22
www.chaumont-jardins.com
Orléans Jazz Festival
02 38 24 05 05
www.tourisme-orleans.fr

June–late August
Amboise "At The Court of King François". 02 47 57 14 47
Toulouse Classical, jazz and rock music. 05 62 27 60 60

July
Aix-en-Provence International Music Festival. 0820 922 923
Albi Classical music.
05 63 49 48 80
Ambert Festival de Folklore
04 73 82 66 34
www.livradoue-dansaire.com
Auvergne Thermathlon du Sancy: Fun trek along the Route des Villes d'Eaux of the Massif Central
04 73 31 20 32

Avignon Theatre Festival
04 90 27 66 50

Béziers Classical music
04 67 36 82 30

Cap d'Agde *Fête de la Mer*
(sea festival; last weekend)
04 67 01 04 04
www.capdagde.com

Carcassonne Festival of the
City: fireworks, classical music
concerts, theatre, opera, dance,
jazz (July 14). 04 68 11 59 15,
www.festivaldecarcassonne.com

Carpentras Music and dance
04 90 60 46 00

Cordes-sur-Ciel *Fête médiévale
du Grand Fauconnnier* (historical
pageant. 05 63 56 34 63,
www.grandfauconnier.com

Forez Classical music in churches
and castles of the region.
04 73 51 55 67

Frontignan *Festival du Muscat*
(mid-month). 04 67 18 31 60
www.tourisme-frontignan.com

Gannat International folk music
04 70 90 12 67

Juan-les-Pins World Jazz Festival
04 97 23 11 10

Lorient Celtic festival
02 97 21 24 29

Luz-St-Sauveur *Jazz à Luz*
(early July) 05 62 92 38 30,
www.jazzaluz.com

Montpellier *Festival de
Radio-France et de Montpellier
Languedoc-Roussillon*: Classical
music and jazz. 04 67 61 66 81,
www.festivalradiofrance
montpellier.com

Nantes International Flower
Show. 02 40 47 04 51

Orcines *Open Golf des Volcans*:
international golf championship
(last week of the month) 04 73 62
15 51, www.golfdesvolcans.com

Perpignan *Estivales* 04 68 66
30 30, www.estivales.com

Quimper Cornouaille Festival,
02 98 55 53 53

Rennes Theatre, music, dance
and poetry 02 99 67 11 11

St-Guilhem-le-Désert Musical
season, 04 67 96 86 19,
www.st-guilhem-le-desert.com

Vollore *Festival des Concerts de
Vollore*: 04 73 51 55 67,
http://concertsdevollore.com

July and August

Sète Festival of St Louis:
jousting, fireworks. 04 67 74 48
44, www.fiestasete.com

St-Bertrand-de-Comminges
Festival du Comminges, classical
music, chamber music. 05 61 88
32 00. www.festival-du-
comminges.com

Vaison-la-Romaine Theatre
and dance 04 90 36 02 11

Mid-July–Mid-September

Arles International Photo
Festival, 04 90 96 76 06

St-Rémy-de-Provence Organ
music, 04 90 92 05 22

Sceaux Classical music,
01 46 60 07 79

August

Aurillac Street Theatre Festival.
04 71 45 47 45, www.aurillac.net

Allanche Secondhand market:
the most important in the
Auvergne. 04 71 20 48 43

Bayonne Corrida and Street
Festival, 0820 42 64 64

Colmar Alsatian Wine Festival,
03 89 20 68 92

Béziers Bullfighting Festival,
04 67 76 13 45,
www.languedoc-france.info

Chamonix Mountain Guides
Festival, 04 50 53 00 88

Entrecasteaux Chamber music,
04 94 72 91 62

Pomarez Running of the Cows, 05 58 89 30 28

Pont de Salers and other villages, International Folklore Festival, 05 65 46 80 67, www.festival-rouergue.com

Prades Festival Pablo Casals: chamber music 04 68 96 33 07

Monteux Fireworks Festival, 04 90 66 97 52

Montesquieu-Volvestre British Film Fest. 05 61 90 65 74

St-Pourçain-sur-Sioule Wine and Food Festival, 04 70 45 32 73, www.tourisme saintpourcinois.com

St-Donat-sur-l'Herbasse 04 75 45 10 29 Bach Festival

Sablé-sur-Sarthe Festival of Baroque music, 02 43 62 22 22, www.sable-sur-sarthe.fr

Salon-de-Provence Music Festival, 04 90 56 27 60

September

Besançon Young Conductors Competition, 03 81 25 05 85

Deauville American Film Festival, 02 31 14 14 14, www.festival-deauville.com

Dinan Ramparts Festival 02 96 39 75 40

Divonne Chamber music 04 50 90 17 70

Lyon Music, dance, modern art 04 72 77 69 69

Le Puy-en-Velay *Les Fêtes du Roi de l'Oiseau*: 6 000 people in Francois 1 period costume. 04 71 09 38 41 www.roideloiseau.com

September–December

Beaujolais, Coteaux du Rhône and du Forez Grape Harvest and Wine Festivals

Puy-de-Dôme Les Automnales: theatre and music throughout

the Auvergne. 04 73 42 23 29 www.puydedome.com

October

Lannion Organ and choral music 02 96 35 14 14

Montpellier International fair. 04 67 17 67 17 www.foire-montpellier.com

Mourjou Chestnut Festival 04 71 49 69 34, www.mourjou.com

Perpignan Jazz Festival. 04 68 86 08 51 www.jazzebre.com

St-Malo Comedy, 02 99 40 39 63, www.quaidesbulles.com

Sauveterre-de-Rouergue Chestnut and cider festival 05 65 72 02 52

November

Beaune Auction sale of the wines of the Hospices de Beaune 03 80 24 47 00

Belfort Cinema. 03 84 22 94 44

Le Puy-en-Velay Hot-Air Balloon Rally. 04 71 09 38 41 www.ot-lepuyenvelay.fr

December

Marseille Santons Fair 04 91 54 91 11

Mont-Ste-Odile Pilgrimage (the most important in Alsace) 03 88 95 80 53

Strasbourg Christmas Market (Chriskindelsmarik) 03 88 52 28 28

December 25

Azay-le-Rideau The Imaginary World of the Château d'Azay-le-Rideau, 02 47 45 44 40

Blois The Story of Blois

Les-Baux-de-Provence Shepherds' Midnight Mass and Son et Lumière in the Loire Valley

PRACTICAL INFORMATION

WHEN TO GO

For relaxing outdoors, high summer can be beautiful, but resorts and the principal sightseeing areas are much more crowded. A better time to travel is May, June or September when French children are at school. Many visitors may prefer the moderate warmth of these early and late summer months to the higher temperatures of July and August, especially in the southern half of the country.

In general the French climate is moderate; extremes of either heat or cold are rare for the most part. Inland the winters are chilly and darkness comes early, especially in the northern latitudes. As spring turns to summer, the days become long and warm and by June the sun lingers well into the evening. Spring and autumn provide opportunities to explore the outdoors and enjoy the lovely countryside and coastal areas of France. In winter, snowfall in the mountainous regions, permits winter sports, including downhill skiing and snowboarding.

KNOW BEFORE YOU GO
Useful Websites

www.franceguide.com – The French Government Tourist Office/Maison de la France site is packed with practical information, advice and tips, including choosing package tours and even buying a property. The homepage has a number of links to more specific guidance, for American and Canadian travellers for example, or to the FGTO's London pages.

www.ambafrance-uk.org – The **French Embassy**'s website provides basic information (geography, demographics, history), a news digest and business-related information. It offers special pages for children, and pages devoted to culture, language study and travel. You can reach other selected French sites (regions, cities, ministries) via its hyperlinks.

www.francekeys.com – This site has plenty of practical information for visiting France. It covers all the regions, with links to tourist offices and related sites. Very useful for planning all the details of your tour in France!

www.franceway.com – This is an online magazine that focuses on culture and heritage. For each region, there are also suggestions for activities and practical information on where to stay and how to get there.

www.ViaMichelin.com – This site has maps, tourist information, travel features, suggestions on hotels and restaurants, and a route planner for numerous locations in Europe. In addition, you can look up weather forecasts, traffic reports and service station location, particularly useful if you will be driving in France.

www.F-T-S.co.uk – The French Travel Service specialises in organising holidays in France using the rail network and can organise travel and hotels.

www.fngic.fr (Tour Guides) – Looking for a professional tour guide? The FNGIC represents and promotes licensed tourist guides.

It is a professional non-profit organisation with about 700 members, all of whom are qualified and have professional accreditation from both the Ministry of Tourism and the Ministry of Culture and Communication. FNGIC, 43, rue Beaubourg, 75003 PARIS. 01 44 59 29 15.

Tourist Offices abroad
◆ **Australia & New Zealand**
Level 13, 25 Bligh Street, 2000 NSW, Sydney, Australia, 61 (0)2 9231 5244, Fax 61 (0)2 9221 8682, http://au.franceguide.com
◆ **Canada**
1800 av. McGill College, Suite 1010, Montreal, Quebec H3A 3J6, (514) 288-2026, Fax (514) 845-4868, http://ca-en.franceguide.com
◆ **Republic of Ireland**
No office +15 60 235 235 (Irish information line); http://ie.franceguide.com
◆ **United Kingdom**
Lincoln House, 300 High Holborn, London WC1V 7JH, 09068 244 123 (60p/min), http://uk.franceguide.com
◆ **United States**
There are three offices, but the quickest way to get a response to any question or request is by phone. http://us.franceguide.com
◆ **New York** – 825 Third Avenue, 29th floor (entrance on 50th Street), New York, NY 10022, France-on-Call Hotline (514) 288 1904
◆ **Los Angeles** – 9454 Wilshire Blvd, Suite 210, 90212 Beverly Hills, CA 310-271-6665
◆ **Chicago** – Consulate General of France, 205 N Michigan Ave., Suite 3770, 60601 Chicago, Illinois, 312 327 0290

National Tourist offices
A national network of regional and local tourist offices provides more precise information useful in planning your trip and answering your questions.
◆ **Fédération Nationale des Comités Régionaux de Tourisme**
11 rue du Faubourg Poissonnière, 75009 Paris, 01 47 03 03 10 www.fncrt.com
◆ **Réseau National des Destinations Départementales**
74–76 r. de Bercy, 75012 Paris 01 44 11 10 20, www.rn2d.net
◆ **Fédération Nationale des Offices de Tourisme et Syndicats d'Initiative**
11 r. du Faubourg Poissonnière, 75009 Paris www.tourisme.fr

Regional Tourist Offices
Alsace Lorraine Champagne
◆ **Alsace**
20a r. Berthe-Molly, BP 50247, Colmar 03 89 24 73 50 www.tourisme-alsace.com
◆ **Lorraine**
Abbaye des Prémontrés, BP 97, 54704 Pont-à-Mousson, 03 83 81 10 32, www.tourisme-lorraine.fr
◆ **Champagne-Ardenne**
50 av. du Général Patton, 51000 Châlons-en-Champagne, 03 26 21 85 80, www.tourisme-champagne-ardenne.com

Atlantic Coast
◆ **Aquitaine**
4/5 place Jean Jaurès, CS31759, 33074 Bordeaux Cedex, 05 56 01 70 00, www.tourisme-aquitaine.fr
◆ **Poitou-Charentes**
8 r. Riffault, BP 56, F-86002 Poitiers Cedex 05 49 50 10 50 www.poitou-charentes-vacances.com

PRACTICAL INFORMATION

Rhône Alps
♦ **Rhône-Alpes**
8 r. Paul Montrochet
69002 Lyon 04 26 73 3159
www.rhonealpes-tourisme.com

Brittany
1 r. Raoul-Ponchon,
35000 Rennes 02 99 67 11 11
www.brittanytourism.com

Burgundy Jura
♦ **Bourgogne**
5 av. Garibaldi, 21006 Dijon Cedex
03 80 28 02 80, www.bourgogne-tourisme.com
♦ **Franche-Comté**
La City, 25044 Besançon Cedex
03 81 25 08 00,
www.franche-comte.org

Chateaux of the Loire
♦ **Centre-Val de Loire**
37 av. de Paris, 45000 Orléans,
02 38 79 95 00,
www.visaloire.com
♦ **Pays de la Loire**
2 r. de la Loire, BP 20411, 44204
Nantes Cedex 02, 02 40 48 24 20,
www.enpaysdelaloire.com

French Alps
♦ **Rhône-Alpes**
8 r. Paul Montrochet
69002 Lyon 04 26 73 3159
www.rhonealpes-tourisme.com

French Riviera
400 Promenade des Anglais,
BP 3126, 06203 Nice Cedex 3
04 93 37 78 78
www.frenchriviera-tourism.com

Languedoc Roussillon Midi-Pyrénées
♦ **Languedoc-Roussillon**
954 av. Jean Mermoz,
34960 Montpellier Cedex 2

04 67 20 02 20
www.sunfrance.com
♦ **Midi-Pyrénées**
1 r. Rémusat, BP78032, 31080
Toulouse Cedex 6
05 34 44 18 18
www.tourism-midi-pyrenees.com

Normandy
14 r. Charles Corbeau, 27000
Evreux 08 10 44 84 48
www.normandie-tourisme.fr

Northern France and the Paris Region
♦ **Île-de-France**
11 r. du Faubourg Poissonnière
75009 Paris 01 73 00 77 00
www.new-paris-idf.com
♦ **Nord-Pas-de-Calais**
6 pl. Mendès-France,
BP 99, 59028 Lille Cedex
03 20 14 57 57
www.tourisme-nordpasdecalais.fr
♦ **Paris**
Paris Convention and Visitors
Bureau, 25 r. des Pyramides, 75001
Paris, http://en.parisinfo.com
♦ **Picardie**
3 r. Vincent Auriol,
80011, Amiens Cedex 1
03 22 22 33 66
www.picardietourisme.com

INTERNATIONAL VISITORS
Embassies and Consulates
Australia Embassy 4 r. Jean-Rey,
75724 Paris, 01 40 59 33 00.
www.france.embassy.gov.au
Canada Embassy 35 av.
Montaigne, 75008 Paris,
01 44 43 29 00,
www.amb-canada.fr
Ireland 4 r. Rude, 75116 Paris
01 44 17 67 00,
www.embassyofireland.fr

New Zealand Embassy 7ter r. Léonard-de-Vinci, 75116 Paris, 01 45 01 43 43, www.nzembassy.com
UK Embassy, 35 r. du Faubourg-St-Honoré, 75363 Paris Cedex 08, 01 44 51 31 00, www.ukinfrance.fco.gov.uk/en
UK Consulate, 18bis r. d'Anjou, 75008 Paris, 01 44 51 31 00, There are also UK Consulates in Bordeaux and Marseille.
USA Embassy, 2 av. Gabriel, 75008 Paris, 01 43 12 22 22, http://france.usembassy.gov
USA Consulates in Lyon, Strasbourg, Marseille, Rennes, Toulouse and Nice and **American Presence Post** in Bordeaux.

Entry Requirements

Passport – Nationals of countries within the European Union entering France need only a national identity card (for UK citizens this means a passport, and most airlines require passports). Nationals of other countries must be in possession of a valid national **passport**.
Visa – No **entry visa** is required for Canadian, US or Australian citizens travelling as tourists and staying less than 90 days, except for students planning to study in France. If you think you may need a visa, apply to your local French Consulate.

Customs Regulations

See the UK Customs website (www.hmrc.gov.uk) for information on allowances, travel safety tips, and to consult and download documents and guides.
There are no limits on the amount of duty and/or tax paid **alcohol and tobacco** that you can bring back into the UK as long as they are for your own use or gifts and are transported by you. If you are bringing in alcohol or tobacco goods and UK Customs have reason to suspect they may be for a commercial purpose, an officer may ask you questions and make checks.

Health

It is advisable to take out comprehensive travel insurance cover, as tourists receiving medical treatment in French hospitals or clinics have to pay for it themselves. **Nationals of non-EU countries** should check with their insurance companies about policy limitations. Remember to keep all receipts. **British and Irish citizens**, if they are not already in possession of an **EHIC** (European Health Insurance Card), should apply for one before travelling. The card entitles UK residents to reduced-cost medical treatment. Apply at UK post offices, call 0845 606 2030, or visit www.ehic.org.uk. Refer to the leaflet *Health Advice for Travellers*, available from post offices, for full details. All prescription drugs taken into France should be clearly labelled; it is recommended to carry a copy of prescriptions.

Accessibility

On French TGV and Corail trains there are wheelchair spaces in 1st-class carriages available to holders of 2nd-class tickets. On Eurostar and Thalys special rates are available for accompanying adults. All airports are equipped to receive physically disabled passengers. **Disabled drivers** may use the EU blue card for parking entitlements.

PRACTICAL INFORMATION

Information about accessibility is available from French disability organizations such as **Association des Paralysés de France** (1 pl. de Rungis, 75013 Paris. 01 53 80 92 97; www.apf.asso.fr), who also maintain a nationwide network of branches throughout the country. The guide Michelin Camping France indicates campsites with facilities suitable for the physically disabled.

GETTING THERE
By Plane

Air travel to either of Paris' two airports is easy (Roissy-Charles-de-Gaulle to the north, and Orly to the south). Contact airline companies and travel agents for details of package tour flights with a rail link-up or Fly-Drive schemes.
Visitors arriving in **Paris** who wish to reach the city centre or a train station may use public transportation or reserve space on the **Airport Shuttle** (for Roissy-Charles-de-Gaulle 01 45 38 55 72, for Orly 01 43 21 06 78);
www.aeroportsdeparis.fr
Many European airlines also operate services to **Nice**, **Lyon** and **Marseille**, as well as other major provincial cities.
Most North American airlines fly to Paris only, but France's regional airports are well connected to both the Parisian airports and to each other.

By Ship

There are numerous **cross-Channel services** (passenger and car ferries) from the United Kingdom and Ireland. To choose the most suitable route between your port of arrival and your destination use the Michelin Tourist and Motoring Atlas France, Michelin map 726 (which gives travel times and mileages) or Michelin maps from the 1:200 000 series (with the orange cover). For details apply to travel agencies or direct to:

♦ **Brittany Ferries**
0871 244 0744 (in the UK),
0825 828 828 (in France), www.brittanyferries.com. Services from Portsmouth, Poole and Plymouth.

♦ **Condor Ferries**
01202 207216,
www.condorferries.co.uk. Services from Poole and Portsmouth.

♦ **LD Lines**
0844 576 8836, www.ldlines.co.uk. Services from Newhaven, Portsmouth and Dover.

♦ **DFDS Seaways**
0871 574 7235 (in the UK),
02 32 14 68 50 (in France), www.dfdsseaways.co.uk. Services between Dover and Dunkerque, and Calais.

♦ **P & O Ferries**
08716 64 21 21 (in theUK),
or 0825 120 156 (in France), www.poferries.com. Service between Dover and Calais.

Eurotunnel

The fastest way across the English Channel is to drive straight under it on a rail shuttle through the Channel Tunnel between the M20 near Folkestone (junction 11A) and the A16 near Calais (junction 42). (**Le Shuttle-Eurotunnel**, 08443 35 35 35 (reservations – UK only); 0810 63 03 04 (from France); www.eurotunnel.com).

BY COACH/BUS

Eurolines (part of National Express), operates regular services between all parts of the UK and towns throughout France. The main UK terminus is Victoria Coach Station, in central London.

◆ **Eurolines (National Express)**
4 Cardiff Rd, Luton, Beds, LU1 1PP.
08717 818178.
www.eurolines.co.uk

By Car

France has an excellent road network, including *autoroutes* – motorways or major highways, often with a toll to pay.

By Train

All rail services throughout France can be arranged through **Rail Europe** in the UK, online (www.raileurope.co.uk; www.facebook.com/RailEuropeUK; www.twitter.com/RailEuropeUK), by telephone 08448 484 064, or call into the **Rail Europe Travel Centre** at 193 Piccadilly, London W1J 9EU. Rail Europe can also book Eurostar travel.
Eurostar runs from **London** (St Pancras) to **Paris** (Gare du Nord) in under 3hr (up to 20 times daily). In Lille and Paris it links to the high-speed rail network (TGV) which covers most of France.
Bookings and information 08432 186 186 in the UK, www.eurostar.com. **Citizens of non-European Economic Area countries** will need to complete a landing card for UK immigration before checking-in. These can be found at desks in front of the check-in area, or ask Eurostar staff. Various versions of the **Eurailpass** may be purchased by residents of countries outside the European Union. www.eurail.com
In the US, contact your travel agent or **Rail Europe** 44 South Broadway,

White Plains, NY 10601; www.raileurope.com 1-800-622-8600

GETTING AROUND
By Train

Comfortable, punctual and good value trains make rail travel a pleasure in France. The state-owned SNCF rail network, covers almost the entire country. Their sleek, fast TGV trains run between main towns, with door-to-door journey times that easily rival air travel, especially Paris–Lyon (2 hours) and Paris–Marseille (3 hours). TGVs must always be booked in advance, and all seats are reserved. However, it is often possible to reserve a TGV seat up to just a few minutes before the train departs.
The main city-to-city lines are also served by other comfortable modern trains, which do not require advance booking. Away from these major lines, SNCF operates a reliable stopping service within each region.
Before booking rail tickets, be sure to enquire at the station whether you are entitled to obtain one of the many rail **discount passes**. For example, groups of friends travelling together, or families with a young child, may be eligible. When first starting any journey by train, remember that rail tickets **must be validated** (*composter*) by using the orange automatic date-stamping machines at the platform entrance.

By Car

Driving in France should not present much difficulty. For British drivers unaccustomed to driving on the right, extra care will be needed at first, but the rules of the road are otherwise similar to those in other Western countries. Road signs generally use easy-to-understand international visual symbols.

Documents

Driving licence

Travellers from other European Union countries and North America can drive in France with a valid national or home-state driving licence. An **international driving licence** is useful but not obligatory. These can be obtained from motoring organisations, e.g. AA and RAC.

Registration papers

It is compulsory to carry the vehicle registration papers (logbook); vehicles registered outside France should display a nationality plate or sticker of approved size close to the registration plate on the back of the vehicle, unless this already forms part of the registration plate.

Insurance

Insurance cover is compulsory, and you must carry a current insurance certificate. Check with your insurance company before leaving to ensure you are fully covered in the event of an accident, as many British insurance policies give only the minimum third-party cover required while in France.
Ensure you have adequate breakdown cover before arriving in France. UK motoring organisations, for example the **AA** and the **RAC**, offer accident insurance and breakdown service programmes, either on a yearly basis or for temporary periods, for both members and non-members. These offer an emergency phone number in the UK, and approved repair services locally. Note that French autoroutes are privately owned, so your European Breakdown Cover service does not extend to breakdowns on the autoroute or its service areas – you must use the emergency telephones or drive off the autoroute if you are able to do so.
Members of the **American Automobile Association** should obtain the free brochure *Offices To Serve You Abroad*. The affiliated organisation for France is the **Automobile Club National** (9 r. d'Artois, 75008 Paris; 01 40 55 43 00).

Road Regulations

Police may check documents at any time. The regulations on drinking and driving (limited to 0.50g/l) and speeding are strictly enforced by on-the-spot fines or confiscation of the vehicle. New regulations introduced in July 2012 require all drivers to carry a breath testing device (ethylotest) in the vehicle. If paying an on-the-spot fine, you should be given a copy of the officer's report form, a receipt for any money paid, and information on how to proceed if you wish to plead not guilty.

Highway code

In France the minimum driving age is 18. Traffic drives on the right. All passengers must wear **seat belts. Children** under the age of 10 must ride in the back seat.
In the absence of stop signs at intersections, cars must **give way to the right**. Traffic on main roads outside built-up areas (priority indicated by a yellow diamond sign) and on roundabouts has right of way. Vehicles must stop when

the lights turn red at road junctions and may filter to the right only when indicated by an amber arrow. Traffic within a roundabout (traffic circle) has priority over vehicles entering the roundabout, unless signs indicate otherwise.

Pedestrian priority
Under legislation introduced in 2010, **pedestrians** now always **have priority over cars** when crossing a road. Until recently, they had priority only at specially designated crossings. They need to "show a clear intention to cross" a road – described as "an ostensible step forward or a hand gesture" – and vehicles are required to stop for them. The only exception is where a designated pedestrian crossing is less than 50m away. Drivers who ignore the rules face a fine of P135.

Lights
Full or dipped headlights must be switched on in rain, poor visibility and at night; use sidelights only when the vehicle is stationary. If driving a UK vehicle, headlight beams should be adjusted for driving on the right. It is illegal to drive with faulty lights in France, so it is advisable to take a spare set of bulbs with you.

Breakdown
Since 2008, it has been compulsory to carry a safety jacket for each passenger and a warning triangle in the vehicle to be used in the case of a **breakdown.** Hazard warning lights are obligatory.

Parking regulations
In built-up areas there are zones where parking is either restricted or subject to a charge; tickets should be obtained from nearby ticket machines (*horodateurs* – small change necessary) and displayed inside the windscreen on the driver's side; failure to display may result in a fine, or towing away and impoundment. Other parking areas in town may require you to take a ticket when passing through a barrier. To exit, you must pay the parking fee and insert the paid-up card in another machine which will lift the exit gate.

Route planning
The road network is excellent and includes many motorways. The roads are very busy during holiday periods (particularly weekends in July and August), and to avoid traffic congestion it is advisable to follow the recommended secondary routes (signposted as *itinéraires bis*).

The motorway network includes simple rest areas (*aires*) every 10–15km/6–10mi and service areas (*aires de service*), with fuel, restaurant and shopping, about every 40km/25mi. The rest areas are fairly basic, often having no more than just toilets. The main service areas are more fully equipped, but vary in size and complexity from perfectly adequate "pit stop" facilities with mini-supermarkets, coffee machines and newspaper kiosks, to extensive complexes often with restaurants and overnight accommodation, too.

For **24hr motorway information** the website www.autoroutes.fr gives real-time information on the whole network.

For general information on traffic and *itinéraires bis*, contact Bison

Futé; 0800 100 200; www.bison-fute.equipement.gouv.fr.

Tolls

In France, most motorway sections are subject to a toll (péage). You can pay in cash or with a credit card.

Car rental

There are car rental agencies at airports, railway stations and in all large towns throughout France. European cars generally have manual transmission so reserve in advance if you need an automatic car. Drivers must be over 21; between ages 21 and 25, drivers are required to pay an extra daily fee; some companies allow drivers under-23 only if the reservation has been made through a travel agent. It is relatively expensive to hire a car in France. Look online for the best prices on car rental around the globe.

BASIC INFORMATION
Business Hours

Offices and other businesses are open Mon–Fri, 9am–noon, 2–6pm. Many also open Saturday mornings. Town and village shops are generally open Tue–Fri; there are local variations. Midday breaks may be much longer in the South. However, in cities, tourist centres or resorts, businesses may keep longer hours or stay open all day, seven days a week, especially if they primarily serve the tourist market.

Electricity

The electric current is 220 volts/50 Hz. Circular two-pin plugs are the rule. Adaptors should be bought before you leave home; they are on sale in most airports.

Emergencies

First aid, medical advice and chemists' night-service rotas are available from chemists/drugstores (*pharmacie,* identified by a green cross sign).

Mail/Post

Look for the bright yellow *La Poste* signs. Main post offices are generally open Mon–Fri 8am–7pm, Sat 8am–noon. Smaller branches generally open 9am–noon, 2–4pm weekdays. There are often automatic tellers (*guichets automatiques*) inside, which allow you to weigh and post items and avoid a queue. You may also find that you can change money, make copies, send faxes and make phone calls in a post office.

To post a letter from the street look for the bright yellow postboxes. Stamps are also sold in newsagents and cafés that sell cigarettes (*tabac*). Stamp collectors should ask for *timbres de collection* in any post office (there is often a *philatélie* counter).

France uses a five-digit postal code that precedes the name of the city or town on the last line of the address. The first two digits indicate the *département* and the last three digits identify the *commune* or local neighbourhood. www.laposte.fr.

Currency

There are no restrictions on the amount of currency visitors can take into France. Visitors wishing to export currency in foreign banknotes in excess of the given allocation from France should complete a currency declaration form on arrival.

Coins and notes – The unit of currency in France is the **euro** (€).

One euro is divided into 100 cents or *centimes d'euro*.

Banks and currency exchange

Banks are generally open Mon–Fri 9am–5.30pm. Some branches are open for limited transactions on Saturday. Opening hours are shorter on the day before a bank holiday.

A passport or other ID may be necessary when cashing cheques in banks. Commission charges vary and hotels usually charge considerably more than banks for cashing cheques.

By far the most convenient way of obtaining French currency is the **24hr cash dispenser** or **ATM** (*distributeur automatique de billets* in French), found outside many banks and post offices and easily recognisable by the CB (Carte Bleue) logo. Most accept international credit cards (don't forget your PIN) and almost all also give instructions in English. Note that many ATMs will dispense only up to a certain limit, which may be lower than the daily limit set by your bank.

Do not attempt to top up funds the same day (although you can continue to use the card to pay bills in restaurants, for example); this may work with some banks, but at others your card may be declined or, worse, retained. Foreign currency can also be exchanged in major banks, post offices, hotels or private exchange offices found in main cities and near popular tourist attractions.

Credit cards

Major credit cards (Visa, Mastercard, Eurocard) are widely accepted

in shops, hotels, restaurants and petrol stations.

If your card is lost or stolen call the appropriate 24hr hotlines:
- American Express 0805 540 524
- Visa 0800 90 11 79
- Mastercard 0800 90 13 87

You should also report any loss or theft to the local police who will issue you with a certificate (useful proof to show the credit card company).

Emergency numbers

Police (*Gendarme*) 17
Fire (*Pompiers*) 18
Ambulance (*SAMU*) 15
European-wide Emergency Number 112

Public Holidays

There are 11 public holidays in France, as well as other religious and national festival days, and a number of local saints' days, etc. On all these days, museums and other monuments may be closed or may vary their opening hours.

School Holidays

French schools close for holidays five times a year. These are: one week at the end of October, two weeks at Christmas, two weeks in February, two weeks in spring, and the whole of July and August. In these periods, all tourist sights and attractions, hotels, restaurants, and roads are busier than usual.

Smoking Regulations

Since the beginning of 2008, smoking has been forbidden in all public places in France, notably bars, restaurants, railway stations and airports. Ironically, this has created a problem for non-smokers who want to sit outside on a terrace to enjoy the open air, where smoking is not prohibited.

Tax refunds

Non-EU residents can claim back sales tax (*TVA*) on goods when spending more than €175 at one store on the same day. Ask for your receipts and a form when at the sales desk, and take these and your purchases to the local customs office at the airport before you check in for your flight.

Telephones

The telephone system in France is still operated largely by the former state monopoly France Télécom. They offer an English-language enquiries service on
09 69 36 39 00 (in France),
or 0800 364 775 (in UK).
The French **ringing tone** is a series of long tones; the engaged (busy) tone is a series of short beeps. To use a **public phone** you need to buy a prepaid phone card (*télécartes*). Some telephone booths accept credit cards (Visa, Mastercard/Eurocard). *Télécartes* (50 or 120 units) can be bought in post offices, cafés that sell cigarettes (*tabac*) and newsagents, and can be used to make calls in France and abroad. Calls can be received at phone boxes where the blue bell sign is shown. The phone will not ring audibly, so keep your eye on the little message screen.

Mobile/cell phones

While in France, all visitors from other European countries should be able to use their mobile phone as normal. Visitors from some other countries need to ensure before departure that their phone and service contract are compatible with the European system (GSM). The three main mobile phone operators in France are SFR (www.sfr.fr), Orange (www.orange.fr) and Bouygues (www.bouygues telecom.fr).
International roaming rates can be expensive. If you are staying for an extended period, consider buying a pay as you go SIM card, or renting a mobile phone locally, including Blackberries and iPhones – www.cellhire.fr.

National Calls

French telephone numbers have 10 digits. Numbers begin with 01 in Paris and the Paris region; 02 in northwest France; 03 in northeast France; 04 in southeast France and Corsica; 05 in southwest France. However, all 10 numbers must be dialled even within the local region.

International Calls

To call France from abroad, dial the country code 33, omit the initial zero of the French number, and dial the remaining 9-digit number. When calling abroad from France dial 00, followed by the country code (see above), followed by the local area code (usually without any initial zero) and the number of your correspondent.
To use the personal calling card of a telephone company, follow

the card instructions, dialling the access code for the country you are in, e.g.

- **AT&T** 0800 99-0011
- **BT** 0800 99-0244
- **MCI/Verizon** 0800 99-0019
- **Sprint** 0800 99-0087
- **Canada Direct** 0800 99-0016

Cheap rates with 50 percent extra time are available from private telephones to the UK on weekdays 9.30pm–8am, from 2pm on Saturdays and all day on Sundays and holidays. Cheap rates to the USA and Canada are from 2am–noon all week, and to Australia Mon–Sat 9.30pm–8am and all day Sunday.

Toll-free numbers in France (also known as Numéro Verte) begin with 0800. For more information about using phones in France, visit **www.orange.fr**.

TIME

France is in the Central European time zone. During the winter months, from 2am on the last Sunday of October to 2am on the last Sunday of March, France is one hour ahead of GMT.

From 2am on the last Sunday of March to 2am on the last Sunday of October, it adopts daylight saving time and is two hours ahead of GMT. However, the UK changes its clocks to British Summer Time (i.e. daylight saving time) at the same times and on the same dates, so France always remains one hour ahead of the UK. In France the 24-hour clock is widely used.

TIPPING

Since a service charge is automatically included in the prices of meals and accommodation in France, it is not necessary to tip in restaurants and hotels. However, if the service in a restaurant is especially good or if you have enjoyed a fine meal, an extra tip (this is the *pourboire,* rather than the *service*) will be appreciated. Usually €5–10 is enough, but if the bill is big (a large party or a luxury restaurant), it is not uncommon to leave more. In bars and cafés you could leave any small change that remains after paying the bill, but this generally should not be more than 5 percent. Taxi drivers do not have to be tipped, but again it is usual to give a small amount, not more than 10 percent. Attendants at public toilets should be given a few cents. Hairdressers are usually tipped 10–15 percent. Tour guides and tour drivers should be tipped according to the amount of service given: from €2–5 is about right.

PRACTICAL INFORMATION

FRANCE'S MOST FAMOUS PLACES

There's a perfect side of France for every visitor to discover in this extraordinarily diverse country, from the flat plains of the Pas de Calais in the north to the majestic Alps and Pyrénées mountain ranges in the south; from a sleepy village pétanque game to the high fashion and buzzing cultural scene of Paris; splendid châteaux, stunning beaches, world-class skiing, justly famous food and wine – la Belle France offers months of memorable travel, wherever and whenever you decide to visit. Bienvenue!

Paris (pp30–51)

Paris earns a special place in the heart of visitors not just because of its artistic and cultural treasures, but also because of its diverse atmosphere, its smells and noises, its inhabitants and its landmarks. The curvaceous Seine is still the heart of the city: Paris shows off many of its great monuments along the river, so a stroll along the embankments or a boat trip are charming ways to get a feel for the layout of the city. Paris boasts three of the world's great art collections, a centuries-deep legacy of artistic and intellectual achievement, and history that reels in less than 200 years from revolution to empire, from belle-époque to German occupation. And Paris is not just about high culture – there are superb restaurants, cafés and bars, and great shopping.

Normandy & Brittany (pp52-67)

Famous for its ciders, cheeses and calvados, the former dukedom of Normandy boasts elegant coastal resorts, while cows, orchards and hedgrows provide rural charm. Rouen's Gothic cathedral and the ruins of the abbey at Jumièges are two of France's most impressive

and important historic sights. More recent history is preserved at Caen's Mémorial peace museum and the Normandy Landing Beaches. The rugged Celtic peninsula of Brittany in the northwest, with its indented coastline and islands battered by the Atlantic, narrow inlets and sandy bays, has a mysterious past, which is reflected in the many prehistoric remains scattered around the region, such as the menhirs at Carnac. The identity and culture of the Bretons make this a fascinating region.

Châteaux of the Loire (pp68-75)

Renowned for its magnificent Renaissance châteaux such as Chambord and Chenonceau, the Loire Valley in the Centre Region is also referred to as the "Garden of France" due to the cultivation of vines, flowers and horticultural crops. The many châteaux actually sit on the banks of the River Loire's tributaries, the Indre and the Cher, and date from the 16C onwards.

Alsace Lorraine Champagne (pp76-91)

Alsace has a very Germanic character and many of its towns and villages reflect this. To the west of the Vosges mountains is Lorraine, which despite once being part of Germany, is more French. Further west is Champagne, well known for its sparkling wine, and to the north, the heavily wooded Ardennes region.

Burgundy (pp92-99)

Formerly a great dukedom, Burgundy is placed on the great trade route linking the north with the Mediterranean. Coupled with the proceeds of its viticulture, this led to great wealth that funded amazing buildings like the Hôtel-Dieu at Beaune.

French Alps - Rhône
(pp100-113)

In the southeast of France, stretching from the Mediterranean to Lac Léman (Lake Geneva), the Alps are beloved by winter sports fans, but they also provide dramatic and beautiful mountain landscapes to explore when the snows are confined to the highest peaks. There are National and Regional Parks, which reflect the richness of this environment and allow access to these amazing landscapes. To the east of the Auverne region, the land slopes down to the Rhône Valley, where the rivers Rhône and Saône converge on their journey south towards the great city of Lyon and eventually the Mediterranean Sea.

Bordeaux & Dordogne
(pp114–125)

Of all the world's wine regions, few can match the Bordelais for quality. One of France's oldest trading ports, Bordeaux grew wealthy on the English taste for claret, leaving as its legacy a handsome 18C centre.

Nearby are the vineyards of Cognac. Further inland, the Dordogne, or the Périgord, is known for its agreeable climate, its impressive castles and cave systems, not to mention the meandering Dordogne river itself.

Languedoc-Roussillon
(pp126-135)

Stretching in an arc from the Rhône Delta to the Pyrénées and characterised by vineyards and popular beaches, the Languedoc Roussillon is steeped in history from the Roman era to the medieval. The Gorges du Tarn (Tarn Gorges) to the north are cut into the Grand Causses, from which there are amazing views from the corniche roads.

Provence (pp136–147)

Centred around the impressive Rhône Delta in the south, this ancient region, blessed with sunshine and occupied successively by Celts, Romans and Franks, retained its independence from the French Crown until the 15C. Fascinating cities such as Nîmes, Marseille, Aix-en-Provence and Arles, and the astonishingly well-preserved Roman remains, such as those at St-Rémy-de-Provence, ensure the ongoing popularity of this region.

Côte d'Azur (pp148–157)

The Côte d'Azur – or French Riviera – runs along the Mediterranean coastline of southeast France from Menton to Cassis. What started as a popular winter health resort in the late 18C continues to draw thousands of tourists each year. Resort towns here include Cannes, Beaulieu-sur-Mer and St-Tropez. You can't beat its 300 days of sunshine per year and holiday atmosphere.

PARIS★★★

The brilliance and greatness of Paris – its evocative spirit, the imposing dignity of its avenues and squares, its vast cultural wealth and unique flair and style – are known the world over. The dominance of Paris in France's intellectual, artistic, scientific and political life can be traced back to the 12C when the Capetian kings made it their capital.

A BIT OF HISTORY
Origins

When the Roman Empire fell at the end of the 5C, Paris was a modest township. The **Romans** had extended the settlement south of the river to what is now the **Quartier Latin**. Clovis, King of **the Franks**, settled in Paris in 506. In 885, the Norsemen sailed up the river and attacked Paris; Odo, son of Robert the Strong, bravely led the local resistance, and was elected first king of "France" in 888.

The Capetian Dynasty (987–1328)

In 1136, the abbey church of St-Denis was rebuilt in the revolutionary Gothic style, followed by the iconic Notre-Dame. Between 1180 and 1210, **Philippe Auguste** surrounded the growing city with a ring of fortifications anchored on the Louvre fortress.

The House of Valois (1328–1589)

In 1370 **Charles V** built himself a stronghold in the eastern part of the city, the Bastille.

Paris was taken by the English in 1418. **Joan of Arc** was wounded in front of Porte St-Honoré trying to retake the city in 1429. Paris was won back for France eight years later by Charles VII.

After **Charles VIII**'s campaigns in Italy, the influence of the Renaissance became apparent. The Pont Neuf (New Bridge) was built, which today is the city's oldest surviving bridge.

In 1589, Henri III was assassinated, marking the end of the Valois line.

The Bourbons (1589–1789)

In 1594 Paris opened its gates to **Henri IV**, the new king who had renounced his Protestant faith and

The Louvre and the pyramid

Practical Information

Getting Around Paris

▶**TGV**: *Paris Est/Lyon/Montparnasse/Nord*. Paris is France's capital and its largest city. It lies in the middle of the Île-de-France region, which sits between the Centre, Bourgogne, Champagne-Ardennes, Picardie and Haute Normandie regions. Paris is 85.6km/53mi SW of Compiègne; 69km/42.8mi NW of Fontainebleau; 104km/64.6mi SE of Les Andelys. The **Seine River** flows east–west across the city. Places north of the river are on the *rive droite*, while those to the south are on the *rive gauche*. Paris is divided into 20 arrondissements (districts or neighbourhoods), each one with its own local government and characteristics. Each *arrondissement* is further divided into a number of neighbourhoods determined by history and the people who live there. **The métro** is the easiest and most economical way of moving around the city. **Line 1**, which crosses Paris east–west, services many of the most famous attractions: the Louvre, the Champs-Élysées and the Arc de Triomphe. **Line 4** is useful for travelling across the city from north–south. The metro also services the immediate suburbs of Paris, but for those a bit farther out, use the **RER** suburban trains.

succeeded in pacifying the country. But on 14 May 1610, in the Rue de la Ferronnerie, this monarch too fell victim to an assassin.

Louis XIII (1610–43) may have been king, but Cardinal Richelieu ran France throughout his reign, founding the Académie Française and commissioning architectural projects such as the **Palais Royal** and the **Sorbonne**.

When Paris fell prey to the uprising known as the Fronde in 1648, **Louis XIV** was just a boy. He began his long reign as the 'Sun King' aged 23 in 1661. During his reign, the extraordinary advancement of the arts and literature gave Paris and France huge prestige in Europe; writers, painters, sculptors and landscapers flourished as never before. France's "Century of Greatness" came to an end with Louis XIV's death in 1715.

The country now found itself under the rule of a five-year-old, **Louis XV**, so a regent, Philippe d'Orléans, took the reins. A long period of peace accompanied the years of corruption. Literary salons flourished, spreading new ideas in what became known as the **Age of Enlightenment**.

The personal rule exercised by **Louis XV** was discredited by his favourites, but Paris nevertheless witnessed a number of projects by great architects: the magnificent façades fronting the Place de la Concorde, the École Militaire (Military Academy), and the dome which crowns the Panthéon.

Revolution and Empire (1789–1814)

On **14 July 1789**, in the space of less than an hour, the people of Paris took over the Bastille. The feudal system was abolished on 4 August, and the Declaration of the Rights of Man adopted on 26 August. The king was stripped of power and held with his family in the tower of the

PARIS

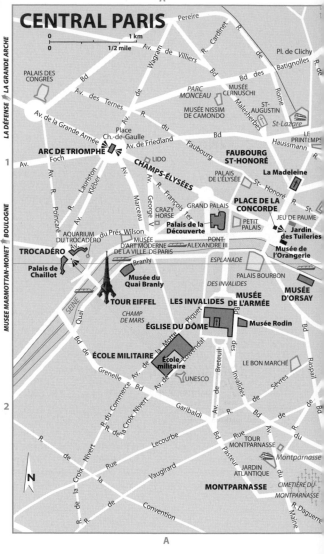

CENTRAL PARIS

0 ——————— 1 km
0 ——————— 1/2 mile

LA DÉFENSE · LA GRANDE ARCHE

MUSÉE MARMOTTAN-MONET · BOULOGNE

Pereire

R. Cardinet R.

Av. de Villiers

Wagram

de

Pl. de Clichy

Batignolles

R. de

PALAIS DES CONGRÈS

Bd

Av. des Ternes

Av. de la Grande Armée

de

PARC MONCEAU

Bd des

Rome

MUSÉE CERNUSCHI

MUSÉE NISSIM DE CAMONDO

Malesherbes

ST-AUGUSTIN

St-Lazare

LE PRINTEMPS

Haussmann

R.

Place Ch.-de-Gaulle

Av. du

Bd

ARC DE TRIOMPHE

Foch

Av. de Friedland

Faubourg

FAUBOURG ST-HONORÉ

Av.

CHAMPS-ÉLYSÉES

Lauriston

Kléber

Av.

Poincaré

R.

LIDO

PALAIS DE L'ÉLYSÉE

St-Honoré

La Madeleine

Av.

Marceau

Av. George V

R. François 1er

CRAZY HORSE

GRAND PALAIS

PLACE DE LA CONCORDE

R.

St-

AQUARIUM DU TROCADÉRO

du Prés. Wilson

Palais de la Découverte

PETIT PALAIS

JEU DE PAUME

TROCADÉRO

MUSÉE D'ART MODERNE DE LA VILLE DE PARIS

PONT ALEXANDRE III

Jardin des Tuileries

Palais de Chaillot

Branly

ESPLANADE

Musée de l'Orangerie

SEINE

Musée du Quai Branly

PALAIS BOURBON

MUSÉE D'ORSAY

TOUR EIFFEL

LES INVALIDES

DES INVALIDES

MUSÉE DE L'ARMÉE

Quai

CHAMP DE MARS

Piquet

ÉGLISE DU DÔME

Bd

Musée Rodin

Bd de Grenelle

ÉCOLE MILITAIRE

Av. de la Motte

Lowendal

Av.

des

Breteuil

LE BON MARCHÉ

Raspail

École militaire

UNESCO

Av. de

Invalides

Sèvres

de

Bd

de

R. du Commerce

R. de la Croix Nivert

Garibaldi

R.

Av.

du

Ba

R.

de

Croix

Nivert

Lecourbe

Bd Pasteur

TOUR MONTPARNASSE

Montparnasse

N

Rue

Vaugirard

JARDIN ATLANTIQUE

du

CIMETIÈRE DU MONTPARNASSE

R.

de la

R.

de

Convention

MONTPARNASSE

R. Daguerre

Maine

A

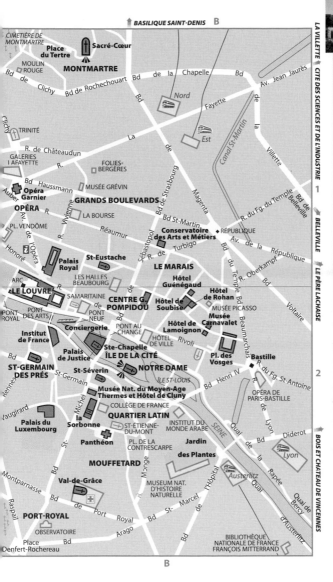

🚆 BASILIQUE SAINT-DENIS   **B**

CIMETIÈRE DE MONTMARTRE

Place du Tertre

⛪ **Sacré-Cœur**

MOULIN ROUGE

MONTMARTRE

Bd de Clichy   Bd de Rochechouart   Bd de la Chapelle   Bd

Av. Jean Jaurès

Nord

Fayette

Clichy

TRINITÉ

R. de Châteaudun

FOLIES-BERGÈRES

GALERIES LAFAYETTE

Bd   Haussmann

Auber   **Opéra Garnier**

OPÉRA

MUSÉE GRÉVIN

GRANDS BOULEVARDS

Bd de Strasbourg

Canal St-Martin

Villette

de la Villette

de

la

Magenta

Est

R. du Fg. du Temple   Bd de Belleville

PL. VENDÔME

LA BOURSE

Vivienne

R.

Réaumur

Bd St-Martin

Bd St-Denis

Conservatoire des Arts et Métiers

◆ **RÉPUBLIQUE**

Av. de la République

R. du Temple

R. Oberkampf

Voltaire

Honoré

Av. de l'Opéra

R.

de   Turbigo

Sébastopol

Palais Royal

St-Eustache

LE MARAIS

Hôtel Guénégaud

ARC

LE LOUVRE

LES HALLES BEAUBOURG

SAMARITAINE

de

CENTRE G. POMPIDOU

Hôtel de Soubise

Hôtel de Rohan

MUSÉE PICASSO

Musée Carnavalet

Beaumarchais

PONT NEUF

PONT DES ARTS

PONT ROYAL

Conciergerie

PONT AU CHANGE

Hôtel de Lamoignon

Institut de France

Palais de Justice

HÔTEL DE VILLE

Rivoli

Ste-Chapelle

ÎLE DE LA CITÉ

Pl. des Vosges

Bastille

R. du Fg. St-Antoine

ST-GERMAIN DES PRÉS

Bd

Rennes

St-Germain

St-Séverin

NOTRE DAME

ÎLE ST-LOUIS

Bd Henri IV

2

Quai de Lyon

OPÉRA DE PARIS-BASTILLE

Vaugirard

Michel

Musée Nat. du Moyen-Age Thermes et Hôtel de Cluny

COLLÈGE DE FRANCE

QUARTIER LATIN

INSTITUT DU MONDE ARABE

SEINE

Lyon

Diderot

Palais du Luxembourg

la **Sorbonne**

ST-ÉTIENNE-DU-MONT

St-

Panthéon

PL. DE LA CONTRESCARPE

Jardin des Plantes

Bd   de   la   Rapée

MOUFFETARD

Monge

Austerlitz

Montparnasse

Val-de-Grâce

Bd

de

Port

MUSEUM NAT. D'HISTOIRE NATURELLE

St-

Marcel

l'Hôpital

Quai

Quai

d'Austerlitz

Raspail

PORT-ROYAL

Royal

Quai de Bercy

OBSERVATOIRE

Place Denfert-Rochereau

Bd

Arago

Bd

BIBLIOTHÈQUE NATIONALE DE FRANCE FRANÇOIS MITTERRAND

B

Templar Prison (Tour du Temple). The revolutionaries then fought among themselves, blighting the following years with instability, fear and massacres. The monarch was guillotined on **21 January 1793** in Place de la Concorde as a prelude to **the Terror**. Robespierre the "Incorruptible" oversaw the Great Terror, a two month orgy of bloodletting when the "national razor", as the guillotine was known, was to slice off 2 561 heads.

The Empire – The Revolution gave way to dictatorship when Napoleon I was proclaimed Emperor of the French on 18 May 1804. Napoleon ordered the erection of a great column in the Place Vendôme; cast from the melted-down metal of guns taken at the Battle of Austerlitz (Slavkov), it commemorated the victories of his *Grande Armée,* and plans began for a great triumphal arch (Arc de Triomphe). But it was not to last. On 31 March 1814, the Allies occupied Paris. On 11 April, the Emperor, "the sole obstacle to peace in Europe", signed the document of abdication at Fontainebleau.

The Restoration (May 1814–February 1848)
The reign of Louis XVIII –
1814–24 The period of rule of Louis XVI's brother was interrupted by the Hundred Days of Napoleon's attempt to re-establish himself between his sojourn on Elba and his final exile to St Helena.

The reign of Charles X – **1824–30** Charles X banned press freedom, causing rioting and fighting in the streets which led to his abdication.

Reign of Louis-Philippe – **1830–48** During the 1830s, Victor

Hugo wrote *Notre-Dame de Paris* and Chopin became the darling of Parisian society. The 1840s saw the publication of the *Count of Monte Cristo* and The *Three Musketeers* by Dumas. On 23 February in 1848, the barricades went up on the streets again after soldiers fired on a crowd of the unemployed, and the monarchy fell.

Second Republic and Second Empire (1848–1870)
Second Republic
In 1849, Léon Foucault proved the rotation and spherical nature of the earth by means of a pendulum (the experiment was repeated in 1855 from the dome of the Panthéon). On 2 December 1851 the short life of the Second Republic was ended by a *coup d'état.*

Second Empire – **1852–70**
Two great exhibitions (in 1855 and 1867) proclaimed the prosperity France enjoyed under the rule of Bonaparte's nephew, Napoleon III. **Baron Haussmann** transformed the capital, giving it many of the features that now seem quintessentially Parisian. The Baron is remembered above all for the ruthless surgery he performed on the capital's ancient urban tissue, opening up new focal points (Place de l'Opéra) and linking them with wide avenues (Grands Boulevards) that were more hygienic and, crucially, harder to barricade.

Republican Continuity (1870 to the present day)
In 1870, Paris prepared for the advancing Prussian army. The ensuing siege subjected the population of Paris to terrible hardships; food ran out and

the winter was exceptionally severe. The city surrendered on 28 January 1871. The revolutionary **Commune** that ensued was ruthlessly suppressed, but not before the Communards had burnt down the City Hall, the Tuileries, pulled down the column in the Place Vendôme and shot their prisoners at the Hostages' Wall in the Rue Haxo. They made their last stand in the Père-Lachaise Cemetery, where the survivors were summarily executed at the Federalists' Wall (Mur des Fédérés). But political institutions were re-established and the nation revived thanks to colonial expansion, an economic boom time that led to the **Belle Epoque** era.

Third Republic – In 1874, Degas painted *The Dancing Class* and Monet *Impression: Rising Sun*, which led to the coining of the initially derisive term Impressionism. The engineer Gustave Eiffel completed his great tower, centrepiece of the Universal Exhibition of 1889. In the century's final decade, Toulouse-Lautrec painted cabaret scenes, and Pissarro Parisian townscapes. In 1898, the 21-year-old Louis Renault built his first car, and Pierre and Marie Curie explored radioactivity. The Théâtre des Champs-Élysées opened in 1913 with a performance of Stravinsky's *Rite of Spring*; its music and choreography outraged an unprepared public. In 1914, on the evening of 31 July, the eve of general mobilisation, Jean Jaurès was assassinated.

The World Wars
World War I (1914–18) Paris was never taken in the Great War, but France as a whole paid a terrible price for the conflict. In 1920,

the interment of an unknown soldier at the Arc de Triomphe marked France's recognition of the sacrifices made by her ordinary soldiers, the unshaven *poilus* of the trenches.

Paris became the epicentre of avant-garde art - Cubism and Surrealism - during the interwar years. In 1934, André Citroën brought out the Traction Avant (Front-Wheel Drive) car, while political violence erupted between fascists, communists and socialists. In 1940, during **World War II**, Paris was **occupied** by the German army within weeks of the start of conflict. Between 16 and 17 July 1942, French Jews, victims of the Nazi racial myth, were rounded up at the Vélodrome d'Hiver prior to their deportation eastwards for extermination; 4 500 members of the Resistance also met their deaths in the clearing on Mount Valérien where the National Memorial of Fighting France now stands. Paris was **liberated** on 19 August 1944.

Fourth and Fifth Republics – The influence of Le Corbusier has reshaped the city's architecture: new forms (Maison de Radio-France), structures on piles (UNESCO), sweeping rooflines (CNIT building), and the exposed ducting of the iconic Centre Georges-Pompidou. The Mitterrand years also brought in grand projects: the Opera house at la Bastille, the Ministry of Finance buildings at Bercy, the Grande Arche at la Défense and the Bibliothèque Nationale de France François-Mitterrand at Tolbiac - distinctive modern landmarks that have changed the cityscape of Paris.

CIVIL ARCHITECTURE

Palais du Louvre★★★

Open Wed–Mon 9am–6pm (Wed and Fri 9.45pm). Various tariffs from €10–€14. 01 40 20 53 17. www.louvre.fr.

When the Grand Louvre was opened to the public in 1994, the different art collections were divided into three departments; **Sully**, **Denon** and **Richelieu**, which are located in the two wings and around the Cour Carrée.
François I had the original Louvre, which then lay beyond the city, pulled down, and in 1546 commissioned Pierre Lescot to build the Renaissance-style residence of the kings of France. When Charles IX came to the throne at age ten, the Florentine **Catherine de' Medici** was made Regent. At first she lived in the Louvre on the floor since known as the Queens' Lodging (Logis des Reines), but ordered the new Tuileries palace to be built and linked with the Louvre. **Charles IX** completed the southwestern part of the Cour Carrée, the courtyard which is the most impressive remaining part of the Old Louvre. **Henri III** was responsible for the southeastern part of the Cour Carrée. **Henri IV**, from 1595, had the work on the Great Gallery (Grande Galerie) continued. **Louis XIII** continued with the construction of the Cour Carrée. The young king **Louis XIV** moved into the Tuileries in 1664 for three years, but in 1682, left Paris for Versailles. The Louvre housed the Academy as well as a less desirable population. In 1715, the Court returned to Paris for seven years;

the young King Louis XV lived in the Tuileries. After the **Revolution**, the Convention used the Louvre theatre for its deliberations. **Napoleon I** took up residence in the Tuileries, enlarging the Place du Carrousel in order to be able to review his legions and embellishing it with a triumphal arch. All of the "restored" monarchs lived in the Tuileries, as did **Napoleon III**, who enclosed the north courtyard. During the night of 23 May 1871, the **Communards** burnt down the Tuileries and severely damaged parts of the Louvre.
In 1875, under **President MacMahon**, the North Wing (Aile Nord) was restored and extended, and refurbishing and rebuilding work carried out on the Riverside Gallery (Galerie du Bord de l'Eau) and the Pavillons de La Trémoille and de Flore.
In 1883, under **President Jules Grévy**, the Palais des Tuileries was demolished; and the city lost one of its key historic buildings.
In 1984 **President Mitterrand** embarked on the "Grand Louvre and Pyramide" project. He commissioned the architect Ming Pei to expand the services and reception area of the now world-famous art museum. Beneath the Cour Napoléon, a vast hall offering information services is lit up by the glass pyramid (**Pyramide★★**) which marks the main entrance to the museum.

Hôtel National des Invalides★★★

Open daily Oct–Mar 10am–5pm (5.30pm Sun); Apr–Sept 10am–6pm (6.30pm Sun). Closed 1st Mon of the month in Oct–Jun, 1 Jan, 1 May,

1 Nov, 25 Dec. €9 incl. audioguide (price includes Église du Dôme, Musée de l'Armée, l'Historial de Gaulle, Musée des Plans-Reliefs and Musée de l'Ordre de la Libération). 0810 11 33 99. www.invalides.org.

The plans for the vast edifice were drawn up between 1671 and 1676. Napoleon used to parade his troops in the main courtyard (Cour d'honneur); here the South Pavilion (Pavillon du Midi) forms the façade of the Église St-Louis, the resting-place of some of France's great soldiers; the interior is hung with flags taken from the enemy. It was here, in 1837, that Berlioz' *Requiem* was performed for the first time.

Église du Dôme★★★

The church of Les Invalides, was begun in 1677. With its beautiful gilded dome, it is one of the great works of the Louis XIV style, On the far side are the guns captured at Vienna in 1805 by Napoleon, still used for ceremonial salvoes on national occasions. The church became a military necropolis after Napoleon had Marshal Turenne (d. 1675) buried here. Note the memorial to Vauban, the great military architect, and the tomb of Marshal Foch.
In Visconti's crypt of green granite from the Vosges stands the "cloak of glory", the unmarked **Tombeau de Napoleon** completed in 1861 to receive the Emperor's mortal remains. Also housed in Hôtel nacional des Invalides is the **Musée de l'Armée**.

Arc de Triomphe★★★

pl. Charles-de-Gaulle. Open daily Apr–Sept 10am–11pm; Oct–Mar 10am–10.30pm. €8. 01 55 37 73 77. www.arcdetriompheparis.com

Together with the **Place Charles de Gaulle★★★** and its 12 radiating avenues, the great triumphal arch makes up one of Paris' principal focal points, known as the **Étoile** (Star). The façades of the buildings around it were designed in a harmonious style as part of Haussmann's plans.
The Arc de Triomphe was the scene on 14 July 1919 of the great victory parade and, on 11 November 1920, of the burial of the Unknown Soldier. Three years later the flame of remembrance was kindled for the first time. The arch is ornamented with sculpture, notably Rude's masterpiece of 1836 known as the *Marseillaise,* depicting volunteers departing to defend France from the invading Prussians (1792).

Place de la Concorde★★★

A perfect expression of the Louis XV style, it was designed by Ange-Jacques Gabriel in 1755 and completed over a period of 20 years. On 21 January 1793, near where the statue of Brest now stands, the guillotine was set up for the execution of Louis XVI and other victims of the Terror.
Two great urban **axes★★★** intersect here: one runs from the Église de la Madeleine to the Palais-Bourbon, the other from *Coysevox's Winged Horses* (*Chevaux ailés*), which mark the entrance to the Tuileries, to the magnificent marble sculptures (copies) by Nicolas and Guillaume Coustou that flank the Champs-Élysées. The pink granite Luxor obelisk (Obélisque de Louksor), 3 300 years old, covered with

hieroglyphics, was brought here from Egypt in 1836.

Eiffel Tower★★★

7 r. de Belloy. Open daily: Lift: mid-Jun–Aug 9am–12.45am; Sept–mid-Jun 9.30am–11.45pm. €8.50 (children, €6.50 (elevator to 2nd floor), €13.50 and €12 (elevator to Top floor); Stairs 1st and 2nd floors only, €5 and €4. 01 44 11 23 23. www.eiffel-tower.com.

The Eiffel Tower is Paris' most famous symbol. Built in just 26 months, the tower opened in March 1889 for the Universal Exhibition (Exposition universelle). In spite of its weight of 7 000 tonnes, height of 320.75m/1 051ft and 2.5 million rivets, it is a masterpiece of lightness. The tower weighs less than the volume of air surrounding it and that the pressure it exerts on the ground is that of a man sitting on a chair.

Palais de Justice and Conciergerie★★

2 bd du Palais. Palais open daily 8.30am–6pm. Closed public holidays. 01 44 32 52 52. Conciergerie Open daily 9.30am–6pm. €8.50. 01 53 40 60 80. http://conciergerie.monuments-nationaux.fr/

Known as the Palace (Palais), this is the principal seat of civil and judicial authority. Before becoming the royal palace of the rulers of medieval France, it had been the residence of Roman governors, Merovingian kings and the children of Clovis, the mint of Dagobert and Duke Eudes' fortress.
The original building has been added to over the centuries.

The First Civil Court is in the former Parliamentary Grand Chamber (*Grand'chambre du parlement*), the place where the kings dispensed justice, where the 16-year-old Louis XIV dictated his orders to Parliament, where that body in its turn demanded the convocation of the States-General in 1788, and where the Revolutionary Tribunal was set up under the public prosecutor, Fouquier-Tinville. The **Conciergerie** served as ante-chamber to the guillotine during the Terror, housing up to 1 200 detainees at any one time. The Galerie des Prisonniers (Prisoners' Gallery), Marie-Antoinette's cachot (cell) and the Chapelle des Girondins (Girondins' Chapel) are particularly moving.

Palais-Royal★★

6 r. de Montpensie.

In 1632, Richelieu ordered the building of the huge edifice that was renamed as the Palais Cardinal (Cardinal's Palace) when it was extended in 1639. On his deathbed, Richelieu bequeathed it to Louis XIII, whereupon its name was changed to the Palais-Royal. In 1783, Victor Louis laid out the charming formal gardens, enclosed by arcades that house a number of specialist shops and boutiques.

École Militaire★★

ave de Lowendal.

The Military Academy by Jacques-Ange Gabriel is one of the outstanding examples of French 18C architecture. It was begun in 1752, financed in part by Mme de Pompadour, and completed in 1773. True to its original function, it now houses the French Army's Staff College.

Panthéon★★

pl. du Panthéon. Open daily Apr–Sept 10am–6.30pm; Oct–Mar 10am–6pm. Closed 1 Jan, 1 May, 25 Dec. €7. 01 44 32 18 00. Guided tours (1hr30min); reservations required. 01 44 54 19 30.

Successively a church, a necropolis, headquarters of the Commune, and a lay temple, the Panthéon is crowned by Soufflot's dome, and built in the shape of a Greek Cross, It has a fine portico with Corinthian columns and a pediment carved by David d'Angers in 1831. In the crypt are the tombs of the famous.

Opéra Garnier★★

1 pl. de l'Opéra. Open daily 10am–5pm (mid Jul–Aug, 6pm). €9. Closed 1 Jan, 1 May and for special events. 0892 89 90 90. www.operadeparis.fr.

This is the National Academy of Music, and was until 1990 France's premier home of opera. It opened in 1875 under the direction of Charles Garnier, who had dreamed of creating an authentic Second Empire style. But the huge edifice, "more operatic than any opera" (Ian Nairn), magnificent though it was, lacked sufficient originality to inspire a new school of architecture.

Palais de Chaillot★★

pl. du Trocadéro.

Built for the 1937 Exhibition, the Palais houses a variety of museums. From the wide terrace with its statues in gilded bronze, there is a wonderful **view**★★★ of Paris; in the foreground are the Trocadéro Gardens with their spectacular fountains, and beyond the curving river, the Eiffel Tower, the Champ-de-Mars and the École Militaire.

ECCLESIASTICAL ARCHITECTURE

Cathédrale Notre-Dame★★★

r. du cloître Notre-Dame. Open daily 8am–6.45pm, Sat–Sun 8am–7.15pm. No charge. 01 53 10 07 00. www.notredamedeparis.fr.

People have worshipped at Notre Dame for 2000 years and the present building has witnessed the greatest events of French history. Notre-Dame was started in 1163; the bulk of the structure was completed by 1245 when St Louis knighted his son and placed the Crown of Thorns in the cathedral, until the Sainte-Chapelle was ready to receive it. In 1430, the cathedral was the setting for the coronation of Henry VI of England as King of France; in 1558, Mary Stuart was crowned Queen of France by her marriage to François II. It was in a much-dilapidated building that Napoleon Bonaparte crowned himself Emperor. In 1841 Viollet-le-Duc restoration it in an idealised, Gothic style.

Sainte-Chapelle★★★

4 bd du Palais. Open Mar–Oct 9.30am–6pm; Nov–Feb 9am–5pm. €8.50. 01 53 40 60 80. www.monum.fr.

The lightness and clarity of the chapel built by St Louis to house the recently acquired relics of the

Upper chapel, Sainte-Chapelle

© Jeff Schultes/Dreamstime.com

Passion is striking; it was completed in an astonishing 33 months.

Abbaye de St-Germain-des-Prés★★

pl. Saint-Germain des Prés.

The Merovingian kings are buried here in this most venerable of the city's churches. Destroyed by the Normans, it was restored in the 10C and 11C. Around 1160, the nave was enlarged and the chancel rebuilt in the new Gothic style. In 1822 a somewhat over-zealous restoration took place.

Église St-Séverin-St-Nicolas★★

www.saint-severin.com.

This much-loved Latin Quarter Church straddles various architectural styles from High Gothic to the Flamboyant style.

Église St-Eustache★★

2 Impasse Saint-Eustache. suggested donation €3.01 42 36 31 05. http://saint-eustache.org.

This was once the richest church in Paris, its layout modelled on that of Notre-Dame when building began in 1532. St-Eustache took over a century to complete, and the Gothic skeleton is fleshed out with Renaissance finishes and detail.

Église Notre-Dame-du-Val-de-Grâce★★

1 pl. Laveran. Open Mon–Sat 2–6pm, Sun 9am–noon, 2–6pm. 01 43 29 12 31.

Commissioned by Anne of Austria in thanksgiving for the birth of Louis XIV in 1638, the church recalls the Renaissance architecture of Rome; the dome is obviously inspired by St Peter's.

URBAN DESIGN

Since much of medieval Paris was swept away in the 19C, three central districts typify particular stages in the city's evolution.

Le Marais★★★

When Charles V moved to the Hôtel St-Paul in the Marais district in the 14C, the area soon became chic, and Rue St-Antoine the city's finest street. The classic French town house, the *hôtel*, took on its definitive form here. Look for: the

Hôtel Lamoignon★ (24 r. Pavée), the arcaded **Place des Vosges★★★**, the **Hôtel de Sully★** (62 r. Saint-Antoine), **Hôtel Guénégaud★★** (60 r. des Archives), **Hôtel Carnavalet★** (23 r. de Sévigné), **Hôtel de Rohan★★** (87 r. Vieille-du-Temple) and **Hôtel de Soubise★★** (60 r. des Francs-Bourgeois).

La Voie Triomphale (Tuileries to the Arc de Triomphe)★★★

The "Triumphal Way" was laid out under Louis XVI, Napoleon III and during the Third Republic.

Jardin des Tuileries★

Le Nôtre's archetypal French garden; the Riverside Terrace (Terrasse du Bord de l'Eau) became the playground of royal princes and of the sons of the two Napoleons, then of all the children of Paris.

Champs-Élysées★★★

In 1667, the avenue was a service road for the houses facing the Rue du Faubourg-St-Honoré, but very soon refreshment stalls were set up and crowds flocked to the area. In 1836, the **Arc de Triomphe★★★** was completed; the Champs-Élysées became fashionable during the reign of Louis-Napoleon, when high society flocked to restaurants (like Ledoyen's), theatres or to receptions in grand houses (like No 25, with its bronze doors and onyx staircase). Nowadays, luxury shops, expensive cafés, and motor showrooms are more showy, but it remains the capital's rallying point for key national events.

La Défense★★

The skyscrapers and walkways of La Défense are unlike traditional

business districts elsewhere. A 200m/3 937ft terraced podium, punctuated with gardens, fountains and shaded spots; lined with huge towers and works by modern sculptors, it runs from the Seine up to La Grande Arche.

La Grande Arche★★

Open daily Sept–Mar 10am–7pm; Apr–Aug 10am–8pm. €10. 01 49 07 27 27. www.grandearche.com.

The Cathédrale Notre-Dame with its spire could fit into the space between the walls of the arch of Danish architect Johan Otto von Spreckelsen's vast hollow cube.

La Villette★★

The 55ha/135-acre **Parc de la Villette★** houses an impressive urban complex featuring the **Cité des Sciences et de l'Industrie**

POLITICAL AND INTELLECTUAL LIFE

There are a number of buildings and districts that resonate with the history of Parisian political and intellectual life.

Institut de France★★

quai Conti. 01 44 41 44 41. www.institut-de-france.fr.

Dating from 1662, the Institute was founded by Mazarin for scholars from the provinces incorporated into France during his ministry.

Montmartre★★★

Artists and bohemians moved into the steep, narrow lanes and stairways of the "Martyrs' Hill" village in the late 19C. At its centre is the **Place du Tertre★★** with its touristy "art market".

Rising above an incomparable **panorama★★★** over the city, is the exotic outline of the, **Basilique du Sacré-Cœur★★** (*r. du Chevalier-de-la-Barre; 01 53 41 89 00; www.sacre-coeur-montmartre.com*).

Palais du Luxembourg★★

The seat of the Senate, the French Upper House, was built in the early 17C by Marie de' Medici, who wanted a palace to remind her of Florence's Pitti Palace.

Quartier Latin★★★

The Sorbonne, the country's most illustrious university, founded in 1253, lies on the left bank of the Seine in the "Latin" Quarter (so-called because Latin was the language of instruction until the Revolution). Don't miss iconic terrace cafés, including Flore (*172 bd St Germain*), Deux-Magots (*6 pl. St Germain des Prés*) and Procope (*13 r. Ancienne Comédie*).

Quartier de St-Germain-des-Prés★★

Antique dealers, literary cafés, and the night-life of side streets all combine in this former centre of international bohemian life.

MUSEUMS

Most museums are free 1st Sun of month and closed 1 May, 25 Dec.

Musée d'Orsay★★★

62 r. de Lille. Opening times vary. €9 / €12 permanent/ temporary. 01 40 49 48 14. www.musee-orsay.fr.

The upper floor is dedicated to one of the world's finest collections of Impressionist art.

Musée National d'Art Moderne (Centre Georges Pompidou)★★★

pl. Georges-Pompidou. Open daily 11am–9pm. €11-13 01 44 78 12 33. www.centrepompidou.fr.

The renovated and enlarged galleries of the inside-out Pompidou centre encompass a head-spinning array of modern art.

Hôtel de Cluny (Musée national du Moyen Âge)★★

Hôtel de Cluny, 6 pl. Paul Painlevé. Open Wed–Mon 9.15am–5.45pm. €8. 01 53 73 78 16. www.musee-moyenage.fr.

A medieval mansion housing a world-class collection of medieval arts and crafts.

Musée de l'Orangerie★★

Jardin des Tuileries. Open Wed–Mon 9am–6pm. . €7.50. 01 44 77 80 07. www.musee-orangerie.fr.

Monet's vast water lily paintings were conceived specially for the two oval ground floor galleries in the Orangerie.

Musée de l'Armée (Hôtel National des Invalides)★★★

0810 11 33 99. www.invalides.org.

Compelling collections from centuries of military campaigns.

Cité des Sciences et de l'Industrie★★★

30 ave Corentin-Cariou. Open daily 10am-6pm (Sun 7pm).€8–15. 01 40 05 80 00. www.cite-sciences.fr.

La Gare Saint Lazare (1877) by Claude Monet, Musée d'Orsay

This vast science and technology museum offers plenty of hands-on displays for minds of all ages.

Musée du Quai Branly★★

37 quai Branly. Opening times vary. €8.50. 01 56 61 70 00. www.quaibranly.fr.

Modern purpose-built museum near the Eiffel Tower, exhibiting indigenous art from Africa, Asia, Oceania and the Americas.

🍃 Palais de la Découverte★★

ave Franklin-D.-Roosevelt. Opening times vary. €8 (children, €6; under 6yrs free); Planetarium €3. 01 56 43 20 20.

This children's museum is a marvel of ingenuity and interest; clever animators bring the exhibits to life.

Musée des Arts et Métiers★★

60 r. Réaumur. Open Tue–Sun 10am–6pm. €6.50. 01 53 01 82 00. www.arts-et-metiers.net.

National repository of scientific instruments, machines and gizmos housed in an ancient abbey.

Musée Rodin★★★

Open 10am-5.45pm Tue-Sun. €9. 01 44 18 61 10. www.musee-rodin.fr.

The sculptor's most famous works, including The Thinker, the Kiss, and the Burghers of Calais are displayed in a beautiful 18C mansion and its tranquil grounds.

Musée Carnavalet★★

Open Tue–Sun 10am–6pm. 01 44 59 58 58. http://carnavalet.paris.fr/.

A treasure trove of Parisian history in a pair of Marais mansions.

Musée Marmottan-Monet★★

Open Tue–Sun 10am–6pm. €10. 01 44 96 50 33. www.marmottan.com.

The most important body of work by the Impressionist master Monet, is housed in a purpose-built underground gallery.

PARKS AND GARDENS

The city has around 450 parks, public gardens and green spaces. **Bois de Vincennes**, 995ha/4 458 acres including the Parc Floral; **Bois de Boulogne,** 846ha/2 090 acres with the Bagatelle, iris and rose gardens; **Jardin des Plantes**, historic Botanic Gardens of Paris; **Jardin des Tuileries**, with its ancient and modern statuary; **Jardin du Luxembourg**, lovely Latin Quarter park with a circular pond by a palace, and with big play areas for children; **Jardin du Palais-Royal**, a haven of peace and elegance in the heart of Paris.

PARIS

CHÂTEAU DE VERSAILLES★★★

Versailles was the creation of the French monarchy at the moment of its greatest splendour. Consisting of the château, the gardens, and the **Trianon★★**, it is a wonderfully harmonious composition of building and landscape, the definitive monument of French Classicism.

Practical Information

Getting There

▶**TGV**: *Versailles-Chantiers.*
Versailles is only 18km/11mi from Paris, easily reached by road or train (take line C of the RER to Versailles-Rive gauche, or SNCF rail link from St-Lazare to Versailles-Rive droite or from Montparnasse to Versailles-Chantiers). The château and park form one side of the town of Versailles. Place du Marché is the town's focal point, with its delightful restaurants, shops, cafés, brasseries and weekly markets.

A BIT OF HISTORY

Built originally in 1624 as a modest hunting lodge, the young Louis XIV saw Versailles as the perfect place to build his own opulent château far from the mobs of Paris, whilst showcasing the glory of the French arts and the absolute power of the Sun King. Construction began in 1661, and continued for almost a century.
Revolution and Restoration – .
When the Revolution drove Louis XVI from Versailles, the artworks were moved to the Louvre and the furnishings auctioned off. Today, the palace is listed as a UNESCO World Heritage Monument.

HIGHLIGHTS

Grands Appartements★★★
(*Open Tue–Sun Apr–Oct 9am–6.30pm; Nov–Mar 9am–5.30pm. Closed 1 Jan, 1 May, 25 Dec. €18. 01 30 83 78 00. www.chateauversailles.fr*)
–The king held court in the Grands Appartements three times a week.
Cour de Marbre★★ – The marble paved heart of Louis XIII's chateau was for the King's private use.
Galerie des Glaces (Hall of Mirrors)★★★ – The mirrors in this splendid reception room catch the rays of the setting sun.
Appartement de la Reine★★ – The Queen's suite was constructed for Louis XIV's wife Queen Marie-Thérèse, who died here in 1683.
Chambre de la Reine – In France, royal births were public events: in this room 19 children of France were born, among them Louis XV and Philip V of Spain.
The Gardens (Jardins)★★★ (open daily 8am–8.30pm) – A masterpiece of French landscape, celebrating the monarch's supreme authority through Classical symbolism.
Domaine de Marie-Antoinette★★ (*Open daily except Mon: Apr–Oct, noon–6.30pm (8.30pm for the gardens); Nov–Mar, noon–5.30pm (8pm for gardens). €10. 01 30 83 76 20. www.chateauversailles.fr*) – A visit to Marie-Antoinette's Estate located on the northern edge of the Grand Park is unmissable: here Louis XVI's wife would relax, away from the Court's rigorous etiquette.
Château★★ – This pink marble and porphyry palace is widely regarded as the most refined set of buildings within the Versailles compound.
Ville de Versailles★★ – The town of Versailles was built as an annex to the château to house the numerous people who served the court.

CHÂTEAU DE CHANTILLY★★★

A synonym for elegance, Chantilly is home to wonderful art collections, a great park and forest, and the cult of the horse as well as the château itself.

Practical Information

Getting There

▶**TER/RER**: *Chantilly-Gouvieux.* Chantilly is 50km/31mi N of Paris. When you arrive, the château is well signposted.

CHÂTEAU★★★

Open Apr–Oct 10am–6pm; Nov– Mar 10.30am–5pm. €14-18. Guided tours (30min). 03 44 27 31 80. www.chateaudechantilly.com.

Anne de Montmorency, the great Constable of France who served six monarchs (from Louis XII to Charles IX), had a Renaissance castle built here in 1528 on the foundations of an earlier 14C building. In 1560 a charming little château (Petit Château) was built to the south of the main building.

Louis II of Bourbon, known as the Great Condé, and his descendants later made the state rooms of the Petit Château into their living quarters; there is much to delight the eye here, including Rococo woodwork, manuscripts, silver caskets and icons.

The greatest treasure is in the Library (*Cabinet des Livres. Open daily 9.15am–5pm*); this is the **Limbourg** brothers' sumptuously illuminated *Book of Hours for the Duke of Berry* (*Les Très Riches Heures du Duc de Berry*) dating from about 1415 (on display in reproduction). During the Revolution, the château was dismantled to first-floor level, the Petit Château was ruined and the park laid waste.

When Louis-Joseph de Condé died, the Duke of Aumale rebuilt the great edifice (1875–83) in a neo-Renaissance style.

The château houses a **museum★★** (*open same hours as château; (park and gardens) €6; 03 44 62 62 62*) with a wealth of manuscripts, furniture, paintings, and sculpture. The landscaped **English-style garden★** (*Apr–Oct, 10am–8pm (last admission 6pm),Nov–Mar, 10.30am–6pm; €7 (under-18s €3); 03 44 27 31 80*) was laid out on the surviving relics of Le Nôtre's park in 1820.

Grandes Écuries★★

Open Mar–Nov 10am–5pm.

Built in 1721 by Jean Aubert for Louis-Henri of Bourbon, the Great Condé's great-grandson, the stables house the **Musée Vivant du Cheval et du Poney★** (⊙‒closed for restoration until 2014. 03 44 27 31 80; www.museevivantducheval.fr), which has stalls from the time of the Duke of Aumale, historic harnessing, costumes, and all kinds of objects associated with horse riding. Riding displays take place in the central rotunda.

Over 3 000 horses are stabled and trained in and around Chantilly; race meetings and hunts carry on the tradition begun on 15 May 1834 when France's first great official race meeting was held, and maintain Chantilly's reputation as the country's thoroughbred capital. The French Derby (*Prix du Jockey Club*) is held here every April.

CHÂTEAU DE CHANTILLY

DISNEYLAND RESORT PARIS★★★

Opened in 1992 under the name EuroDisney, Disneyland Paris is an enormous holiday resort outside the city with hotels, a 27-hole golf course, Disney Village entertainment and shopping complex, and campsite.

Practical Information

Getting There

▶**TGV**: *DisneyLand Paris.*
The resort is located 30km/18.6mi east of Paris in Chessy. RER: (line A) Marne-la-Vallée–Chessy; by shuttle from Orly and Roissy-Charles de Gaulle Airports; by car via autoroute A 4 direction Metz; exit at junction 14 and follow sign to Disneyland.

ENTRANCE

Entry – Hours and prices vary - see www.disneylandparis.co.uk.
Tips – To avoid long queues visit popular attractions during the parade, or get a **Fast Pass** with a 1hr time slot.
Booking a show – head for City Hall, Town Sq, Disneyland Park.
Disabled guests – see City Hall (Disneyland Park) or info desk inside Walt Disney Studios Park.
Lockers and storage – At the entrance and Main Street Station.
Rental – Photography, pushchairs and wheelchairs in Town Square Terrace (Disneyland Park) and in Front Lot (Walt Disney Studios Park).
Animals – Must be left in the Animal Care Center by the car park.
Baby Care Center, Lost Children, Near the Plaza Gardens Restaurant (Disneyland Park) or in Front Lot (Walt Disney Studios Park).

DISNEYLAND PARK★★★

The 55ha/136 acre-Disneyland Paris site comprises five themed territories or lands. A daily **Disney Parade★★**, carries all the favourite Disney cartoon characters on a procession of floats. The Main Street Electrical Parade★★ adds extra illuminations to the fairy-tale setting. **Main Street USA**, the core of the resort, is styled as a late 19C American town. A steam train, the **Euro Disneyland Railroad★**, travels across the park and through the **Grand Canyon Diorama**. **Frontierland** – **Big Thunder Mountain★★★** is the classic Old West rollercoaster, while **Phantom Manor★★★** conceals hundreds of mischievous ghosts.
Adventureland – Marauders at **Pirates of the Caribbean★★★**, is the biggest draw, followed by an Indiana Jones experience and **La Cabane des Robinson★★**.
Fantasyland – Favourite fairy tales come alive beneath the gaze of **Le Château de la Belle au bois dormant★★**.
Discoveryland – Past discoveries and future dreams carry you through **Space Mountain★★★ – Mission 2**, **Star Tours★★★** and other rides

DISNEY STUDIOS PARK

Dedicated to the wonders of the cinema this park takes you backstage at **Animagique★★★** and other rides.

DISNEY VILLAGE★

Shops, restaurants and bars, plus **La Légende de Buffalo Bill★★**, a cabaret dinner that tells the story of the Wild West, complete with horses, bison, cowboys and Indians.

CHÂTEAU DE VAUX-LE-VICOMTE★★★

This splendid château, one of the masterpieces of the 17C, lies at the heart of French Brie, a countryside of vast fields broken with occasional copses.

Practical Information
Getting There

▶**RER:** *Melun.* Châteaubus shuttle from station. Vaux-le-Vicomte is 60km/37mi SE of Paris.

A BIT OF HISTORY

Nicolas Fouquet had been Superintendent of Finances since the days of Mazarin and built a vast personal fortune. In 1656, he decided to construct at Vaux a palace to symbolise his success; as architect he chose Louis Le Vau, as interior decorator Charles Le Brun, as landscaper André Le Nôtre. By 1661, Vaux looked as it does today. Fouquet was a man of lavish tastes, but sadly lacking in political judgement. He had counted on taking Mazarin's place right up to the moment when Louis XIV took power into his own hands. Furthermore, he had alienated Colbert, and, even worse, had made advances to one of the king's favourites, Mlle de La Vallière. By May, the decision to place him under arrest had already been taken. On 17 August, the unwitting Fouquet threw the most sumptuous of festivities among the Baroque splendours of Vaux. Hoping to impress the young Louis, he succeeded only in offending the king more deeply by the extravagance of the proceedings. Dinner arrived on a solid gold service, at a time when the royal silverware had been melted down to repay the expenses of the Thirty Years' War. On 10 September, Fouquet was arrested, his property confiscated, and his brilliant team of designers put to work on Versailles.

CHÂTEAU

Open mid-Mar–mid-Nov 10am–6pm. Day pass €16 (children, €13). 01 64 14 41 90. www.vaux-le-vicomte.com.

Le Vau's château is the definitive masterpiece of the early Louis XIV style. It is to be understood as the central feature of a grandiose designed landscape. Le Brun's talent is typified in his king's Bedroom, which rivals the splendour of the Royal Apartments at Versailles. In the **gardens★★★**, Le Nôtre showed himself to be a master of perspective.

Château de Vaux-le-Vicomte

© Arthus Bertrand/Château de Vaux-le-Vicomte

FONTAINEBLEAU★★★

The 12C Capetian kings' hunting lodge in a vast forest, grew into an extraordinarily majestic palace and park listed as a World Heritage site.

Practical Information

Getting There

▶TER: *Fontainebleau-Avon.* Fontainebleau and its château are in the midst of a large forest, 64km/39.7mi S of Paris.

A BIT OF HISTORY

The woodland covers 25 000ha/ 62 000 acres, much of it is a forest of sessile oaks, Norway pines and beeches, traversed by a network of well-signposted footpaths.
In spite of the forest's fame and popularity, it is the palace begun by François I that has made the reputation of Fontainebleau.

CHÂTEAU★★★

77300 Fontainebleau. **Château open Wed–Mon: Oct–Mar 9.30am–5pm; Apr–Sept 9.30am–6pm. Closed 1 Jan, 1 May, 25 Dec. €10. Gardens open daily Nov–Feb 9am–5pm; Mar–Apr and Oct 9am–6pm; May–Sept 9am–7pm. 01 60 71 50 60. www.musee-chateau-fontainebleau.fr.*

From the days of the Capetian kings to the time of Napoleon III, the Palace of Fontainebleau has been lived in, added to and altered by the sovereigns of France. Napoleon Bonaparte called Fontainebleau "the house of Eternity" and furnished it in Empire style. In 1528, François I commissioned more alterations bringing in gifted and prolific artists who are known as the **First School of Fontainebleau**. He also acquired works of art including Leonardo's Mona Lisa and paintings by Raphael. This era endowed the palace with many of its most splendid features: on the outside, the Court of the White Horse or Farewell Court (**Cour du Cheval-Blanc ou des Adieux★★**), the famous horseshoe staircase, where Napoleon bade his men farewell on 20 April 1814, after abdicating; on the inside, the François I Gallery (**Galerie François I★★★**) and the Ballroom (**Salle de Bal★★★**).

Musée Napoléon I★

Exhibits include portraits, silverware, arms, medals, ceramics, coronation robes, uniforms and personal memorabilia from the Emperor's military campaigns and daily life (guided tour only).

Gardens★

Open daily Nov–Feb 9am–5pm; Mar–Apr and Oct 9am–6pm; May–Sept 9am–7pm. Closed 25 Dec, 1 Jan. 01 60 71 50 70. www.musee-chateau-fontainebleau.fr.

Highlights are the **Grotte du Jardin des Pins★** (ponds and bucolic landscapes); the **Jardin anglais★** where the Bliaut or Blaut fountain, which gave its name to the palace, plays in the middle of the garden; and the **park,** created by Henri IV, sixty years before the installation of the Grand Canal at Versailles. This dazzling sight was a great novelty for the *Ancien Régime.*

CHARTRES★★★

Chartres' magnificent cathedral, the "Acropolis of France" (Rodin), has beckoned pilgrims across the endless cornfields of the Beauce for 800 years. Druids once worshipped here; there is also evidence of the pagan cult of a holy spring, and possibly also of a mother-goddess, whom the first missionaries may have Christianised as a forerunner of the Virgin Mary.

Practical Information
Getting There
▶**TER**: *Chartres*.
The cathedral dominates the old quarter, Quartier St-André.

A BIT OF HISTORY
In the picturesque old town (**le Vieux Chartres★**) the old mill-races and laundry-houses have been restored, and 17C houses have kept their embossed doorways topped by a bull's-eye. The most attractive townscape is to be found in the St-André quarter, by the riverbanks, and in Rue des Écuyers and Rue du Cygne. Chartres attracted pilgrims at an early date, first of all to Our Lady of the Underground Chapel (*Notre-Dame-de-Sous-Terre*), then to the cathedral.

HIGHLIGHT
Cathédrale Notre-Dame★★★

Open daily 8.30am–7.30pm. Guided tours Nov–Mar 2.45pm; Apr–Oct Sun–Mon 2.45pm, Tue–Sat noon and 2.45pm. 02 37 21 75 02.

Reconstructed in just 25 years after the Romanesque edifice burnt down in 1194, the building has a unity of style possessed by few other Gothic churches. However, the architect wisely kept two Romanesque masterworks, the Old Bell Tower (Clocher vieux) of 1145 and the Royal Doorway, **Portail**

Royal★★★, of the west front, with its expressive sculpted figures. The cathedral's interior is lit by its superb 12C and 13C stained glass (**vitraux★★★**) depicting 5 000 figures. The windows are the greatest achievement of this art form. "Chartres blue" is famous for its clarity and depth, seen at its best in the wonderful Notre-Dame-de-la-Belle-Verrière Window (*first window on the south side of the ambulatory*).

ADDITIONAL SIGHTS
Musée des Beaux-Arts★ (*29 cloître Notre Dame*). **Église St-Pierre★** – **stained glass★** (*5 pl. St-Pierre*)

EXCURSIONS
Rambouillet

53km/33mi SW of Paris, via the A 13 and A 12. i Hôtel de Ville, pl. de la Libération, 78120 Rambouillet. 01 34 83 21 21. www.rambouillet-tourisme.fr.

The combination of château, park and forest makes Rambouillet one of the main sights in the Île-de-France. Since 1883 it has been the official summer residence of the President of the French Republic.

Forêt de Rambouillet★
Wildlife thrives in this vast forest wit its huge network of walking and cycle tracks, over 20 lakes, and villages with old houses.

COMPIÈGNE★★★

In 1429, Philippe le Bon (the Good), Duke of Burgundy, hoped to incorporate Picardie into his realm by means of a joint operation with the English. Disgusted with the inertia of the French Court in the face of this threat, Joan of Arc came to Compiègne on her own initiative and ordered the French line of defence along the Oise to be reinforced. But on 23 May 1430, she was seized by the Burgundians. Wary of possible consequences, Philip the Good sold her on to the English; one year later she was burnt at the stake in Rouen.

Practical Information

Getting There

▶**TER**: *Compiègne*. Hidden in the Forest of Compiègne, the town is 60km/37mi E of Beauvais.

CHÂTEAU★★★

Open Wed–Mon 10am–6pm. Closed 1 Jan, 1 May, 25 Dec. €6.50 (free 1st Sun in the month). 03 44 38 47 02. www.musee-chateau-compiegne.fr.

Louis XV was dissatisfied with the crumbling buildings inherited from his great-grandfather, and in 1738 he had the château reconstructed. While the place was still a building site, it formed the background to the first meeting (1770) between Louis XVI and Marie-Antoinette.

Musée de la Voiture et du Tourisme★★

In addition to 18C and 19C coaches, the vehicles exhibited include: the **Mancelle** of 1898, a steam mail-coach designed by Amédée Bollée; the **Jamais Contente** ("Never Satisfied") of 1899, an electric car with tyres by Michelin, the first to reach 100kph/62mph; a Type C **Renault** of 1900, one of the first cars to have enclosed bodywork (by Labourdette); and a **Citroën** half-track of 1924.

EXCURSIONS

Clairière de l'Armistice★★

8km/5mi E.

This is the place where, on 11 November 1918, the armistice was signed that put an end to WWI at 11am on the same day. The Musée Wagon de l'Armistice displays the railway carriage where the document was signed.

Château de Pierrefonds★★

14km/8.7mi SE.

The stronghold looks every bit the medieval castle as it looms over the village crouching at its feet. However, it is mostly 19C. It was dismantled during the reign of Louis XIII, and Napoleon I bought the castle ruins. In 1857 Louis Napoleon, inspired by romantic ideals, commissioned **Viollet-le-Duc** (1814–79) to restore it

Beauvais★★

Beauvais lies on the A 16 in southern Picardy 03 44 15 30 30. www.beauvaistourisme.fr.

An extraordinary spire-less Gothic **cathedral★★★** stands at the centre of this fortified city. Built over three centuries, its roof collapsed several times and was never completed.

LILLE★★★

Lively, convivial capital of French Flanders and close to the Belgian border, the city successfully combines vibrant forward-looking appeal with its splendid Baroque heritage.

Practical Information

Getting There

▶**TER**: *Lille Europe/Flandres.*
Lille is a large city close to the Belgian border, 220km/138mi N of Paris, and 110km/69mi from Calais. It is easily reached by high-speed TGV and Eurostar trains, which arrive in the centre, or by road on A 1 from Paris and A 25 from the English Channel.

A BIT OF HISTORY

A trading city from medieval times, Lille grew rich on the wool and cloth trade. In the 15C Lille belonged to Burgundy, but in 1667, it fell to Louis XIV, and became the capital of France's northern provinces. In October 1914 Lille surrendered to the Germans; some 900 buildings were destroyed. During WWII, the French troops capitulated on 1 June 1940. From the 1960s to 1990s, a plan to restore the old district successfully preserved its artistic heritage.

LA CITADELLE★

The Citadel is a military base. Guided tours only. May–Aug Sun 3pm. Contact tourist office for details and reservation.

Vauban's "Queen of citadels" was part of Louis XIV's defences along the Flemish border.

LE VIEUX LILLE★★★

Beautiful façades of 17–18C buildings line the bustling old streets where there are numerous little shops and brasseries.

VIEILLE BOURSE★★

The ornate Old Exchange was built in 1652–3 and presents a Flemish take on the Louis XIII style. The building proclaims the importance of textile manufacturing in the city

MUSÉE DES BEAUX-ARTS★★★

Open daily except Tue: Mon 2–6pm, Wed–Sun 10am–6pm. Closed public holidays. €6.50 (free 1st Sun in the month). 03 20 06 78 00. www.palaisdesbeauxarts.fr.

Important collection includes masterpieces of French Flemish, Italian, and Spanish art from the Middle Ages to the 20C, Highlights include works by Goya, and Rubens' vast 'Descent from the Cross".

HOSPICE COMTESSE★

Open daily except Tue: Mon 2–6pm, Wed–Sun 10am–6pm. 03 28 36 84 00.

Dating from 1237, the old poorhouse hospital houses a collection of Flemish and Dutch paintings from the 15–17C.

MUSÉE D'ART MODERNE★★

Open Sun at 10.30am. Consult website for individual exhibitions. 03 20 19 68 68. www.musee-lam.fr.

Set in a verdant sculpture park in the suburb of Villeneuve d'Ascq the huge structure of brick and glass cubes houses works by Braque, Picasso in Cubist mode, Miro', and Modigliani's almond-eyed ladies.

NORMANDY & BRITTANY

The old dukedom of Normandy extends from the edge of the Paris Basin towards the Breton peninsula. To many it is reminiscent of southern England with its shared heritage of Norman architecture and pastoral countryside. There is great diversity in the buildings here; masons carved the fine Caen limestone into great churches while humbler structures demonstrate diverse construction. Long populated by Celts, Brittany has affinities with the other Celtic lands fringing the Atlantic. Its identity is expressed in the Breton language (akin to Welsh), traditions and landscape. The province's mysterious past makes itself felt in the prehistoric remains, menhirs, dolmens and megaliths. Granite distinguishes Breton building and is used to great effect.

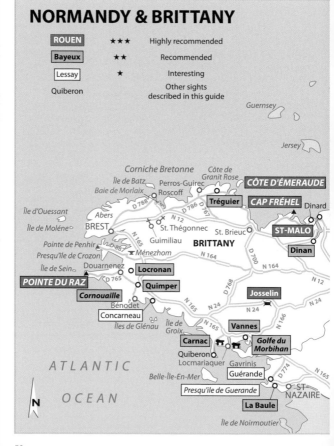

NORMANDY & BRITTANY

ROUEN	★★★	Highly recommended
Bayeux	★★	Recommended
Lessay	★	Interesting
Quiberon		Other sights described in this guide

NORMANDY

On either side of the Seine Valley extends Upper Normandy (Haute-Normandie), centred on the historic city of Rouen. In northern Lower Normandy is the Cotentin Peninsula, which projects into the English Channel dividing the Bay of the Seine from the Gulf of St-Malo. To the southeast lies the *bocage* (pasture) and the Pays d'Auge, famous for its ciders, cheeses and calvados.

BRITTANY

Brittany's rugged, indented coastline is known as "Armor" (country near the sea) by the Gauls. Its cliffs, rocky headlands and offshore islands are battered by Atlantic breakers, while its narrow drowned valleys, *abers*, and sandy bays are washed by tides of exceptional range. Inland is the "Argoat" (country of the wood), once thickly forested, now a mixture of *bocage*, heath and moor.

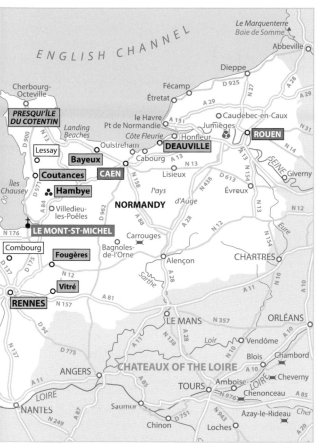

ROUEN★★★

Rouen, capital of Upper Normandy, has undergone a remarkable campaign of restoration that has given new life to the old city's network of narrow, winding streets lined with magnificent half-timbered houses. With its skyline of towers, spires and fine buildings, it offers a wealth of artistic delights and is a city of first-rate museums – the Musée de Beaux-Arts alone is worth the trip. Rouen sits in a lovely valley surrounded by high hills, from which there are extensive views over the city and the Seine. Established at the lowest point on the Seine that could be successfully bridged, Rouen developed into a hugely successful port and industrial centre.

Practical Information

Getting There

▶**TER**: *Rouen-Rive-Droite.*
The city stands on both banks of a curve in the River Seine, 133km/83mi NW of Paris.

A BIT OF HISTORY

Rouen has been important since Roman times owing to its position as the lowest bridging point on the Seine; the alignment of its two main streets (Rue du Gros-Horloge and Rue des Carmes) still reflects the layout of the early city.

Although Rouen is the birthplace of a number of scientists, it is men of letters and artists who have contributed most to Rouen's fame. Gustave Flaubert (1821–80) lived in and around the city. His major works include *Madame Bovary* (1857), in which the village of Ry (20km/12.4mi east) is described under the name of Yonville.

HIGHLIGHTS

Cathédrale Notre-Dame★★★

Open Apr–Oct Mon 2–6pm, Tue–Sat 9am–7pm, Sun 8am–6pm; Nov–Mar closes noon- 2pm. www.cathedrale-rouen.net.

This is one of the finest achievements of the French Gothic; it was rebuilt after a fire in 1200. Thanks to the generosity of John Lackland, Duke of Normandy, as well as the king of England, reconstruction was swift. The spaciousness of the interior is striking. The great edifice seems to have been under repair for most of its existence, and restoration work is perpetually underway.

Vieux Rouen★★★

The cathedral and the Rue du Gros Horloge are at the heart of Vieux Rouen. The old town's narrow streets, many of them pedestrianised, are lined with more than 800 timber-framed houses, large and small, elegant or picturesquely askew. Until 1520, the upper floors jutted out for reasons of economy and greater floor-space. Bustling **Rue du Gros-Horloge★★**, lined with old houses, is one of the city centre's main attractions. The Gros-Horloge clock on its arch has only one hand; next to it is the belfry, from the top of which there is a fine view over the city.

Rue St-Romain★★ is one of the most fascinating streets, with many timber-framed houses dating

Houses in Vieux Rouen

from the 15–18C. No 74 is a Gothic building with 15C windows.

Place du Vieux-Marché★

This modern complex on the edge of the Old Town is the site where Joan of Arc, aged 19, was burned at the stake as a heretic; 25 years later she was rehabilitated. In the centre of the square, the great Cross of Rehabilitation, marks the spot where Joan of Arc was burned. There is also a covered market and a church incorporating **stained-glass windows★★** of 16C date.

Église St-Maclou★★

When compared with the cathedral, the church shows how the Gothic style evolved. It was begun in 1437 and is a fine example of pure Flamboyant style. At the north corner of the west front is a fountain with two manikins performing the same act as their counterpart at Brussels, albeit with somewhat less finesse.

Aître St-Maclou★★

This is a rare example of a medieval plague cemetery, enclosed by half-timbered buildings decorated with macabre Dance of Death carvings.

Église St-Ouen★★

Built in the 14C, this former abbey church is the peak of achievement of the High Gothic style.

Musée des Beaux-Arts★★★

Open Wed–Mon 10am–6pm. Closed public holidays. €5. 02 35 71 28 40. www.rouen-musees.com.

The museum has a magnificent collection of 15–20C painting, as well as fine sculpture.

Musée de la Céramique★★

Open Wed–Mon 10am–1pm, 2–6pm. €3. 02 35 07 31 74. www.rouen-musees.com.

Rouen pottery was hugely popular in the 18C. The 17C Hotel d'Hocqueville houses its outstanding faïence collections.

ROUEN

Palais de Justice★★

This splendid 15C and early 16C Renaissance building housed the Exchequer of Normandy (law courts). It was badly damaged in August 1944. The **main court** excavations have revealed a 12C Jewish place of worship. Note the Renaissance façade.

Musée Le Secq des Tournelles★★

Open Wed–Mon 10am–1pm, 2–6pm. €3. 02 35 88 42 92. www.rouen-musees.com.

The Wrought Ironwork Museum is housed in old Église St-Laurent, a fine Flamboyant building, and contains an exceptionally rich collection of ironmongery.

Jardin des Plantes★

2.5km/1.5mi. Leave Rouen by avenue de Bretagne. Open daily 8.30am-8pm in summer; 8am–5.45pm in winter. No charge. 02 35 88 48 35. www.rouen.fr/jardinplantes

This beautiful 10ha/25-acre park, contains around 3 000 plant species inside the conservatories and **tropical hothouses** and a further 5 000 out in the open air. A star attraction is the **Victoria Regia**, a giant water lily.

CAEN★★★

Tough and enduring, the city of Caen rebuilt itself after near destruction by bombing during WWII. Today the city proudly preserves an impressive historical legacy, while being committed to peace and the future.

Practical Information
Getting There

▸**TER**: *Caen*. 15km/9mi inland from the ferry terminal at Ouistreham; 94km/59mi from Le Havre.

A BIT OF HISTORY

After the invasions of the Norsemen in the 9C and 10C, and the establishment of the duchy of Normandy, Benedictines built the first major religious buildings in Normandy. Caen owes its architectural heritage to William, Duke of Normandy, and his wife Mathilda, who chose it as their residence. They married in 1053, against papal opposition, which arose because they were cousins. This led to their excommunication

until they made amends by William founding the Abbey for Men, and Mathilda the Abbey for Women.

HIGHLIGHTS
L'Abbaye-aux-Hommes★★

Guided tours (1hr30min) daily 9.30am, 11am, 2.30pm and 4pm. €3. 02 31 30 42 81.

The abbey church was founded by William the Conqueror; begun in 1066, it took 12 years to build. The great lantern-tower over the crossing is probably the work of Lanfranc and William themselves; in its simple perfection, it is a masterpiece of Romanesque art.

Église St-Étienne, Abbaye-aux-Hommes

© Robby Verschueren/iStockphoto.com

Château Ducal★

Guided tours Jul–Aug Fri.
No charge. 02 31 27 14 14.

This great fortress, perched on a bluff overlooking the city, was built by William in 1060, and subsequently strengthened and extended. From its ramparts there are extensive views over Caen. The château houses **Caen's Musée des Beaux-Arts★★**.

Abbaye-aux-Dames★★

Open daily 2–5.30pm. Guided tours (1hr) daily 2.30pm and 4pm. No charge. 02 31 06 98 98.

The Norman building was founded by Mathilda in 1062 as the church of the Abbey for Women.

Le Mémorial★★

Open mid-Feb–mid-Nov daily 9am–7pm; rest of year hours vary slightly. €18.80. 02 31 06 06 45.
www.memorial-caen.fr.

The WW2 memorial erected by the city, which was destroyed in 1944 in the Battle of Normandy, takes the form of a Museum for Peace. The façade of the sober building of Caen stone, facing Esplanade Dwight-Eisenhower, is marked by a fissure that evokes the destruction of the city and the breakthrough of the Allies in the Liberation of France and Europe from the Nazi yoke. It stands on the site of the bunker of W Richter, the German general, who on 6 June faced the British-Canadian forces. The **Mur de la Liberté** (Wall of Freedom) pays tribute to the hundreds of thousands of American soldiers who fought for freedom in Europe.

Musée de Normandie★★

Château. Open daily 9.30am–6pm. Closed Tue (Nov–May) and public holidays. 02 31 30 47 60.
www.musee-de-normandie.caen.fr.

This great museum displays the history of the Normandy region, its culture and people.

Église St-Pierre★

A mix of Gothic and Renaissance architecture make this church quite fascinating. The main church was built in the 13–14C and the Renaissance **east end★★** was added in the early 16C.

CAEN

Sailing in Deauville

© OT Deauville–Patrice Le Bris

Hotel d'Escoville★

The tourist office is is a fine example of a typical 16C Caen townhouse.

Musée des Beaux-Arts★★

Located within the château. Open Wed–Mon 9.30am–6pm. Closed public holidays. €3–7. 02 31 30 47 70. www.mba.caen.fr.

The Fine Arts Museum lies within the precinct of William the Conqueror's castle. Large religious paintings and imposing historical and allegorical scenes hang in vast halls, bathed in light, whereas works of religious fervour and smaller paintings are essentially displayed in the small cabinets.

EXCURSIONS
Deauville⚱⚱⚱

94km/59mi from Rouen, 43km/27mi from Le Havre, Deauville lies on the Côte Fleurie. Place de la Mairie. 02 31 14 40 00. www.deauville.org.

Deauville, a popular resort since the mid-19C, is known for the luxury and refinement of its various establishments and the elegance

of its entertainments. Events of the summer season include racing, the polo world championship, regattas, tennis and golf tournaments, galas, and the international yearling fair. In early September, the city hosts the **American Film Festival**.

La Suisse Normande★★

The Suisse Normande takes in the Orne Valley as well as the Noireau, the Vère, the Rouvre and the Baize. Place du Tripot, Clécy. 02 31 69 79 95. www.ot-suisse-normande.com.

The whimsically-named area straddles the **Orne** and **Calvados** regions. It has neither mountains nor lakes in the Swiss sense and does not even include Normandy's highest points. Instead, the River Orne cuts its way through the ancient rocks of the Armorican Massif, producing steep banks surmounted by rock escarpments, drawing in tourists who come for its landscapes and outdoor pursuits. The Suisse Normande lies between the towns of Condé-sur-Noireau, Thury-Harcourt and **Putanges**. **Clécy★** is the tourist centre of the region, close to some of the most picturesque spots in the Orne Valley.

BAYEUX★★

The Bayeux Tapestry still presents its unique record of the events of 1066 and the Battle of Hastings. Its home, the former capital of the Bessin, was the first French town to be liberated (7 June 1944) in WWII. The town escaped damage during the war, leaving a cathedral and old houses – many tastefully restored – as well as a pedestrian precinct, for explorers in the 21C.

Practical Information

Getting There

▶**TER**: *Bayeux.*
30km/18.6mi from Caen, the town is just inland from the Omaha and Arromanches Landing Beaches.

A BIT OF HISTORY

Bayeux was the "cradle of the Dukes of Normandy" and home of William, who invaded and conquered England.
Almost 900 years later the invasion came the other way when on 6 June 1944 the Allies landed on the Normandy beaches. On 7 June Bayeux became the first French town to be liberated and here on D-Day, General de Gaulle made his first speech on French soil.

BAYEUX TAPESTRY★★★

(Tapisserie de la Reine Mathilde)

Open daily mid-Mar–mid-Nov 9am –6.30pm (May–Aug, 7pm); mid-Nov–mid-Mar 9.30am–12.30pm, 2–6pm. Closed 1 Jan, 2nd week in Jan, 25 Dec. €8 (children, €4). 02 31 51 25 50. www.tapisserie-bayeux.fr.

Beautifully displayed in a specially designed building, it is most likely that this extraordinary masterpiece of embroidery was made by talented nuns – in fact noble Saxon women who had chosen the convent – in England, soon after the Conquest in 1066. Using a style similar to today's strip cartoon, its 72 scenes recount the epic of the Norman invasion with striking storytelling; it is an irreplaceable source of information on the ships, weapons, clothes and ways of life of the mid-11C.

CATHÉDRALE NOTRE-DAME★★

Guided tours of Cathedral 10.30am, 11.45am, 2.30pm, 3.45pm, 5pm. €4. 02 31 51 28 28.

The Romanesque vaulted crypt and lower nave date from the 11C. The 12C added intricate stonework, while later elegant additions include the superb chancel.

MUSÉE-MÉMORIAL DE LA BATAILLE DE NORMANDIE★

Open mid-Feb–Apr 10am–12.30pm, 2–6pm; May–Sept 9.30am–6.30pm; Oct–Dec 10am–12.30pm, 2–6pm. Closed . €7 (children, €4). 02 31 51 46 90.

Situated on the line that separated the British and American sectors in 1944, the Memorial Museum recalls the dramatic events of summer 1944. Two large galleries, named Overlord and Eisenhower, explain the chronology of the Battle of Normandy and give a detailed account of the equipment and uniforms of the various nations involved in the conflict. A great variety of heavy equipment is exhibited.

MONT-ST-MICHEL★★★

Mont-St-Michel has been called "the Wonder of the Western World"; its extraordinary site, its rich and influential history and its glorious architecture combine to make it the most splendid of all the abbeys of France. At the beginning of the 8C St Michael appeared to Aubert, the bishop of Avranches. Aubert founded an oratory on an island then known as Mont Tombe. This oratory was soon replaced by an abbey, which adopted the Benedictine Rule in the 10C, thereby assuring its importance. Two centuries later the Romanesque abbey reached its peak of development. In the 13C, following a fire, a great rebuilding in Gothic style took place, known as *la Merveille* – the Marvel. Even though the English beseiged it during the Hundred Years' War, the Mount did not fall.

Practical Information

Getting There

02 33 60 14 30.
www.ot-montsaintmichel.com.
▶*TGV*: *Dol de Bretagne TGV, then direct bus; or TGV to Rennes then TER to Pontorson, then direct bus.*

123km/76mi SW of Caen via A84, D43, then follow the coast. Mont-St-Michel is a granite island about 900m/984yd round and 80m/262ft high. As the bay is already partially silted up, the mount is usually to be seen surrounded by huge sand banks which shift with the tides and often reshape the mouths of the neighbouring rivers. It is linked to the mainland by a causeway built in 1877. i

L'ABBAYE (ABBEY)★★★

Open May–Aug 9am–7pm; Sept–Apr 9.30am–6pm. Closed 1 Jan, 1 May, 25 Dec. €9. 02 33 89 80 00.

The architecture of the Abbey was determined by the constraints imposed by the rock on which it stands. Crowned as it is by the Abbey church and the buildings of the Merveille (c.1225), the result bears little resemblance

to the conventionally planned Benedictine monastery. Highlights include the **Église★★** and **La Merveille★★★**; the latter is group of buildings on the north side of the mount. The **salle des Hôtes★** is a masterpiece of High Gothic; the **Refectory★** is filled with light from its recessed windows. From the gardens there is a **view** of the north face of the mount.

EXCURSIONS
Coutances★★

76km/47.2mi N of Mont-St-Michel via A84, D9, then D7.

On its hilltop overlooking the woodlands and pastures *(bocage)* of the Cotentin Peninsula, Coutances, the religious and judicial centre of the peninsula, is dominated by its remarkable cathedral.
Cathédrale Notre-Dame de Coutances★★★ – *Open year-round; times vary, http://cathedralecoutances.free.fr.*
The present building (1220–75) made use of some of the remains of Geoffroy de Montbray's Norman cathedral, as well as drawing on the experience gained in the then

Mont-St-Michel

© Vasilyev Dmitry/Fotolia.com

recently-completed abbey at Fécamp. The west front is framed by two towers, whose soaring, slender lines are emphasised by the tall, narrow corner turrets, with very little decoration to distract the eye from its heavenward climb. The interior is as light as it is lofty: light floods in through 16 windows and a magnificent octagonal lantern tower over the crossing.

Jardin des Plantes★ – *Open Jul & Aug 9am–11.30pm; Apr–Jun and Sept 9am–8pm; rest of the year 9am–5pm. No charge. 02 33 19 08 10.*
The garden's entrance is flanked by an old cider press on one side and the **Quesnel-Morinière Museum** on the other. The terraced promenade traverses the sloping gardens with its many flower beds and pine trees. The obelisk in the centre commemorates a former mayor, Jean-Jaques Quesnel-Morinière.

Abbaye d'Hambye★★

25km/15.5mi SE of Coutances.
43 place de la République, Villedieu.
02 33 61 76 92.

The 12C abbey of Hambye is charmingly sited in the green valley of the Sienne. Its ruins evoke the serenity of Benedictine life. The abbey is nearly as complete as Mont-St-Michel. The best-preserved buildings include the chapterhouse, sacristy and parlour.
Église Abbatiale★★ – *Open Apr–Oct Wed–Mon 10am–noon, 2–6pm. €4.50. 02 33 61 76 92.*
The abbey buildings are dominated by the church, with slender columns and sharply pointed arches around the choir (1180–1200). The chapterhouse is a masterpiece of Norman Gothic.

Lessay★

21km/13mi N of Coutances.

Lessay, a small town in the middle of the Cotentin Peninsula, lies on the edge of moorland country whose harsh beauty was sung by Barbey d'Aurevilly (1808–89), who helped establish a distinct Norman literature. The **Église abbatiale**★★, founded in 1056, is one of the most perfect examples of Romanesque architecture in Normandy.

COUTANCES

QUIMPER★★

Quimper is in Brittany's far west and is the capital of Finistère. It lies in a pretty valley at the junction (*kemper* in Breton) of two rivers, the Steir and the Odet.

Practical Information

Getting There
▶TGV: *Quimper.*
72km/45mi SE of Brest, and 69km/43mi NW of Lorient.

A BIT OF HISTORY

The town was first of all a Gaulish foundation, sited on the north bank of the Odet estuary. Towards the end of the 5C BC, Celts sailed over from Britain (hence the area's name of Cornouaille, i.e. Cornwall) and drove out the original inhabitants. This was the era of the legendary King Gradlon and of the fabulous city of Ys which is supposed to have sunk beneath the waves of Douarnenez Bay. The town has a long tradition of making faïence (fine earthenware), and is a centre of Breton folk art.

VISIT

The **Cathédrale St-Corentin★★** is dedicated to Saint Corentin, who helped found Brittany after the fall of the Roman Empire. Much of the interior decoration was stripped away during the Revolution and the Reign of Terror (1793), leaving the lime-washed interior with a bright and appealing atmosphere. The **medieval town★** lies between the cathedral, the Odet and its tributary, the Steyr. There are fine old houses with granite ground floors and timber-framed galleries. The **Musée des Beaux-Arts★★** contains a collection of European

painting from the 14C to the present, while the **Musée Départemental Breton★**, housed in the former palace of the Bishops of Cornwall, presents a synthesis of the archaeology, folk and decorative arts of Finistère.

LA CORNOUAILLE★★

Although the area today is limited to the coast and hinterland west of its capital Quimper, Cornouaille was once the Duchy of medieval Brittany, stretching as far north as Morlaix. Brittany's "Cornwall" juts out into the Atlantic just like its counterpart across the Channel. The spectacular coastline with its two peninsulas, **Presqu'île de Penmarch★** and **Cap Sizun★★**, culminates in the breathtaking **Pointe du Raz★★★**.

Locronan★★ used to be a major centre for woven linen used for sails by the French, Spanish and English navies. As a result, the centre of the village is endowed with splendid examples of Breton architecture that mostly date to the 18C, and was largely built at the behest of wealthy sail merchants. In the 19C, competition from Vitré and Rennes, coupled with the general economic downturn of the period, brought ruin and stagnation for Locronan.

Raz Point★★★ is one of France's most spectacular coastlines. Its jagged cliffs, battered by the waves and seamed with caves, rise to over 70m/220ft. The growth of **Concarneau★** was based on its importance as a fishing port. Trawlers and cargo-boats moor in the inner harbour, while the outer harbour is lively with pleasure craft. The **walled town★★** was one of the strongholds of the ancient county of Cornouaille.

RENNES★★

This city of artistic, architectural and historical interest, founded by the Gauls, became capital of Brittany in the 16C.

Practical Information

Getting There

▶**TGV**: *Rennes.*
Rennes lies 105km/66mi N of Nantes, and 152km/95mi W of Le Mans.

A BIT OF HISTORY

Famous Breton knight **Bertrand Du Guesclin** entered a tournament at Rennes at age 17 and later defended the city against an English siege in 1356. In December 1720 an accidental fire caused by a lamp falling into a carpenter's wood shavings destroyed much of the town.

HIGHLIGHTS
Palais du Parlement de Bretagne★★

Brittany's Parliament initially had its seat in Rennes for part of the year and Nantes for the other, before finally the decision was taken in 1561 to establish a single seat in Rennes.

Le Vieux Rennes★

The old town was devastated in 1720 by a great fire that raged for eight days and engulfed almost 1 000 houses. Enough buildings were spared to make a walk through the old part of Rennes an architecturally rewarding experience. The medieval houses crowd together in the narrow streets, identifiable by their timber construction, their projecting upper floors and their sculptured decoration. No 3 r. St-Guillaume,

called the **Du Guesclin House**, has a deeply carved door flanked by figures of St Sebastian and one of his tormentors. The **Hôtel de Brie★** (*8 r. du Chapitre*) is of such refinement that it has been attributed to Mansart.

Les Champs Libres★

This cultural centre brings together three institutions: the Musée de Bretagne, the Espace des Sciences and the library.

Musée des Beaux-Arts★

The permanent collection rooms at the Museum of Fine Arts have recently been restyled, extended and enriched with new works that have never been shown. It now contains fine examples of painting, sculpture, drawing, prints and objects from the 14C to the present.

EXCURSIONS
Fougères★★

A large town on the border with Normandy, Fougères was a traditional centre for shoemaking. Today, the main attraction is its massive 11–15C fortress beside the River Nançon.

Vitré★★

This is the best-preserved "old world" town in Brittany; its fortified castle, its ramparts and its small streets have remained just as they were 400 or 500 years ago, giving the town a picturesque and evocative appeal.

Combourg★

This picturesque old town stands at the edge of Lac Tranquille, a large lake, and is dominated by an imposing feudal castle.

ST-MALO★★★

The site★★★ of the walled town of St-Malo on the east bank of the Rance is unique in France, making the ancient port one of the country's great tourist attractions.

Practical Information

Getting There

▶**TGV**: *Saint Malo.* 70km/44mi NNW of Rennes.

OLD TOWN★★

The town's prosperity began in the 16C. In 1534, **Jacques Cartier** had set out from here on the voyage which led to the discovery and naming of Canada; very soon a thriving commerce had begun, based on furs and fish. In 1689, Vauban was commissioned to strengthen the defences of St-Malo. Within the walls is the old town, almost entirely rebuilt in its original form after near-total destruction in 1944. The houses along the Rue de Dinan and those facing the walls are particularly fine.

Sights of interest in town include the **aquarium★★** and a **museum★** exploring the history of the town

CÔTE D'ÉMERAUDE★★★

Brittany's picturesque northern shore from Cancale (**headland – Pointe du Grouin★★**) to **Le Val André★★** is known as the **Emerald Coast** and includes some famous beaches at Dinard, St-Lunaire, Paramé and St Malo. The Emerald Coast scenic road runs through major resorts (Dinard, St-Malo) and offers detours to the tips of the numerous headlands, including **Fort de Latte★★**, **Cap Fréhel★★★** and **Cap d'Erquy★** from which the views of the jagged coastline are in places quite spectacular.

Dinard★★★ – On the magnificent estuary of the River Rance opposite

St-Malo, Dinard, once a small fishing village, is an elegant resort with sheltered sandy beaches and luxuriant Mediterranean vegetation flourishing in the mild climate. The resort took off when a wealthy American called Coppinger built a château here in 1850. He was followed two years later by a British family, who attracted many of their fellow-countrymen. By the end of the 19C its reputation rivalled that of Brighton; classy villas and chic hotels sprang up to serve an international smart set.

Promenades lead from **Plage de l'Écluse★** (or **Grande Plage**), a fine beach bordered by hotels, the casino and convention centre, to the **Plage du Prieuré**. From the **Pointe du Moulinet★★**, the view extends as far as Cap Fréhel to the west and the ramparts of St-Malo to the east. In summer, the **Promenade du Clair de Lune★** with its pretty parterres and Mediterranean plants forms an attractive setting for evening concerts.

Fort La Latte★★ – This stronghold, built originally in the 14C, and restored in the early 20C, has kept its feudal appearance. It stands on a spectacular **site★★**, separated from the mainland by two gullies, which are crossed by drawbridges.

Dinan★★ – Dinan is a gem of a town, surrounded by ramparts and guarded by a castle. The houses of the old town cluster together behind the long circuit of walls, built by the Dukes of Brittany in the 14C.

VANNES★★

Vannes is a pleasant city in the shape of an amphitheatre at the highest point to which tides flow at the head of the Morbihan Gulf. The picturesque old town, enclosed in its ramparts and grouped around the Cathedral, is a pedestrian zone of elegant shops in old half-timbered town houses.

Practical Information

Getting There
▶**TGV**: *Vannes*. Vannes is a lively, popular resort on the SE coast of Brittany. The historic centre is by the cathedral and Pl. Henri IV.

A BIT OF HISTORY

Vannes was the capital of the **Veneti** tribe, one of Gaul's most powerful peoples, intrepid sailors who crossed the seas to trade with the inhabitants of the British Isles. After they suffered a terrible defeat at sea in 56 BC at the hands of the Romans, losing 200 ships in a single day, Brittany remained a backwater for a very long time. In the 9C, Vannes became Nominoé's capital of a united Brittany.

OLD TOWN★★

The walled area (**remparts★**) around the cathedral still has the air of a medieval town with its old half-timbered houses built over a granite ground floor with pillars, arcades and lintels. Among these, is a 14C market hall known as **La Cohue★**. Its upper floor was the ducal law-court right up until 1796, the ground floor as a market until 1840. There are fine houses with granite pilasters and 16C slate-hung gables bordering **Place Henri IV★** and in the adjoining streets.

GOLFE DU MORBIHAN★★

The indented coastline and the play of the tides around the countless islands make this one of Brittany's most fascinating maritime landscapes. The best way to see the gulf is therefore by boat. About 40 islands are privately owned and inhabited. The largest are Île d'Arz and the Île aux Moines, both communes. The Île d'Arz is about 3.5km/2mi long and has several megalithic monuments. The Île aux Moines is 7km/4.3mi long and the most populous. It is a quiet and restful resort where camellias and mimosas grow among palm trees.

Aquarium du Golfe★ – More than 50 pools house about 1 000 fish from all over the world

Château de Suscinio★ – The former summer residence of the Dukes of Brittany.

Port-Navalo★ – The little port and seaside resort guards the entrance to the Gulf. There are fine views.

Locmariaquer★★ – This group of megaliths is an important part of a programme of conservation and restoration of megalithic sites.

Presqu'île de Quiberon★ Quiberon used to be an island, but over the years, sand has formed an isthmus linking it to the mainland.

Château de Josselin★★ – This famous stronghold of the Rohan family, who have owned the castle for more than 500 years and still live here in the private apartments, has stood guard over the crossing of the Oust for 900 years.

Carnac★ – In the bleak Breton countryside just north of the little town of Carnac (pop 4 150) are some of the world's most remarkable **megaliths★★**.

BELLE-ÎLE★★★

The name alone is enticing, but the island's beauty surpasses expectations. This, the largest of the Breton islands, is a schist plateau measuring about 84sq km/32sq mi; 17 km/10.5mi long and 5–10km/3–6mi wide. Valleys cut deep into the high rocks, forming beaches and harbours. Farmland alternates with wild heath, and whitewashed houses stand in lush fields.

NORMANDY & BRITTANY

MUST SEE

Practical Information

Getting There

▶**TGV**: *Auray.* Regular car ferries link Quibéron (Brittany) and Le Palais in 45min are operated by SMN (*08 20 05 60 00. www.smn-navigation.fr*).
Passenger-only 🚤 **boats** operate in summer between Le Palais and Lorient (Brittany).

A BIT OF HISTORY

Belle-Île's interest lies as much in its history as in its wonderful coastline. In the Middle Ages the island belonged to the Counts of Cornouaille and was often raided by pirates (French as well as Dutch and English). From the 16C the island was constantly in danger of an English attack, as its proximity to the French coast gave it great strategic importance. The fortifications were substantially increased, but the English fleet eventually took Belle-Île's citadel in the Seven Years' War.

HIGHLIGHTS
Le Palais

The island's capital – "Palais" to its friends – is the hub of island life. The natural harbour is dominated by the star-shaped citadel and fortifications, known as **Citadelle Vauban★** (*open daily Apr, June, Sept–Oct 9.30am–6pm; Jul and Aug 9am–7pm; Nov–Mar: 9.30am–5pm. €6.50 (child €3.50). 02 97 31 85 54).* The proximity of Belle-Île to the

ports of the south coast of Brittany and the mouth of the Loire gave it great importance in the fight for the control of the high seas conducted by England and France. In 1658, chancellor Fouquet consolidated the defences and installed 200 new batteries.
From 1682, the great military engineer Vauban adapted the citadel to the latest technology of war, converting an old chapel into a powder-magazine with a projecting roof to fend off broadsides, rebuilding the old arsenal as well as laying out an officers' walk with a gallery giving fine sea views.

Côte Sauvage★★★

The Côte Sauvage, literally "wild coast", runs from the Pointe des Poulains to the Pointe de Talud. Battered by the Atlantic waves, the schist has been sculpted into spectacular coastal scenes.
Port-Donnant★★ has a splendid sandy beach between high cliffs but is known for its great rollers and perilous currents.
The **Aiguilles de Port-Coton★★** are pyramids hollowed out into caverns and grottoes. The different colours of the rock have been exposed by the action of the sea.

ADDITIONAL SIGHTS
Sauzon★
Pointe des Poulains★★
Port-Goulphar★

NANTES★★★

Nantes is Brittany's largest city, sited at the point at which the mighty Loire becomes tidal. Islets in the river facilitated the building of bridges, making Nantes the focus of trade between Lower Brittany and Poitou.

Practical Information
Getting Around
▶**TGV**: *Nantes.*
Three tramway lines and over 60 bus routes make for easy exploration.

A BIT OF HISTORY

Nantes was a sizeable trading port from medieval times, reaching its full importance in the 15C under Duke François II. On 13 April 1598, Henri IV signed the **Edict of Nantes** in its cathedral, establishing equality between Catholics and Protestants. Louis XIV revoked the Edict in 1685, provoking the Huguenot exodus to England, Holland and Germany.
In the early 18C Nantes grew to be France's premier port by trading sugar and slaves between the West Indies and Africa, until the loss of French territories abroad and the abolition of slavery led to decline. In the 19C and 20C, the construction of large downstream harbour facilities has ensured Nantes' continuing prosperity.

CHÂTEAU DES DUCS DE BRETAGNE★★

4 pl. Marc Elder. Museum €5. 02 51 17 49 48. www.chateau-nantes.fr.

"God's teeth! No small beer, these dukes of Brittany!" exclaimed Henri IV on seeing this massive stronghold for the first time. Much rebuilt and strengthened by Duke François II, the interior reflects the castle's role as a palace of government and residence, known for its high life of feasts and jousting.

ADDITIONAL SIGHTS
Other sights of interest include the **Musée des Beaux-Arts★★**, **Muséum d'Histoire Naturelle★★**, the 19C **town★**, **Palais Dobrée★**, **Musée Jules-Verne★**, **Musée archéologique★**, **Jardin des Plantes★** and **Ancienne Île Feydeau**.

EXCURSIONS
Planète Sauvage★★ – Over 1500 animals roam this 140ha/350-acre safari park. There are two circuits: one on foot, the other by car.
La Baule☖☖☖ – Water-sports, tennis, a casino, golf, and a crescent of sandy beach, make this one of the most popular resorts on the Atlantic. 19C houses hide behind modern development. Other nearby resorts such as **La Baule-les-Pins★★**, **Le Pouliguen★** and **Pornichet★**, with their pleasure boat harbours, make ideal bases for exploring the **"Côte d'Amour"** and the **Guérande Peninsula**.
La Côte Sauvage – This 'Wild Coast' stretches from Pointe du Croisic in the west to Pointe de Penchâteau in the east. A road and footpaths skirt the rocky coastline; its sandy bays and caves, such as the cave of the Korrigans (the little elves of Breton legends), are accessible only at low tide.
Guérande★ – A well preserved medieval walled town overlooking the salt marshes.

CHÂTEAUX OF THE LOIRE

Rising far to the southeast in the Massif Central, France's longest river, the Loire, was once a busy waterway. Many of the towns along its banks – Orléans, once the Loire's foremost port, Blois, Tours, Langeais and Saumur – all bear traces of this heritage. But river navigation was never easy and, once the railways came, the Loire was sidelined. Nowadays the region is famous for its magnificent Renaissance châteaux adorning the banks of the Loire's tributaries, the Indre and the Cher.

GEOGRAPHY

The Loire Valley has been called "a home-spun cloak with golden fringes", a reference to the fertile valleys of the Loire and its tributaries and the low plâteaux that separate them. From Orléans onwards the Loire is at its best, with gentle landscapes and soft light.

HISTORY

After the Romans left, the Franks occupied the region. Until the 12C most of the area was held by powerful barons. After 1202 King Philippe-Auguste took charge, after seizing the territory from King John of England. In the late medieval period the region was involved in the Hundred Years' War, with much of the Loire falling into English hands again. However, during the 16C the great château-building period began, driven by the new ways of thinking about art and architecture spawned by the Renaissance and exemplified by the magnificent edifices at Chenonceau, Azay, Blois and Chambord, their elegance and exuberance contrasting with the stern fortresses of an earlier age, such as the great castle at Angers. Around Amboise and Tours are troglodytic dwellings.

ECONOMY

The Loire Valley is a major agricultural region, cultivating vines, cereals, rapeseed, sugar beet and sunflowers. Manufacturing plays its part, as does tourism, based on the châteaux and the cathedrals of Orléans and Tours.

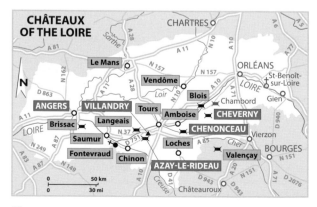

ANGERS★★★

This dynamic and cultured city on the River Maine was once the capital of a mighty Plantagenet kingdom encompassing all of England and half of France.

Practical Information

Getting There

▶**TGV**: *Angers-Saint-Laud.*
Anger is mid-way between Nantes (88km/55mi SW) and Le Mans (94km/59mi NE).

CITY

On 9 June 1129, Geoffrey Plantagenet married William the Conqueror's granddaughter Mathilda, whose inheritance of both Normandy and England made her quite a catch. Twenty-three years later another significant marriage took place, between Henry II, Geoffrey's son, and Eleanor of Aquitaine, the divorced wife of Louis VII. Two months later Henry became king of England, thereby extending the frontiers of the Angevin state to Scotland in the north and the Basque country in the south. By contrast, Paris seemed little more than an overgrown village in comparison with Angers. In 1203, King Philippe Auguste incorporated Anjou into the French kingdom, together with Normandy, Maine, Touraine and Poitou.
Château★★★ – Built by Louis IX from 1228 to 1238, this splendid fortress was designed to deter any threat from the nearby Dukes of Brittany. Its 17 towers in alternating courses of dark schist and white freestone are suitably forbidding. A purpose-built gallery at the heart of the château displays the **Tenture de l'Apocalypse**★★★ tapestry.
Cathédral★★ – The cathedral stands in a charming district.
Musée Jean-Lurçat et de la Tapisserie contemporaine★★ –

The former St John's Hospital, founded in 1174, now houses a series of tapestries known as **Le Chant du Monde**★★ in the vaulted hospital ward.
Monastery buildings★ – The abbey buildings, extensively restored in the 17C and 18C, house local government offices.

EXCURSIONS

Château de Brissac★★ – The château, set in a fine park shaded by magnificent **cedar trees**★, was damaged during the Wars of Religion.
Château de Serrant★★★ – Built over a period of three centuries, 16–18C, this sumptuous moated mansion has massive domed towers and magnificently furnished **apartments**★★★
Le Mans★★ – Le Mans is renowned as the home of the 24hr Grand Prix, the "*24 Heures de Mans*". The walled old town was part of the Plantagenet estates, and has long been the site of trade fairs and festivals, including a Spring Fair (late Mar–early Apr), a great Four-Day Fair (mid-Sept) and an Onion Fair (first Fri in Sept). As a result, Le Mans has a fine gastronomic tradition. The **historic centre**★★ lies within its 4C Gallo-Roman ramparts, some of the few extant in western France. The **cathedral**★★ is magnificent. Rebuilt in 1991, the **Musée des 24 Heures du Mans – Circuit de la Sarthe**★★ displays 110 vehicles, celebrating the history of the race. The race circuits are south of Le Mans between N 138 and D 139.

SAUMUR★★

Lying on the banks of the Loire, beneath its imposing fortress, Saumur is famous for its Cavalry School, its wines (especially sparkling wines), its medal makers and its mushrooms (production of which is 42 percent of the national total).

Practical Information

Getting There

▶**TGV**: *Saumur.*
Saumur lies 65km/40mi SE of Angers, 32km/20mi NE of Chinon.

A BIT OF HISTORY

In the 11C Saumur was fought over by the Count of Blois and the Count of Anjou. In 1203, the town was captured by Philippe Auguste. In the late 16C and early 17C the town became a great centre of Protestantism. In 1611, a general assembly of the Protestant churches was held there after the death of Henri IV. Louis XIII grew alarmed at the Protestant danger and had the town walls demolished in 1623. The Revocation of the Edict of Nantes in 1685 dealt Saumur a fatal blow; many inhabitants emigrated and the Protestant church was demolished.
École d'application de l'arme blindée et de la cavalerie (EAABC) – Saumur is home to the famous Cadre Noir cavalry unit, who now put on displays of formation horse riding. In the museum are armoured vehicles and interesting mementoes of officers who served in the cavalry of the African Army between 1830 and 1962.

OLD TOWN★

The narrow twisting streets between the castle and the bridge still follow their original course. Along the main shopping street, rue St-Jean, and in the square, **place St-Pierre**, half-timbered houses and 18C mansions with wrought-iron balconies stand side by side. The **town hall★** and **Église Notre-Dame-de-Nantilly★** are both worth a look. The sturdy **château** is surprisingly decorated in the style of a country house.

EXCURSIONS

Fontevraud l'Abbaye★★★ – The Order of Fontevraud was founded in 1099, and despite the ravages of history, Fontevraud Abbey remains the largest group of monastic buildings in France; note the lofty vaulting of the abbey church and the impressive kitchen.
Chinon★★ – Chinon occupies a sunny site on the Vienne, surrounded by fertile countryside. The **old town★★** has kept its medieval and Renaissance appearance. The spur overlooking the town was the site of a fortress long before Henry II of England built the present **castle★★**.
Château de Langeais★★ – Seen from outside, the château still looks like a medieval fortress, with drawbridge, towers, battlement sentry-walk and almost windowless walls. Inside, the **apartments★★★** have kept their medieval layout. The great Angevin ruler Foulques Nerra built a sturdy keep here in 994 to command the Loire Valley; now in ruins in the park of the château, it is arguably the oldest such building in France. The château itself was built to protect France from Brittany. In 1491, the marriage of Charles VIII of France and Anne of Brittany ended the threat.

TOURS★★

With a civilised air, under dazzling Loire Valley skies, built in bright white tufa and roofed in black slate, the ancient city of Tours makes a perfect base for excursions into the château country.

Practical Information
Getting There
▶TGV: *Tours.*
127km/79mi E of Angers.

A BIT OF HISTORY
The place originated in Gallic times, becoming an important centre of trade and administration under the Romans in the 1C AD. Throughout the Middle Ages it was an important religious centre and was the capital of Tours (Touraine) county; indeed, Tours became the capital of France under Louis XI.

HIGHLIGHTS
Château★

25 ave André Malraux.

Not comparable in grandeur to the more typical Loire châteaux, this is a heterogeneous collection of buildings from the 4–19C.
The lower parts of the wall on the west side go back to Roman times and here too is the 11C residence of the Counts of Anjou; the Guise Tower (Tour de Guise) with its machicolations and pepper-pot roof is of the 13–15C, while the dormer-windowed Governor's Lodging (Logis du Gouverneur) is 15C and other additions were made as recently as the 17–19C.

Cathédrale St-Gatien★★
Following a fire, the cathedral was rebuilt from 1235 onwards. The work lasted all of 250 years. As a result it demonstrates the complete evolution of the Gothic style, from a chevet in the early phase, to a Flamboyant west front, and even a lantern crowning the twin towers that is characteristic of the Early Renaissance. The stained glass ranges in date from the 13C (high windows in the chancel) via the 14C (transept rose windows) to the 15C (rose window of the west front).

La Psalette★

Open Apr daily 10am–12.30pm, 2–5.30pm (Sun am by appointment); May–Aug daily 9.30am–12.30pm, 2–6pm (Sun am by appointment); Sept–Mar daily except Mon, Tue and Sun am, 10am–12.30pm, 2–5.30pm. Closed 1 Jan, 1 May and 25 Dec. €3. 02 47 47 05 19.http://la-psalette. monuments-nationaux.fr.

This is the name given to the cathedral cloisters where canons and choir-master used to meet. The tiny Archive Room (Salle des Archives) of 1520 and the vaulted Library (Librairie) are reached by means of a spiral staircase, Gothic in structure but Renaissance in the way in which it is detailed.

Place Plumereau★
This busy and picturesque square is located at the old "meeting of the ways" (carroi); it is bordered by fine 15C residences built of stone and timber. On the corner with the Rue du Change and the Rue de la Monnaie is a carved corner post with a somewhat mutilated depiction of the Circumcision.

MuséedesBeaux-Arts★★

18 pl. François Sicard. Open daily except Tue 9am–6pm. Closed 1 Jan, 1 May, 14 Jul, 1 and 11 Nov, 25 Dec. €4. 02 47 05 68 73.

In the former Bishops' Palace (17–18C), its rooms are decorated with Louis XVI panelling and silk hangings made locally. It houses works of art from the châteaux at Richelieu and Chanteloup (now the site of the Parc de la Pagode), as well as from the great abbeys of Touraine. The collection of paintings consists mostly of French works of the 19–20C, but there are also two outstanding Mantegnas, a Resurrection and Christ in the Garden of Olives (late 15C).

Musée du Compagnonnage★★

8 r. Nationale and a walkway. Open daily 9am–12.30pm, 2–6pm (Jan–Jun and mid Sept–Dec daily except Tue). Closed public holidays. €5. 02 47 21 62 20.

The city long prided itself on its craftsmen, and even at the end of the 19C there were still three guilds jealously guarding their traditions. The museum contains many fine examples of the work of master craftsmen, such as roofers and slaters, blacksmiths and locksmiths, saddlers and carpenters.

EXCURSIONS
Amboise★★

The busy town centre rises from the south bank of the Loire. 02 47 57 09 28. www.amboise-valdeloire. com. On the edge of town kids will love the Parc des Mini-Châteaux (La Menaudière; 0 2 47 23 44 57;

www.mini-chateaux.com) and the Parc de la Pagode de Chanteloup (Route de Blere. 02 47 57 20 97. www.pagode-chanteloup.com).

Amboise lies at the foot of an escarpment, on which stand the fragmentary but still substantial remains of one of the great royal châteaux – best viewed from the north side of the river.
The **château★★** was part of the 15C Golden Age of Amboise. Charles VIII was born here in 1470; from his 22nd year onwards he carried on the work begun by his father, Louis XI. In 1496 Charles returned from his Italian campaign, bringing with him artisans and a taste for antiquity and a decorative sense unknown at the time in France. However, his castle suffered later at the hands of Louis XIII's troops, and on orders of Napoleon's Senate.

Clos-Lucé★

Very near the château. Open daily: Jul–Aug 9am–8pm; Sept–Oct 9am–7pm; rest of year times vary. €13.50 (winter €11). 02 47 57 00 73. www.vinci-closluce.com.
To this manor house of red brick with stone dressings François I invited **Leonardo da Vinci** in 1516. At Amboise, Leonardo devoted his time to organising royal festivities, designing a château at Romorantin, planning the drainage of the Sologne and amusing himself designing mechanical inventions, some of which have now been constructed and are in a display of "fabuleuses machines".

Château de Chenonceau★★★

14km/8.7mi S of Amboise, the château straddles the River Cher.

Open daily: Jul–Aug 9am–8pm; rest of year times vary. €11-16. 02 47 23 90 07. www.chenonceau.com.

Chenonceau is a jewel of Renaissance architecture, built 1513–21 on the site of a fortified mill on the River Cher by Thomas Bohier, François I's treasurer. It is a rectangular building with corner-towers; it stands on two piers of the former mill resting on the bed of the Cher. The highlight is Catherine de Medici's two-storey gallery, built on the elegant 60m/197ft multi-arched bridge spanning the river and provides one of the region's iconic views.

Loches★★

Loches lies on the River Indre, 49km/30.4mi SE of Tours. pl. de la Marne. 02 47 91 82 82. www.loches-tourainecotesud.com

Modern Loches lies mostly on the left bank of the Indre, at the foot of the fortified bluff that dominates the valley and that set natural limits to the growth of the medieval town.
The **medieval town★★** is contained within a continuous wall some 1 000m/1 100 yd long. To the south, the great square **keep ★★** was built by the Counts of Anjou in the 11C on even earlier foundations. To the north is the **château★★**, begun at the end of the 14C as an extension of a 13C watchtower. Part of the royal apartments are medieval (Vieux logis), part Renaissance (Nouveau logis). It was in the great hall of the Vieux Logis on 3 and 5 June 1429 that Joan of Arc persuaded the Dauphin to undertake his coronation journey to Reims.

Château d'Azay-le-Rideau★★★

Azay lies about 25km/15.5mi from Tours in the direction of Chinon. Open daily: Oct–Mar 10am–5.15pm; Apr–Jun and Sep 9.30am–6pm; Jul–Aug 9.30am–7pm. €9.50. 02 47 50 02 09. http://azay-le-rideau.monuments-nationaux.fr.

In a sylvan setting, moated by and reflected in the waters of the Indre, this castle is one of the most gracious and beguiling of Loire châteaux. It was built for financier Gilles Berthelot from 1518–29 in French Gothic style. Its defences – Disneyesque pepperpot towers and turrets – are purely decorative.

Jardins et Château de Villandry★★★

Coming from Langeais, take D 16. Coming from Tours, take D 288, which crosses the Loire at Savonnières.Open: château and gardens open daily, all year, from 9am, closing hours vary; €9.50 (château and gardens); 02 47 50 02 09. www.chateauvillandry.fr.

In 1536, Jean Le Breton, France's former ambassador in Italy, rebuilt the château in Renaissance style. Nowadays, however, Villandry is known more for its terraced **gardens★★★**, which were restored to their Renaissance glory from 1906 onwards by Dr Joachim de Carvallo, founder of the French Historic Houses Association. Inside the **château★★** is Louis XV panelling in the Great Salon and Dining Room, and a surprising 13C Mudejar ceiling from Spain, brought here by Dr Carvallo.

BLOIS★★

Blois looks northwards to the Beauce and south to the Sologne, and is situated at a point on the Loire where the limestone landscapes around Orléans give way to the chalk country of Touraine downstream. The town was transformed from 1503 onwards when the kings moved there from Amboise, bringing with them all the trades devoted to satisfying the royal taste for luxury.

Practical Information

Getting There

▶**TER:** *Blois.*
Blois is roughly mid-way between Tours (66km/41mi SW) and Orléans (61km/38mi NE).

CHÂTEAU★★★

Open daily at 9am, closing times vary. Closed 1 Jan and 25 Dec. €9.50. 02 54 90 33 33. www.chateaudeblois.fr.

The whole development of secular French architecture from feudalism to the Classicism of Louis XIII's reign can be traced at Blois, from medieval round towers and spiral stairways to the transition from the Gothic to the Renaissance, evident in the Louis XII Wing of 1498–1501. Louis had been born at Blois in 1462 and, together with Anne of Brittany, carried out a number of improvements. 15 years later, the François I wing exemplifies the ornamented style of the first phase of the French Renaissance. The much-modified interior includes, on the first floor, Catherine de Medici's study with its secret cupboards, and on the second floor, Henri III's apartments, scene of the murder of Henri de Guise.

Maison de la Magie Robert-Houdin★

1 pl. du Chateau. Opening hours vary. €8 (children 6-17 years: €5). 02 54 90 33 33. www. maisondelamagie.fr.

Set up in a 19C *hôtel particulier* facing the château, the 'Maison de la Magie' dedicated to the great Robert-Houdin, deals with the history of magic and serves as a national centre for the art of illusionism.

EXCURSIONS
Suèvres★

11km/7mi NE along N 152.

The ancient Gallo-Roman city of Sodobrium hides its picturesque façades below the noisy main road on the north bank of the Loire. A huge porch (*caquetoire*) where the parishioners could pause for a chat opens into the roadside **church of St-Christophe.**
The houses at *No 9* and *No 14 bis* in rue Pierre-Pouteau date from the 15C. Turn right into picturesque rue des Moulins, where footbridges span the stream. The washing place is at the corner of rue St-Simon, where there are traces of an old fortified gate. Further on through the trees (*left*) emerges the two-storey Romanesque tower of the **Église St-Lubin**.

Château de Chambord★★★

S of the Loire, between Beaugency and Blois, Open daily: Jan–Mar and Oct–Dec 10am–5pm; Apr–Sept

9am–6pm. Closed 1 Jan, 1 May, 25 Dec. €9.50. 02 54 50 40 00. www. chambord.org. 02 54 33 39 16.

The first of France's great Classical palaces, Chambord stands in a vast park enclosed by a wall within the enormous forest of Sologne. At the age of 21, and flushed with triumph from his victory over the Swiss, François I had a vision of a dream castle to be built as a palace of pleasure and status symbol for a Renaissance prince. Leonardo da Vinci may have helped with the plans for this fabulous château, which was begun in 1519. After the king suffered defeat and captivity at Pavia in 1525, he judged it more suitable for a monarch to live close to his capital, at either Fontainebleau or St-Germain-en-Laye. The château's famous double staircase, undoubtedly conceived by Leonardo da Vinci, is a masterpiece of interlocking spirals opening onto internal loggias. The extraordinary roof terrace was where the king and his entourage spent much of their time watching tournaments and festivals or the start and return of the hunt; its nooks and crannies lent themselves to the confidences, intrigues and assignations of courtly life.

Château de Cheverny★★★

17km/10.5mi S of Blois. Open daily, hours vary. €8.70 (children, €5.70) 02 54 79 96 29. www.chateau-cheverny.com. 02 54 79 95 63. There's also an exhibition on the cartoon character Tintin.

Cheverny was built between 1604 and 1634 with that simplicity and distinction characteristic of the Classical architecture of the reigns of Henri IV and Louis XIII.

Vendôme★★

Rue Poterie runs north–south across the town centre. Hotel du Saillant, Parc Ronsard. 02 54 77 05 07. www.chateaux-valdeloire.com/ Vendome.html.

With its moated centre, Vendôme is a fascinating and picturesque town crowded with bell towers, gables and steep slate roofs. It stands on a group of islands in the River Loire that fit together like a jigsaw puzzle. Its Benedictine **Abbaye de la Trinité★**, founded in 1040, was once an important site for pilgrims, who came to venerate the supposed Holy Tear Christ shed at Lazarus' tomb.

Château de Valençay★★

The château is on D 956, between Tours and Vierzon. Open daily, mid Mar–mid-Nov; Jul & Aug 9.30am–7pm, rest of year hours vary. €11. 02 54 00 15 69. www.chateau-valencay.fr.

Vast and superbly proportioned, this classic 16C Renaissance pile stands in an exquisite park. The defensive features of the original medieval castle were retained as decoration. In 1803, the estate was acquired by **Charles-Maurice de Talleyrand-Périgord**, paid for mostly by Napoleon, as a glittering background to international diplomacy conducted by its owner. Inside are opulent furnishings of the Régence and Empire periods, including 18C Savonnerie carpets and the round table from the Congress of Vienna.

BLOIS

ALSACE LORRAINE CHAMPAGNE

Alsace is France's window onto Central Europe. Its capital, Strasbourg, was part of the Holy Roman Empire; today, it is the seat of the Council of Europe, and as one of the continent's first "Eurocities", Alsace has become a symbol of intranational European economy. Together with the other picturesque towns and villages along this left bank of the Rhine, it has an unmistakably Germanic character. Lorraine owes its name to ancient Lotharingia, once part of Charlemagne's kingdoms.

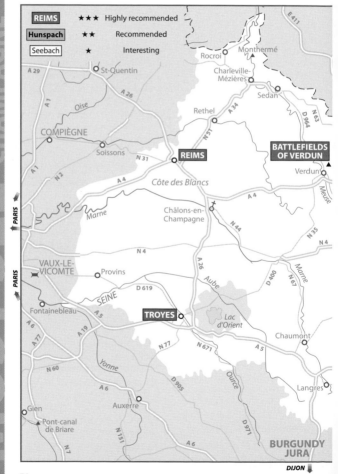

REIMS	★★★	Highly recommended
Hunspach	★★	Recommended
Seebach	★	Interesting

E 411

Rocroi — Monthermé

A 29 — St-Quentin

Charleville-Mézières

A 26

Oise — Sedan — N 63

COMPIÈGNE

Rethel — A 34 — D 964

A 1

Soissons — N 31

N 2 — A 4 — REIMS — BATTLEFIELDS OF VERDUN

Côte des Blancs — Verdun

Marne — Châlons-en-Champagne — A 4 — Meuse

N 44 — N 35

N 4 — A 26 — N 4

VAUX-LE-VICOMTE — Provins — Aube — A 400 — Marne

SEINE — D 619 — N 67

Fontainebleau — A 5 — A 19 — TROYES — Lac d'Orient

A 6 — A 77 — Chaumont

N 60 — N 77 — N 671 — A 5

Yonne — Langres

A 6 — Ource — D 905

Gien — Auxerre — D 971

Pont-canal de Briare — N 151 — A 6 — BURGUNDY JURA

N 7 — DIJON

← PARIS
← PARIS

Its coal, iron-ore and salt deposits led to the development of heavy industry, a prize that France and Germany have long fought over; Alsace and Lorraine have changed hands four times since 1871 – a fact that has influenced everything from the food to people's livelihoods. Today, most residents speak French, German and the Alsatian dialect, which mingles both languages. Alsace also produces splendid wines. The Champagne region to the west is world famous for its sparkling wine, produced on the steep slopes around Reims. The Ardennes to the north is one of Europe's largest forest areas, stretching into Belgium and merging with the German Eifel. Unsurprisingly, the Ardennes has seen many battles, from the Franco-Prussian War to World War II.

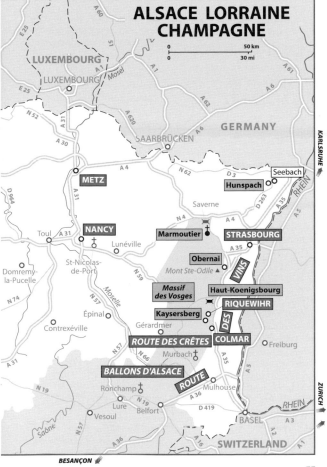

ALSACE LORRAINE CHAMPAGNE

0   50 km
0   30 mi

LUXEMBOURG
LUXEMBOURG
Mosel
GERMANY
SAARBRÜCKEN
KARLSRUHE
METZ
Seebach
Hunspach
RHEIN
Saverne
Toul
NANCY
Marmoutier
STRASBOURG
Lunéville
St-Nicolas-de-Port
Obernai
Mont Ste-Odile ▲
DES VINS
Domremy-la-Pucelle
Massif des Vosges
Haut-Koenigsbourg
Épinal
Kaysersberg
RIQUEWIHR
Contrexéville
Gérardmer
ROUTE DES CRÊTES
COLMAR
Freiburg
Murbach
BALLONS D'ALSACE
ROUTE
Ronchamp
Mulhouse
ZURICH
Lure
Belfort
RHEIN
Vesoul
BASEL
SWITZERLAND
BESANÇON

METZ★★★

The city lies at the confluence of the Moselle with the Seille, a strategic site much appreciated by the Romans; their great highways leading from the Channel coast to the Rhine and from Trier to Italy were linked here, their course marked today by Metz' busy shopping street, Rue Serpenoise.

ALSACE LORRAINE CHAMPAGNE

MUST SEE

Practical Information

Getting There

▶**TGV**: *Metz-Ville.*

Metz is a major junction at the heart of Lorraine, and lies due S of Luxembourg, 50km/31mi from the German border and 160km/100mi NW of Strasbourg.

A BIT OF HISTORY

The history of Metz has always been shaped by the threat posed by the Germanic tribes to the east. Fortified from the 4C, the city later became the capital of the kingdom of Lotharingia (Lorraine), before being attached to the Holy Roman Empire. In 1552, it was annexed by a French kingdom and its role henceforth was that of a fortress-town guarding the border.

1871–1944 – On 6 August 1870, the Prussians took the city, which became part of the German Empire. A quarter of its population chose to resettle in France, and the town took on a Germanic character. Metz was key to the Schlieffen Plan, the strategy that brought the German armies to within 50km/30mi of Paris in WWI. Leading up to WWII, Metz was incorporated into the ineffective Maginot Line. Ironically, its forts were later used against the Allied armies, who took over two months to eject the Germans in 1944.

HIGHLIGHTS

Cathédrale St-Étienne★★★

The cathedral is known as "God's Lantern" (Lanterne du Bon Dieu) due to its stained-glass windows (**verrières★★★**).

Musées de Metz Métropole- La Cour d'Or★★

Open Mon–Fri (except Tue) 9am–5pm, Sat–Sun 10am–5pm. €4.60. 03 87 20 13 20. http://musees. metzmetropole.fr.

Housed in the 17C Petits Carmes abbey, and the 15C **Grenier de Chèvrement★** the museum shows the town's importance, from the Gallo-Roman to Carolingian eras.

Centre Pompidou- Metz★★★

Open daily (except Tue) Mon-Fri 11am–6pm, Sat, 10am–8pm, Sun 10am-6pm. €7. 03 87 15 39 39. www.centrepompidou-metz.fr.

The first offshoot of Paris' famous Centre Pompidou hosts ever-changing exhibitions of 20C and 21C art, mostly taken from the museum's Parisian namesake.

ADDITIONAL SIGHTS

Porte des Allemands★

This massive fortress, once part of the town walls, straddles the River Seille.

Place St-Louis★

In the heart of the old town, place St-Louis is lined with arcaded buildings from the 14C, 15C and 16C that once housed money-changers' shops. On the corner of rue de la Tête-d'Or, note the three gold Roman heads set in the wall.

VERDUN★★

This ancient stronghold occupies a strategic position on the Meuse.
The Upper Town with its cathedral and citadel is poised on an outcrop
overlooking the river.

Practical Information
Getting There

▶**TER**: *Verdun*. Mid-way between
Metz (80km/50mi to the east) and
Reims (120km/75mi to the west).

A BIT OF HISTORY

The Gauls were the first to build
a fortress here on the left bank of
the Meuse. They were followed by
the Romans, but Verdun entered
the mainstream of history with the
signing of the **Treaty of Verdun**
in 843. By its terms, Charlemagne's
realm was divided up among
his grandsons, contrary to their
father's wish for its preservation as
a single unit. The emperor, Lothair,
received the central zone (Northern
Italy, Provence, the Rhineland and
the Low Countries); Louis, the
Germanic countries, and Charles
the Bald, Gaul. The repercussions
have been felt throughout the
centuries, and the treaty has been
referred to as "the most significant
in all the continent's history", partly
because Louis was dissatisfied
with his portion and launched

what might be considered the first
of all Franco-German wars in 858
following the death of Lothair.
The town was besieged in 1870
at the start of the Franco-Prussian
War, then occupied for three years.
In World War I, Verdun was the
scene of some of the bloodiest
fighting of the Western Front, in a
battle that lasted 18 months.

SIGHT
Ville Haute★

The seat of a bishop, the fortified
upper town rises in stages from the
banks of the river. The city's historic
buildings include **Cathédrale
Notre-Dame★**, laid out like the
great Romanesque basilicas of the
Rhineland, and the Bishop's Palace
(**Palais épiscopal★**), constructed
by Robert de Cotte in the 18C.

ADDITIONAL SIGHT
Citadelle Souterraine

(Underground Citadel) – self-
guided vehicle travels 7km/4.3mi
of tunnels equipped to fulfil the
needs of the army.

© R. Mattès/MICHELIN
Palais épiscopal

VERDUN

BATTLEFIELDS OF VERDUN★★★

The name of Verdun is forever linked to the decisive struggle on which turned the outcome of the First World War (1914–18). The gaze of the world was fixed for a year-and-a-half on the violence endured by both sides, in a battle that inspired the utmost steadfastness and courage.

Douaumont Ossuary and the graves, Verdun battlefield

© philippe montembaut/Fotolia.com

ALSACE LORRAINE
CHAMPAGNE

MUST SEE

Practical Information
Getting There
▶**TER**: *Verdun*. The battlefields are 10km/6.2mi NE of Verdun.

A BIT OF HISTORY

At the outbreak of war in August 1914, Verdun lay a mere 40km/25mi from the Franco-German frontier. The 21 February 1916 dawned bright but cold. A devastating bombardment preceded the Germans' frontal assault on the French lines. Within four days Douaumont Fort had fallen.

This was the moment at which General Pétain took effective charge of the battle; by the time of his replacement in April 1917, it was clear that the German attempt to break the staying-power of the French army had failed. Verdun, the hinge of the whole Western Front, could not be taken.

A series of battles raged throughout March and April in the Argonne, around Les Éparges; and, closer to Verdun, on Hill 304 and the other eminence known chillingly as the Mort-Homme (Dead Man's Hill). On 11 July, the final German offensive ground to a halt in front of the Souville fort, a mere 5km/3mi from the city. The French counter-offensive began in October 1916. By 20 August 1917, the Hell of Verdun, the longest continuous battle of the First World War, which had cost the lives of over 700 000 men, was over. A century later, remains of the dead are still being found in the forests; they are kept in the **Ossuaire de Douaumont**, a moving monument that contains the bones of over 130,000 unidentified French and German soldiers.

NANCY ★★★

Capital of the industrial area of Lorraine, Nancy is sited on the low-lying land between the River Meurthe and the Moselle Heights (Côtes de Moselle).

A BIT OF HISTORY

The city was founded in the 11C, but its real history begins in the 15C when the Dukes of Lorraine asserted their independence. In the 17C, the new town (*Ville neuve*) was planned on a regular pattern by the artist **Claude Lorrain** (1600–82). In 1738, Louis XV appointed, as ruler for life, his own father-in-law Stanislas Leszczynski, and by 1766 the Duchy had been painlessly incorporated into the French kingdom. Stanislas was a man of peace, fond of his daughter the Queen of France, a lover of good living and of the opposite sex. A passionate builder, he united the old quarter of Nancy with the "New Town" by means of a great centrepiece in honour of his son-in-law; the project was completed between 1752 and 1755.

HIGHLIGHTS
Place Stanislas ★★★

UNESCO World Heritage-listed Place Stanislas is a space of

Practical Information

Getting There

▶**TGV:** *Nancy-Ville.* Nancy lies 56km/35mi due S of Metz. The historic Old Town is the heart of the city, centred on place St-Epvre.

Getting Around/Tours

◆ **Guided tours** – various guided tours (French only) €8-9. Audioguides €6. Download the free **Zevisit** app for your mobile phone or MP3 player.

◆ **Tourist train** – May–Sept: 40min tours of the historic town depart from place de la Carrière, daily at 10am, 11am, 2pm, 3pm, 4pm. €6 (6–14 years €4). 03 89 73 74 24. *www.petit-train.com.*

◆ **City pass** – This pass covers six museums, transport and an audioguide visit. *€10.*

◆ **Weekends in Nancy** – Contact the tourist office for details of weekend and short break deals. 03 83 3522 41; www.ot-nancy.fr

Place Stanislas – gilded railings and the statue of Stanislas

© Ivan Bastien/iStockphoto.com

NANCY

exceptional elegance and clarity of structure, lined with handsome townhouses and ringed with ornate **gilded railings** of inimitable gracefulness designed by Jean **Lamour**, a metal-worker of genius.

Arc de Triomphe★

This 18C triumphal arch was built to honour Louis XV; it is modelled on Septimus Severus' arch in Rome.

Place de la Carrière★

The square is lined with beautiful 18C mansions. Fountains decorate the corners and at each end there are railings and lanterns by Lamour.

Palais du Gouverneur★

The former residence of the governors of Lorraine faces the Arc de Triomphe across pl. du Général-de-Gaulle and pl. de la Carrière.

Porte de la Craffe★

Once part of the 14C fortifications, the gate displays the thistle of Nancy and the cross of Lorraine. To the north stands the Renaissance **Porte de la Citadelle.**

Palais ducal★★

René II had the 13C ruins rebuilt after his victory over Charles the Bold of Burgundy. In the 16C, Duke Antoine completed the elegant **Porterie★★** (gateway), together with the Galerie des Cerfs (Deer Gallery).

Musée de l'École de Nancy★★

36-38 rue du Sergent Blandan. Open Wed–Sun 10am–6pm. €6. 03 83 40 14 86. www.ecole-de-nancy.com.

A fascinating collection of furniture, glasswork and ceramics made in Nancy between 1885 and 1914 by artisans who became known as the **École de Nancy**.

MuséedesBeaux-Arts★★

3, pl. Stanislas. Open daily except Tue 10am–6pm. €6. 03 83 85 30 72.

Housed in one of the pavilions on pl. Stanislas, the museum contains rich collections of European art from the 14C to the present day.

Musée Lorrain★★★

In the Palais ducal. Open daily except Tue 10am–12.30pm, 2–6pm. €4. 03 83 32 18 74.

The museum illustrates the history of Lorraine, with art and folklore collections and a rich **archaeological gallery**.

Église des Cordeliers★

Open daily except Mon 10am–12.30pm, 2–6pm. €3.50. 03 83 32 18 74.

A restored 15C Franciscan convent and church built by Duke René II.

Jardin botanique du Montet★

Opening times vary . €4.10 (greenhouses only). 03 83 41 47 47. www.cjbn.uhp-nancy.fr.

The botanical gardens contain thematic collections and hot houses with 6 500 species: orchids, insect-eating and succulent plants.

Église Notre-Dame-de Bon-Secours★

Avenue de Strasbourg.

Built in 1738, this church contains **Stanislas' tomb★** and the **mausoleum of Catherine Opalinsk★★**, Stanislas' wife.

STRASBOURG★★★

This important modern city, with a busy river port and renowned university, is not just the lively capital of Alsace. It is also where the Council of Europe and European Parliament are located. The Grande Île, the historic centre around the cathedral, is a UNESCO World Heritage-listed site.

A BIT OF HISTORY

Strasbourg's name comes from the German meaning "City of the roads", and the place is indeed a meeting point for the highways, railways and waterways linking the Mediterranean with the Rhineland, Central Europe, the North Sea and the Baltic.

Strasbourg remained a **free city** within the Holy Roman Empire even after the rest of Alsace was incorporated into France by the Peace of Westphalia in 1648; Louis XIV annexed the city in 1681. In 1870, Strasbourg was seized by Germany after a long siege. It became French at the 1918

Practical Information

Getting There

▶**TGV**: *Strasbourg*. On the banks of the river Ill, Strasbourg is less than 8km/5mi W of the Rhine, and 150km/95mi E of Nancy.

Getting Around/Tours

✦ **Park & Ride** – Eight *Parkings Relais* car parks on the outskirts of town (indicated by a square panel with the letters P+R on a violet background) are linked to the centre by tramway. *(from €3.20, tram ticket inc). For all bus and tram information, contact CTS 03 88 77 70 70. www.cts-strasbourg.fr*

✦ **Tramways** – 6 lines link tourist sights in and around Strasbourg.

✦ **Buses** – 29 bus routes crisscross Strasbourg; intercity buses link the city with the most beautiful and popular Alsatian villages.

Tickets: A wide variety of tickets, carnets, and passes covers services on both the bus and tram network. A single-journey ticket is valid for an hour on the bus and tram network (€1.60); a 24H ticket (€4) allows an unlimited number of journeys within that time frame. A 24H

Trio ticket(€5.70) gives unlimited journeys, for up to 3 people in a 24-hour period.

✦ **Strasbourg Pass** – this 3-day pass allows free or half-price admission to most of the city's highlights. On sale in tourist office information centres (place de la Cathédrale, place de la Gare and Pont de l'Europe). *www.otstrasbourg.fr €14.* Also ask at Tourism Offices about:
Guided tours (1hr 30min) by approved guides. *€6.80;*

✦ **Audio-guided tours** – The 1hr 30min itinerary lets you explore the cathedral, the old town and Petite France at your own speed. €5.50.

✦ **Mini-train** – Departure place du Château, by the cathedral, every half-hour, depending on time of year. €5.50. *03 88 77 70 03. www.cts-strasbourg.fr*

✦ **Boat trips on the Ill** – Guided trips (1hr 10min) taking in the Petite France, past Barrage Vauban, then the Faux Rempart moat as far as Palais de l'Europe. Departure from the Palais Rohan pier every half-hour, depending on time of year. €9.20 (children €4.80). *03 88 84 13 13. www.batorama.fr*

Armistice, but was again taken by Germany from 1940 to 1944.

The old city is a time-warp vision of bygone Alsace - timber-framed houses with wooden galleries, loggias on brackets, windows with tiny panes of coloured glass, and overhanging upper storeys.

LANDMARKS
Cathédrale Notre-Dame★★★

1 r. Rohan. Open daily 7–11.20am, 12.35–7pm; no visits during services. 03 88 21 43 34.
www.cathedrale-strasbourg.fr.

In 1176, the cathedral was rebuilt in red Vosges sandstone, and used bundles of oak piles as a foundation (happily, these were recently reinforced with concrete). Externally, this is still a Romanesque building as far as choir, transept and lantern-tower are concerned. The famous Gothic **spire★★★** (€3) is an architectural masterpiece, and an unmistakable landmark; visible over much of the Alsace plain, it rises to a height of 142m/466ft. The High Gothic west front (**façade★★★**) is decorated with a wealth of sculpture, especially in the central portal (**portail central**). The three lower levels of the tympanum have particularly fine 13C scenes of the Passion and Resurrection, and the Death of Judas; in the arching can be seen the Creation, the Apostles, the Evangelists and the Martyrs. In the south doorway (**portail Sud**) is a famous portrayal of the Seducer about to succeed in tempting the most daring of the Foolish Virgins (she is undoing her dress).

Inside, the nave elevation is a straightforward example of the High Gothic style of the 14C. In the south transept is the 13C Angel pillar (**pilier des Anges★★**) or Last Judgement (**du Jugement dernier**); its delicate statuary, on three levels, raises Gothic art to a peak of perfection. **Stained-glass windows★★★** from the 12C, 13C and 14C are remarkable. The **astronomical clock★** (*clock chimes at 12.30pm; tickets availabl;e from 9am-11.30am*) dating from 1838, continues to draw crowds with its clockwork automata ringing out the quarter-hours (the figure of Death has the privilege of sounding the hours) and the crowd of figures brought out to mark midday (12.30pm).

Musée de l'Œuvre Notre-Dame★★

3 pl. du Château. Open Tue–Fri noon–6pm, Sat–Sun 10am–6pm.
€6. 03 88 52 50 00.
www.musees-strasbourg.org.
This museum greatly enhances the visitor's appreciation of the cathedral. Its great treasure is the famous **Tête de Christ★★** from Wissembourg in northern Alsace. In addition, there is the oldest stained glass in existence, no less, and many of the cathedral's original statues, including the Church and the Synagogue, and the Wise and Foolish Virgins.

Palais Rohan★

2 pl. du Château. 03 88 88 50 50.
www.musees-strasbourg.org.

Residence of the Prince-Bishops of Strasbourg, the palace was built between 1732 and 1742. The Prince-Bishops' state rooms are among the finest French interiors of the 18C. The palace also houses several **museums★★**.

OLD TOWN★★★

The old town nestles round the cathedral, on the island formed by the river Ill. This World Heritage Site is a delight to explore at leisure.

Place de la Cathédrale★

The **Pharmacie du Cerf** on the corner of rue Mercière, which dates from 1268, was the oldest chemist's in France until it closed in 2000. On the north side of the cathedral, the **Maison Kammerzell★** (1589), restored 1954 and now an excellent restaurant, has splendid carved frescoes and wooden sculptures.

Pont du Corbeau

The former "execution" bridge from which the condemned were tied up in sacks and plunged into the water.

Cour du Corbeau★

This pretty 14C courtyard of a once-fashionable inn welcomed illustrious guests, such as Frederick the Great and Emperor Joseph II,

Quai St-Nicolas

The embankment is lined with some fine old Renaissance houses; three are now the **Musée Alsacien**, (*23–25 quai St-Nicolas; open Mon, Wed–Fri noon–6pm, Sat & Sun 10am-6pm; €6; 03 88 52 50 01*), which houses interesting exhibits on Alsatian traditions, arts and crafts. Louis Pasteur lived at No 18.

La Petite France★★

Once the fishermen's, tanners' and millers' district, this is today one of the most interesting and best-preserved areas of the old town. Quai de la Petite France runs alongside the canal, offering a charming **scene★** particularly at dusk, of the old houses reflected in the water, notably in the **Rue du Bain-aux-Plantes★★**.

Ponts Couverts★

This is the name given to three successive bridges spanning the River Ill; each guarded by a massive square tower, remaining from the 14C fortifications. The bridges once had wooden roofs.

Rue du Bain-aux-Plantes★★

The street is lined with timber-framed corbelled houses dating from the Alsatian Renaissance (16–17C). Note, the tanners' house (Gerwerstub, No 42), from 1572, and Nos 31, 33, 27 and 25 (1651).

Rue du Dôme and adjacent streets

The old aristocratic district by place Broglie has several 18C mansions, particularly rue Brûlée: the **Hôtel des Deux-Ponts** (1754) at No 13, the bishop's residence at No 16, and at No 9 the town hall's side entrance.

ADDITIONAL SIGHTS
Musée d'Art Moderne et Contemporain★★

1 place Hans-Jean-Arp. Open Tue–Sun 10am–6pm. €7. 03 88 23 31 31. www.musees-strasbourg.org.

Standing on the bank of the River Ill, the museum is a vision of glass and lightness. The collection covers the period from the late 19C to the present day. A substantial body of works by **Jean Arp** and his

85

wife Sophie Taeuber-Arp include constructivist-inspired stained-glass panels

As a reaction against World War I, the Dadaists signed derisory, even absurd, works (Janco, Schwitters). Following in their footsteps, the Surrealists Brauner, Ernst and Arp tried to introduce the world of dreams into their works.

CAPITAL OF EUROPE
Palais de l'Europe★

Allée Spach, av de l'Europe. Guided tour (1hr) by reservation. Service des visites, Conseil de l'Europe, 67075 Strasbourg Cedex. 03 88 41 20 29.

The palace houses the **European Council**, including the council of ministers, the parliamentary assembly and the international secretariat. The palace contains 1 350 offices, meeting rooms, a library and the largest parliamentary amphitheatre in Europe.

Opposite, the **Parc de l'Orangerie★** was laid out by Le Nôtre in 1692 and includes a lake, a waterfall and a zoo; storks are a familiar sight everywhere.

Palais des
Droits de l'Homme

Nearby, on the banks of the river Ill, stands the futuristic new Palais des Droits de l'Homme, designed by Richard Rogers, which houses the European Court of Human Rights.

WINE VILLAGES

Some of the most picturesque villages in Alsace are a short drive from the city.

Saverne★ – The town at the entrance to the Vosges uplands has **old houses★** and a splendid red sandstone **château★** with a monumental Louis XVI **façade★★**. The 12C former abbey church of the **Église de Marmoutier★★** has a fine Romanesque style **west front ★★** in regional red sandstone.

Hunspach★★ – Close to the Rhine and the German border, Hunspach is one of Alsace's most charming villages. Flowers fill the streets of timber-framed houses with projecting roofs and bull's-eye windows (a Baroque feature). Many of the buildings are old farmhouses, with yards opening off the street; orchards, vines and long-handled pumps complete the picturesque scene.

Nearby, **Seebach★** (*5km/3mi NE by D 249*) is a wonderful example of the flower-decked Alsatian village with its half-timbered houses.

Obernai★★ – Obernai is north of Colmar on the main highway to Strasbourg. With its ruined walls and narrow, winding streets lined with high-gabled houses, the little town of Obernai seems to represent the very essence of Alsace.

A delightful tableau of cheerfully-coloured timber-framed buildings, the picturesque **Place du Marché★★** is Obernai's centrepiece, graced by a fountain with a statue of St Odile. Its Town Hall (**Hôtel de Ville★**, 15-16C) has a fine oriel window, a 16C Corn Hall (**Ancienne Halle aux blés★**) with a stork's nest above its doorway, and the Chapel Tower (**Tour de la Chapelle★**), a 13C bell tower. There are many **old houses★** in the streets around place du Marché.

COLMAR★★★

Since the 13C, Colmar prospered as a river port at the heart of the wine trade and boasts fine monuments in its unspoilt old town centre.

Practical Information
Getting There

▶**TGV**: *Colmar*. Colmar is located 71km/44mi SSW of Strasbourg, 40km/25mi N of Mulhouse.

A BIT OF HISTORY

Between 1871 and 1918 Alsace and Lorraine were part of Germany. In February 1945, the German lines north of Colmar were overrun by American troops, who stood aside to let the French 5th armoured division of General Schlesser enter Colmar.

MUSÉE UNTERLINDEN★★★

1 r. d'Unterlinden. Open May–Oct daily 9am–6pm; Nov–Apr Wed–Mon 9am–noon, 2–5pm. €8. 03 89 20 15 50. www.musee-unterlinden.com.

The museum houses rich collections of paintings and sculpture from the late Middle Ages and the Renaissance.

RETABLE D'ISSENHEIM★★★

The highlight of the museum is **Matthias Grünewald's** 16C **Issenheim altarpiece,** an extraordinary work of emotion and intensity.

VILLE ANCIENNE★★

The heart of the old town is a tangle of picturesque old houses, Particularly striking are the **Maison Pfister★★**and the 15C Old Customs House, **Ancienne Douane★**

PETITE VENISE★ (LITTLE VENICE)

The historic canal quarter is a tangle of waterways, whose narrow lanes and pretty quaysides make for pleasant strolling. Below Pont St-Pierre, **boat trips** (*Apr–Oct 30min trips 10am–7pm; €5.50; 03 89 41 01 94 www.ot-colmar.fr*) on little flat-bottomed boats are available to explore the district further.

EXCURSIONS
Kaysersberg★★

12km/7.4mi NW of Colmar. 39 r. Gén de Gaulle. 03 89 78 11 11. www.ville-kaysersberg.fr.

Kaysersberg is a typically pretty Alsace village of flower-bedecked old houses dating from the 16C. The **Musée Albert-Schweitzer**; *open May–Oct daily 9am–noon, 2–6pm; €2*) is dedicated to the great doctor, theologian and pioneer of Third World aid.

Château du Haut-Kœnigsbourg★★

21km/13mi N of Colmar. Open daily Jun–Aug 9.15am–6pm; rest of year times vary. €8. 03 88 82 50 60. www.haut-koenigsbourg.fr.

This vast, mock-medieval edifice in pink sandstone perching atop a lofty outcrop dates from 1147. Sacked by the Swedes in the 17C, it was a romantic ruin for the next 200 years, until Kaiser Wilhelm II had it restored from 1900 to 1908 as a symbol of power in the now-German territory of Alsace.

RIQUEWIHR★★★

Situated along the Route des Vins, the tiny, beautiful village of Riquewihr is surrounded by medieval walls. It prides itself on its fine Riesling. The town looks pretty much the same today as it did in the 16C.

Practical Information
Getting There
▸**TGV**: *Colmar, then local bus.*
Riquewihr lies 16km/10mi
NW of Colmar.

HIGHLIGHTS
Château des Ducs de Wurtemberg
Completed in 1540, the castle has kept its mullioned windows, its gable decorated with antlers and its stair turret. It houses the **Musée de la Communication en Alsace**.

Maison Liebrich★ (Cour des cigognes)
A well dating from 1603 and a huge wine press from 1817 stand in the picturesque courtyard of this 16C house, surrounded by balustraded wooden galleries. Opposite stands the **Maison Behrel** adorned with a lovely oriel (1514).

Place des Trois-Églises
The square is framed by two former churches, St-Érard and Notre-Dame, and a 19C Protestant church.

Maison Preiss-Zimmer★
The house that belonged to the wine-growers' guild stands in the last but one of a succession of picturesque court-yards. On place de la Sinn at the end of rue du Général-de-Gaulle, is the pretty 1580 **Fontaine Sinnbrunnen**.

Rue et cour des Juifs
Rue des Juifs and the picturesque Cour des Juifs are the old ghetto;

a narrow passageway leads to the ramparts and the **Musée de la Tour des Voleurs**.

Maison Kiener★
No 2. The 16C house has a bas-relief depicting Death getting hold of the founder of the house. Opposite, the **Auberge du Cerf** dates from 1566.

Rue Latérale
Lovely houses include the **Maison du marchand Tobie Berger** at No 6, which has a 16C oriel and a Renaissance doorway in the courtyard.

Maison du Bouton d'Or
No 16. The house goes back to 1566. An alleyway, just round the corner, leads to another tithe court, known as the Cour de Strasbourg.

Musée du Dolder
Open Jul–Aug daily, 1.45–6.30pm. Apr–Jun and Sep–Oct Sat–Sun and holidays 1.45–6.30pm €2.50.

The local history museum houses mementoes, prints, weapons, tools and furniture.

Maison Hansi
Open May–Dec daily 10.30am–6pm, rest of year times vary. €2. 03 89 47 97 00.

Contains watercolours, prints and decorated ceramics by the Colmar artist and cartoonist, JJ Waltz, known as 'Hansi'.

ROUTE DES CRÊTES★★★

In World War I, the French and German armies confronted each other along the old frontier between the two countries formed by the crest-line of the Vosges. Hugging the ridge is the strategic north–south road planned by French military engineers to serve the front; today it forms a fine scenic route, the 🚗 **Vosges Scenic Road**, running for 63km/39mi from the Bonhomme Pass (Col du Bonhomme) in the north to Thann in the south. It offers the visitor a splendid introduction to the varied landscapes of these uplands, which include the sweeping pasturelands of the summits, an array of lakes, and the broad valleys of the Fisch and the Thur.

Practical Information
Getting There
The route starts 30km/18.6mi W of Colmar and heads S to Thann, which lies 25km/16mi W of Toulouse on N66.

COL DU BONHOMME
949m/3 114ft high, this is the pass linking the provinces of Alsace and Lorraine.

COL DE LA SCHLUCHT
1 139m/3 737ft. This is the steepest but also one of the busiest of the routes through the Vosges. The eastern slopes are subject to intense erosion because of the gradient of the torrential rivers; at a distance of only 9km/5.6mi from the pass, the town of **Munster★** lies 877m/2 877ft below, while Colmar, 26km/16mi away, is 1 065m/3 494ft lower.

HOHNECK★★★
1 362m/4 469ft. Rising near the central point of the range, this is one of the most visited of the Vosges summits. From the top there are superb **views★★★**; to the east, the **Munster Valley★★** plunges steeply down towards the broad expanses of the Alsace plain, while to the west is the Lorraine plateau, cut into by the valley of the Vologne.

GRAND BALLON★★★
1 424m/4 672ft. The Grand Ballon forms the highest point of the Vosges. From the top (*30min round-trip on foot*) the magnificent **panorama★★★** extends over the southern part of the range, whose physiognomy can be fully appreciated. The eastern and western slopes are quite unlike each other; the drop to the Alsace plain is abrupt, while to the west the land falls away gently to the Lorraine plateau. Glacial action in the Quaternary era is responsible for many features like the massive rounded humps of the summits (*ballons*), and the morainic lakes in the blocked valleys. Above the tree line, the forest clothing the hillsides gives way to the short grass of the wide upland grazing grounds known as the Hautes-Chaumes.

VIEIL-ARMAND★★
The war memorial (*monument national*) marks one of the most bitterly contested battlefields of World War I, where 30,000 soldiers died fighting for the peak of Hartmannswillerkopf.

REIMS★★★

The ancient university town on the banks of the River Vesle is famous for its magnificent and important cathedral, where French kings were traditionally crowned. It has a wealth of other architectural masterpieces. Reims is also (along with Epernay) the capital of champagne's wine industry. Most of the great 🍷 **champagne** houses' cellars are open to the public.

Practical Information

Getting There

▶**TGV**: *Reims*. Reims is 143km/89mi NE of Paris on the A 4 *autoroute*, and 275km/171mi from Calais on the A 26, which skirts the town. Take any turning for Centre Ville.

A BIT OF HISTORY

It was at Reims, in 496, that Clovis, King of the Franks, was baptised by St Remigius (St Rémi). This significant event made the 35-year-old warrior the only Christian ruler in the chaotic era after the fall of the Roman Empire.

The Carolingian period produced Charlemagne's Talisman (now in the Bishops' Palace) as well as the Épernay Gospel. In 816, Louis I the Pious was crowned here; thereafter, coronations at Reims became an essential part of royal legitimacy. By the time of Charles X, 25 kings had been crowned here. The most moving coronation was that of Charles VII on 17 July 1429, which took place in the middle of the Hundred Years' War in the presence of Joan of Arc. On 7 May 1945, in a technical college near the station, the document was signed that marked the surrender of Germany, and the end of WW2 in Europe.

CATHÉDRALE NOTRE-DAME★★★

Open daily 7.30am–7.30pm

Begun in 1211, this is one of the great cathedrals of France. The west front has wonderfully soaring lines and superb 13C sculpture, whose masterpiece is the world-famous Smiling Angel (in a splay of the north portal). The west end of the nave is best seen towards the end of the afternoon when the sun lights up the two rose windows. Reims was occupied by the German army in September 1914, and for four years remained in the battle zone. By the end of the war, the cathedral was in ruins.

PALAIS DU TAU★★

Open May–Sept Tue–Sun 9.30am–6.30pm; rest of the year 9.30am–2.30pm, 2–5.30pm. €7.50. 03 26 47 81 79. http://palais-tau. monuments-nationaux.fr.

Dating from 1690, the palace of the bishops of Reims houses some of the cathedral's original statuary and two huge 15C Arras tapestries depicting the life of King Clovis. The rich treasury has superb items such as the 9C Talisman of Charlemagne, and the 11C cut-glass Holy Thorn reliquary.

BASILIQUE ST-RÉMI★★

Place Chanoine Ladame. Open daily 8am–7pm. No charge.

This Benedictine abbey church is the oldest church in Reims. In the sombre interior (**intérieur★★★**) the choir provides light Gothic contrast to a dark Romanesque nave.

TROYES★★★

The lively centre of this distinguished old trading town is a charming collection of picturesque half-timbered houses, many beautifully restored.

Practical Information

Getting There

▶TER: *Troyes.* 125km/78mi S of Reims by *autoroute*, and 176km/110mi SE of Paris in the cradle formed by the A 5 and A 26 *autoroutes*.

A BIT OF HISTORY

Troyes is one of the capitals of the province of Champagne (the other being Reims). The town developed in the Seine valley on the great trade route between Italy and the cities of Flanders. It once had a considerable Jewish population, and in the Middle Ages hosted two huge three-month long annual fairs that attracted merchants and craftsmen from all over Europe. But by the end of the 14C, these gatherings fell into decline. Troyes has long been France's most important centre of hosiery manufacture, an industry introduced at the beginning of the 16C. The city's wealth enabled it to overcome the great fire of 1524; houses and churches were rebuilt in a style showing both the Italianate influence of artists who came from Fontainebleau around 1540, as well as the persistence of medieval traditions.

LE VIEUX TROYES★★

The outline of the old town looks amusingly like a champagne cork, with the area around the cathedral forming the head. The majority of the old houses are timber-framed and elegantly infilled with chequer-board patterns made from brick, slate or chalk. The best examples are in Rue Champeaux, Ruelle des Chats, Rue de Vauluisant and the Cour du Mortier d'Or.

Maison de l'Outil et de la Pensée ouvrière★★

7 r. de la Trinité. Open daily 10am–6pm. €6.50. 03 25 73 28 26. www.maison-de-l-outil.com.

The 16C Hôtel du Mauroy is a fine setting for the Tools and Trade Museum, a fascinating collection of objects and tools used in traditional trades.

Musée de Vauluisant★

4 r. Vauluisant. Opening times vary. €3. 03 25 73 05 85.

The 16C Renaissance **Hôtel de Vauluisant★** contains museums of **local art** and **hosiery**.

Cathédrale St-Pierre et St-Paul★★

Built from 1208 until the 17C, the regional Gothic style can be traced over the whole period of its evolution. The superb stained-glass windows (**vitraux★★**) transform the building into a cage of glass.

Musée d'Art Moderne★★

14 Place Saint-Pierre. Open May–Sept: Tue–Fri 10am–1pm, 2–7pm, Sat-Sun 11am–7pm; rest of year times vary €5. 03 25 76 26 80.

The former Bishops' Palace houses an impressive collection of modern art, including a fine showing of **Fauvist** works.

BURGUNDY

Burgundy's unity is based more on history than on geography. Fortunately located on the trade route linking northern Europe to the Mediterranean, Burgundy was consolidated by its great Dukes in the 15C, staying independent of France in the Middle Ages. The powerful Dukes extended their rule to include the Jura, but the Duchy became a province of the Holy Roman Empire, annexed by France in 1674.

It comprises a number of diverse *pays*, though its heartland lies in the limestone plateaux stretching eastwards from the Auxerre area and terminating in escarpments, which drop down to the Saône Valley.

Of the Burgundian escarpments, La Côte is the most renowned, with its slopes producing some of the world's finest wines. To the north is the Morvan, a wild granite massif of poor soils, with scattered hamlets and extensive forests. Further north and west the Nivernais stretches to the Loire, and to the south the lower reaches of the Saône are bordered by the broad Bresse plain. Burgundy has been synonymous with fine wines since the 14C, but the region also produces cheese, cereals and poultry, and tourism is increasingly important.

To the east the Jura's limestone uplands run in a great arc for some 240km/150mi from Rhine to Rhône, corresponding roughly to the old province of Franche-Comté. It is a mountainous region with a different kind of appeal to Burgundy, an out-of-the-way land of lakes, forests, mountains and pastures.

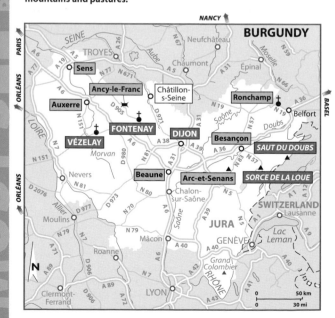

DIJON★★★

Close to some of the world's finest vineyards, Dijon, former capital city of the Dukes of Burgundy has a remarkable artistic heritage.

Practical Information
Getting There
▶**TGV**: *Dijon-Ville*. 46km/29mi N of Beaune. From Charles de Gaulle airport, take TGV via Gare de Lyon.

A BIT OF HISTORY

Dijon had been the capital of Burgundy ever since the rule of Robert the Pious in the 11C. **Philippe le Hardi** (the Bold), first of an illustrious line of Valois Dukes took the title in 1364, just as his brother Charles V acceded to the French throne, closely entwining the two. His marriage in 1369 to Margaret of Flanders made him the most powerful prince in Europe. His successor **Jean sans Peur** (John the Fearless) was assassinated in 1419. **Philippe le Bon** (the Good) inherited the title. During his 48-year reign, the Burgundian state had never been more extensive. Burgundy's alliance with England became unpopular as Joan of Arc awakened nationalism. Philippe submitted himself to the authority of the French king, beginning the end of the Hundred Years' War. **Charles le Téméraire** (the Rash) the last of the Valois Dukes, squandered its resources. In 1477, Charles died, and Mary of Burgundy, Charles' daughter, married Maximilian, Holy Roman Emperor. She was to be the mother of **Philippe le Beau** (the Fair). The recovery of Burgundy and the other lands making up her dowry cost France two and a half centuries of struggle.

PALAIS DES DUCS ET DES ÉTATS DE BOURGOGNE★★

pl. des Ducs-de-Bourgogne. Open Mon–Fri 8.45am–12.15am, Sat 9.30am–12.30pm. No charge. 03 80 74 52 71.

Neglected since the death of Charles the Bold, the ducal palace was restored in the 17C and given a setting of dignified Classical buildings. The exterior of the Great Hall of the States-General (Salle des États) recalls the Marble Court (Cour de Marbre) at Versailles.
Musée des Beaux-Arts★★ – The ducal palace houses a rich and varied collection of paintings and sculptures.
Salle des Gardes★★★ – The centrepiece of the ducal palace's most important interior is formed by two tombs, which before the French Revolution were in the Champmol Charterhouse. The tomb of Philip the Bold features a dramatic procession of hooded mourners making its way around the cloisters formed by the four sides of the monument. Nearby, the tomb (**tombeau★★★**) of John the Fearless and Margaret of Bavaria is similar in style.

ANCIENNE CHARTREUSE DE CHAMPMOL★

Enter at 1 bd Chanoine-Kir. Follow signs for "Puits de Moïse". Open 10am–6pm. No charge. 03 80 42 48 01.

All that is left of the Charterhouse is the elaborately sculpted Moses' Well (**Puits de Moïse★★**) and the chapel doorway (**portail de la chapelle★**).

EXCURSIONS
Châtillon-sur-Seine★

83km/51.5mi N of Dijon.
www.pays-chatillonnais.fr.

The main reason to visit Châtillon is to see the magnificent Vix treasure. **Le Trésor de Vix★★** – Found in the tomb of a young Celtic queen, dating from the 6C BC, grave goods including a remarkable bronze vase are displayed in the **Musée du Pays Châtillonais** (*open daily Jul & Aug 10am-7pm, rest of year 9am-noon, 2pm-6pm; €7; 03 80 91 24 67; www.musee-vix.fr*).

Abbaye de Fontenay★★★

The abbey is next to Montbard, in northern Burgundy.

The Abbaye de Fontenay, founded by **St Bernard** in a lonely valley near the River Brenne, is the most perfect surviving example of a Cistercian abbey, offering a unique window onto the self-sufficient life of a 12C Cistercian monastery

CÔTE DE NUITS★★

Leave Dijon on D 122, known as the Route des Grands Crus.

The Côte de Nuits road follows foothills covered with vines and passes through villages with world-famous names.
Chenôve – The dukes' wine cellar, **Cuverie des ducs de Bourgogne** (*open Jul–Sept 2–7pm; rest of the year by appointment; 03 80 51 55 00*) contains two splendid 13C presses.
Marsannay-la-Côte – Part of the Côte de Nuits, Marsannay produces popular rosé wines.
Fixin – This village produces

some of the best of the Côte de Nuits wines. The small **Musée Noisot** (*open mid-Apr to mid-Oct Sat–Sun 2–6pm. €4.50. 03 80 52 45 62*) houses mementoes of Napoleon's campaigns.
Gevrey-Chambertin – A typical Burgundian wine-growing village whose oldest part huddles around the church and **château**, a square-towered 10C fortress (*open Jun–Sept; guided tours (1hr) 10am–noon, 2–6pm; €6; 03 80 34 36 77. http://chateaudegevrey.free.fr*).
Chambolle-Musigny – The road from Chambolle-Musigny to Curley leads through a gorge, Combe Ambin, to a beauty spot where a small chapel overlooks the junction of two wooded ravines.
Vougeot – The walled vineyard of Clos-Vougeot is one of the most famous of La Côte.
Owned by the **Confrérie des Chevaliers du Tastevin**, the Renaissance **Château du Clos de Vougeot★** is an atmospheric place to visit (*open daily: Apr–Sept 9am–6.30pm; Oct–Mar 9–11.30am, 2–5.30pm; €4.50; 03 80 34 36 77. www.closdevougeot.fr*).
Vosne-Romanée – These vineyards produce legendary red wines, including world-famous Romanée-Conti.
Nuits-St-Georges – The fame of the wines of Nuits goes back to Louis XIV. When the royal doctor advised him to take some glasses of Nuits and Romanée with each meal as a tonic, the whole court wanted to taste it.
The **museum** (*open May–Oct daily except Tue 10am–noon, 2–6pm; €2.30; 03 80 62 01 37*) shows items found in the Gallo-Romansettlement excavated at Les Bolards.

🍇 LEGENDARY VINEYARDS

The lie of the land

The Côte runs along the east-facing slopes of the "mountain", dominating the plains of the Saône Only the east- and south-facing slopes of the combes are planted with vines – around 8 000 hectares of first-quality grapes. Vineyards carpet the limestone slopes, basking in the morning sunlight and well protected from cold winds. This exposure to sunlight is what determines the production of sugar in the grapes and the final alcohol content of the wine. The slopes also ensure that rain runs off, keeping the soil well drained and nicely dry – just how the vines like it – to produce top-class wines.

Burgundy's fine wines – the "grands crus"

For much of its length, the D 974 marks the dividing line between the "noble" grape varieties and the rest, with the grands crus generally planted mid-way up the slopes. Pinot Noir is the king of Burgundy grapes: it is used to make red wines, whereas the great white wines are made from the Chardonnay grape. After the devastation of the phylloxera blight in the 19C, the vineyards were entirely replanted with resistant vines grafted from North American stock. But it's an ill wind that blows no good. Paradoxically, the pesky parasites brought beneficial changes in their wake: small producers were able to buy back land from the big boys, and a reduction in the quantity of wine produced led to much-improved quality. The Côte d'Or divides into two main areas: the superstars are the Côte de Nuits

and the Côte de Beaune. The wines of the Côte de Nuits are prized for their robustness, while those of the Côte de Beaune are admired for their delicacy.

The Côte de Nuits

The Côte de Nuits runs from Fixin to Corgoloin. Planted on limestone slopes, its vineyards cover around 3 740 hectares and produce 104 950 hectolitres annually – that's 14 million bottles, give or take. This is red wine country whose most famous *crus*, running from north to south, are Chambertin, Musigny, Clos-Vougeot et Romanée-Conti. Rich and beefy, these wines need eight to ten years to develop the incomparable body and character of the best Burgundy. To the south, the Hautes-Côtes de Nuits vineyards produce uncomplicated wines on the west-facing slopes.

The Côte de Beaune

The Côte de Beaune stretches over 5 950 hectares from north of Aloxe-Corton to Santenay, producing not only top-notch white wines, but also superb reds. On the upper slopes, the vineyards grow in limestone-rich soil, which changes its character to brown marly earth mingling with pebbles and clay in the lower reaches. The bottom line is an annual production of some 214 335 hectolitres, equating to 28 million bottles. Its most prestigious *crus* are, in the red corner, Corton, Volnay, Pommard and Beaune; in the white camp are Meursault and Montrachet. The reds are muscular and fruity – rather like the whites, which deliver a fabulously rich intensity on the nose and palate.

AUXERRE★★

A port on the River Yonne, the city was once an important staging post on the great Roman highway from Lyon to Boulogne via Autun and Lutetia (Paris).

Practical Information
Getting There

▶**TER**: *Auxerre*. Auxerre lies 149km/93mi NW of Beaune, and 78km/49mi SW of Troyes.

HIGHLIGHTS
Abbaye St-Germain★

Open daily except Tue: May–Sept 10am-6pm; Oct–Apr 10am–noon, 2–6pm. Crypt €6. 03 86 18 05 50. www.auxerre.culture.gouv.fr.

The city's famous Benedictine abbey is named after bishop St Germanus (378–448), born in Auxerre. The abbey **crypt★** Merovingian (6C) remains include two oak beams on Gallo-Roman columns and a 5C monogram of Christ. From the Carolingian period (8–10C) there is a **fresco** of the bishops of Auxerre.

Cathédrale St-Étienne★★

Open 7.30am–6pm. Treasury and crypt Easter–1 Nov daily 9am–6pm (Sun 2–6pm); rest of the year daily except Sun 10am–5pm. €3. 03 86 52 23 29.

This fine Gothic cathedral was built between the 13C and 16C to replace the existing Romanesque one. The **treasury★** has a wealth of precious objects

EXCURSIONS
Briare

The Briare canal is 70km/44mi SW of Auxerre. 02 38 31 20 08. www.briare-le-canal.com.

Briare is a busy port on the banks of the Loire, which was used by river traffic from the 14–19C,. As the navigation companies had trouble with the river's irregular flow and shallowness, Henri IV began building the **Briare Canal** in 1604 to link the basins of the Loire and the Seine via its junction with the River Loing at Montargis. It was the first connecting canal in Europe. The Loire Lateral Canal (1822–38) extends it south to Digoin. It crosses the Loire at Briare on a 19C aqueduct, the **Pont de Canal★**. The channel is the longest in the world and rests on 15 granite piers designed by Gustave Eiffel.

Sens★★

80km/50mi NW of Auxerre. pl. Jean-Jaurès. 03 86 65 19 49. www.office-de-tourisme-sens.com.

In the city centre stands the first of France's great Gothic cathedrals. **Cathédrale St-Étienne★★** – Its foundations were laid in the years 1128–30, though most building took place between 1140 and 1168. Inside, there is a magnificent array of medieval **stained glass★★**; one 12C window tells the story of the murder of Thomas à Becket, who had spent years of exile at nearby Pontigny. The Musées de Sens are housed in the **Old Archbishop's Palace** (16–18C) and the **Palais Synodal★** (Synodal Palace). Collections explore the history of Sens, while the **cathedral treasury (Trésor)★★** is one of France's richest.

Aerial view of Vézelay with Basilique Ste-Marie-Madeleine

© J. Damase/MICHELIN

Chablis

21km/13mi E of Auxerre.
03 86 42 80 80. www.chablis.net.

This small town, with the feel of a big village, is tucked away in the valley of the River Serein, between Auxerre and Tonnerre. Chablis is synonymous with its world-famous flinty white wines made from the Chardonnay grape . Thanks to its many old buildings, it still has a medieval feel. The annual wine fair and the village fairs of November and late January, recall the town's lively commercial past.

Château d'Ancy-le-Franc★★

The château lies SE of Tonnerre. Opening times vary. €9. 03 86 75 14 63. www.chateau-ancy.com.

This dignified château marks the end of the early, Italian-influenced French Renaissance in all its brilliance. The château was begun in 1546 and completed 50 years later.

Vézelay★★★

Vézelay is W of Avallon. www.vezelaytourisme.com.

The quiet and picturesque little village of Vézelay climbs a steep slope among the northern foothills of the Morvan countryside, overlooking the Cure valley.
Its fame is due to the majestic basilica, which numbers among the greatest treasures of France. In 878 an abbey was founded here, and in 1050 it was dedicated to Mary Magdalene, whose remains were supposedly here, and the place soon became one of France's great pilgrimage destinations.
It was here that St Bernard preached the Second Crusade in 1146. In 1279, however, the monks of St-Maximin in Provence claimed to have discovered the bones of Mary Magdalene in a cave; the certification of the relics as authentic led to the decline of Vézelay as a place of pilgrimage.
Basilique Ste-Marie-Madeleine★★★ – First built between 1096 and 1104 and restored following the fire of 1120, this basilica has a fine **view★** over the valley of the river Cure, a marvellous **tympanum★★★** above the central doorway and beautifully decorated **capitals★★★** atop its many pillars.

BESANÇON★★

Just outside Burgundy, the capital of the Franche-Comté occupies a superb **site★★★** on a meander of the River Doubs, overlooked by a rocky outcrop on which Vauban built a fortress, making the town an outstanding example of 17C military architecture. The birthplace of the writer Victor Hugo, Besançon is also known for its many museums and fine architecture.

Practical Information

Getting There

▶**TGV**: *Besançon-Viotte.*
109km/68mi NE of Beaune.

A BIT OF HISTORY

A 2C triumphal arch called the Black Gate (Porte Noire) survives from a Gallo-Roman settlement (Vesontio) which was the home of the Gaulish *Sequani* tribe: the modern Grande-Rue still follows the course of its main street in the heart of old Besançon.

The city is closely connected with the Holy Roman Empire and was given the title of Imperial Free City in 1184. Through inheritance and marriages, in the 15C and 16C the town became part of the Austro-Spanish empire. It marked a high point in the province's commercial life, illustrated by the rise of the Granvelle family. Although born into the humblest of peasant families, the son Perrenot was given an education and rose rapidly, becoming chancellor to Charles V, and built himself the Palais Granvelle. In 1674 Louis XIV conquered the Franche-Comté, made Besançon its capital and had Vauban construct the citadel.

PALAIS GRANVELLE★

Beyond the splendid Renaissance façade of the Granvelle family residence is the fascinating **Musée du Temps** (*open Tue-Sat 9.15am-noon, 2pm-6pm; Sun*

10am-6pm. 03 81 87 81 50), which honours Besançon's heritage as a centre of clock and watch-making with its remarkable collection of timepieces.

CITADEL★★

99 r. des Fusillés-de-la-Résistance. Open daily: Jul–Aug 9am- 7pm, rest of year times vary. €9.20 03 81 87 83 33. www.citadelle.com.

Vauban's mighty 17C fortress is best appreciated from the sentry-walk along the encircling ramparts. The building houses a zoo and the Musée d'Histoire naturelle.

MUSÉE DES BEAUX-ARTS ET D'ARCHÉOLOGIE★★

1 pl. de la Révolution. Open daily except Tue: 9.30am–noon, 2–6pm Sat–Sun,9.30–6pm. €5. 03 81 87 80 49. www.musee-arts-besancon.org.

The museum houses a diverse collection of artistic, historical and archaeological displays, including the priceless 14–17C art collection of the Granvelle family.

EXCURSIONS
Saut du Doubs★★★

On the border 10km/6mi E of Morteau. 03 81 68 00 98. www.villers-le-lac-info.org.

Bursting out of the Chaillexon lake, the waters of the Doubs plunge

MUST SEE BURGUNDY

down in a magnificent drop, known as "le Saut du Doubs", one of the most famous natural phenomena in the Franche-Comté. Frequent **boat trips** (*daily Apr–Oct; €12.90, children €8.90. 03 81 68 13 25; www.sautdudoubs.fr*) leave from Villers-le-Lac, following the river's meanders to the Chaillexon Lake then onwards through a gorge, the most picturesque part of the trip. From the landing-stage, take the path (*30min round-trip on foot*) to the two viewpoints overlooking the Saut du Doubs.

Arc-et-Senans★★

The royal saltworks of Arc-et-Senans lie SW of Besançon and N of Arbois. 03 81 54 45 45. www.salineroyale.com.

The UNESCO World Heritage-listed royal **saltworks**★★ are an extraordinary essay in utopian town planning of the early Industrial Age. In 1773, the King's Counsel decreed that the royal saltworks should be built at Arc-et-Senans, drawing on the salt waters of nearby Salins. The visionary French architect **Claude-Nicolas Ledoux** (1736–1806) set about the task with an ambitious plan; an ideal 18C town laid out in concentric circles. Ledoux's vision makes him one of the forerunners of modern architecture and urban design and while the enterprise was never really viable, being closed down in 1895, the amazing buildings of the *Saline Royale* remain.

Pontarlier

The town lies near the Swiss border. 03 81 46 48 33. www.pontarlier.org.

Between the 13C and 17C Pontarlier was the capital of an independent state, whose regime was ended by Louis XIV's conquest of the Franche-Comté.
Cluse de Pontarlier★★ – *5km/3mi S. of Pontarlier*. The Jura has many such *cluses* – lateral clefts through the high ridges separating two valleys. This example lies along the route to Switzerland and is overlooked by the Larmont and Joux forts (the Cluse de Joux is one of the Jura's most beautiful cluses).
Lac de St-Point★ – *8km/5mi S of Pontarlier*. Nearly 7km/4.3mi long, it is the largest lake in the Jura, in a lovely spot among mountain pastures and pine forests.
Source de la Loue★★★ – *16km/10mi W. of Pontarlier*. In its setting of high cliffs and luxuriant vegetation, the source of the River Loue is one of the region's finest natural sites.
Grand Taureau★★ – *11km/7mi E. Leave Pontarlier S along N 57 and climb to the ski resort of Montagne du Larmont*. This is the highest point (1 323m/4 340ft) of the Larmont mountains, less than 1km/0.5mi from the Franco-Swiss border. The view from here stretches over Pontarlier and the Jura plateaux to the west.

Chapelle de Ronchamp★★

Ronchamp is a small former mining town bordering Alsace. 03 84 20 65 13. www.chapellederonchamp.fr.

Built by **Le Corbusier** (1887-1965), the Chapelle Notre-Dame-du-Haut on its hilltop site is one of few great works of religious architecture produced by the early 20C Modern Movement.

BESANÇON

FRENCH ALPS-RHÔNE

Stretching from the Mediterranean to Lac Léman (Lake Geneva), the French Alps display all the varieties of mountain scenery, from the tranquillity of bare rock and eternal snow to the animation of densely settled valleys. Here, human habitat shows close adaptation to natural conditions. Centuries of endurance and ingenuity have overcome formidable obstacles and brought all possible resources into play, not only settling valley floors, but pushing grazing and cultivation to its highest limits and developing widely varied local traditions of living and building.

Geography – The north of the French Alps is marked by the great sweep of Lac Léman. To the south rise the Alps of Savoy, first the Chablais and Faucigny country and beyond that the famous peaks and glaciers around Mont Blanc. Westward lie other graceful stretches of water, Lake Annecy and Le Bourget Lake. An important communication route is formed by the Sub-Alpine Furrow, a broad and prosperous valley in which Grenoble sits, and the western rampart of the Alps is formed by a succession of massifs including the Vercors. Briançon is close to the Italian border and further south still the scene is often one of striking severity, bare rock rising from vegetation of Mediterranean character.

Geologists divide the French Alps into four main areas: the **Préalpes**, or Alpine foothills, consisting almost entirely of limestone rocks formed during the Secondary Era, except in the Chablais area; the **Alpine trench**, a depression cut through marl, lying at the foot of the central massifs; the **central massifs**, consisting of very old and extremely hard crystalline rocks. The tectonic upheavals of the Tertiary Era folded the ancient landmass, creating "needles" and high peaks, which are the highest of the whole Alpine range. From north to south, these massifs are: the Mont Blanc, Belledonne, Grandes Rousses, Écrins and Mercantour; the **intra-Alpine zone**, forming the axis of the Alps. It consists of sedimentary rocks

Val-d'Isère

©Robert Maxwell/iStockphoto.com

100

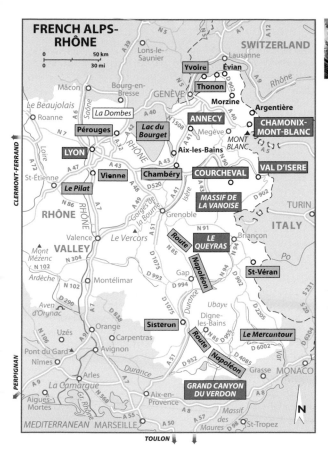

FRENCH ALPS-RHÔNE

0 — 50 km
0 — 30 mi

SWITZERLAND

Lons-le-Saunier
Yvoire
Évian
Mâcon
Bourg-en-Bresse
GENÈVE
Thonon
Morzine
Argentière
Le Beaujolais
La Dombes
Roanne
ANNECY
CHAMONIX-MONT-BLANC
Pérouges
Lac du Bourget
Megève
MONT BLANC
LYON
Aix-les-Bains
VAL D'ISERE
St-Étienne
Vienne
Chambéry
COURCHEVAL
Le Pilat
MASSIF DE LA VANOISE
TURIN
RHÔNE
Grenoble
ITALY
Valence
Le Vercors
Route
LE QUEYRAS
Briançon
Mont Mézenc
VALLEY
Napoléon
Gap
St-Véran
Ardèche
Montélimar
Ubaye
Aven d'Orgnac
Sisteron
Digne-les-Bains
Le Mercantour
Orange
Uzés
Carpentras
Route
Avignon
Napoléon
Grasse
MONACO
Nîmes
Arles
La Camargue
GRAND CANYON DU VERDON
Aigues-Mortes
Aix-en-Provence
Massif des Maures
St-Tropez
MEDITERRANEAN
MARSEILLE
TOULON

CLERMONT-FERRAND
PERPIGNAN
N

transformed and folded by the violent upheavals that took place in the area. It includes the Vanoise, the Briançonnais and the Queyras as well as the upper valleys of the Tarentaise, Maurienne and Ubaye.

History – The Alps have been inhabited since the Stone Age, but it was the Romans who first made an impact on the region as they sought to control the trade routes through the mountains. After the Romans the area was subject to Barbarian invasions before eventually becoming the County of Savoy which, during the 15C, was integrated with Piedmont and became the Duchy of Savoy.

Economy – Traditionally the Alps were an area of cattle rearing, and observed the traditional summer practices of transhumance, when man and beast would head into the high mountain pastures, returning just before the onset of winter. Now year-round tourism is of major importance, with many activities in summer, as well as the traditional winter sports.

ANNECY★★★

Lakeside Annecy enjoys an exquisitely beautiful setting of water and mountains, and has a picturesque old centre clustered around the River Thiou.

Practical Information
Getting There
▶**TGV**: *Annecy*. The town is 39.4km/24.5mi NE of Lac du Bourget.

A BIT OF HISTORY
An ancient lake settlement, then a hillside Gallo-Roman town, Annecy moved back downhill in the Middle Ages to its present site by the Thiou, whose rapid waters powered its many mills. In the 16C Annecy became the regional capital, displacing Geneva, and in the 17C was the home of the influential **St Francis of Sales**, bitter opponent of Calvinism, which had spread throughout the region.

OLD ANNECY★★
The picturesque old town, largely pedestrianised and renovated, lies on the banks of the Thiou as it flows from the lake. Its arcaded houses, Italianate wells and colourful markets (*Tue, Wed and Sun mornings*) give immense charm.

Rue Ste-Claire★ is a delight with its arcades and gabled houses. The **Palais de l'Isle★** rising from the midst of the river offers the most famous view of Old Annecy.

MUSÉE-CHÂTEAU D'ANNECY★

Open Jun–Sept daily 10.30am–6pm; Oct–May, daily except Tue 10am–noon, 2-5pm. Closed public holidays. €5.50. 04 50 33 87 34.

This handsomely restored castle of the lords of Geneva, dates from the 12C to the 16C. It was damaged by fire several times, abandoned in the 17C, then used as a garrison.

LAKE★★★
A road runs around the edge of this lovely lake, giving wonderful views. Fine vista from the **Avenue d'Albigny**, in Annecy. There are several pleasant small resorts on the lakeside, notably **Talloires★★★**, overlooking the narrows dividing the Grand Lac to the north from

Lac Annecy at Talloires

© Pierre Jacques/hemis.fr

the Petit Lac to the south.
For boat trips, contact 04 50 51 08 40,
www.annecy-croisieres.com.

EXCURSIONS
Lac du Bourget★★

The lake is 39km/24.5mi
SW of Annecy.

France's largest, deepest and most celebrated natural lake enjoys an impressive mountain setting. On its eastern shore is the elegant spa town of Aix-les-Bains a famous resort with lively streets, opulent hotels near the spa baths, and an attractive lakeshore.
The lake and its banks form a rich and unusual habitat for wildlife, including 50 species of fish, and crayfish; birdlife includes 300 or so cormorants that winter on the west bank at La Grande Cale.
Jutting into the lake, the **Abbaye royale de Hautecombe★★** (founded 1125) houses the tombs of 42 princely members of the House of Savoy.

Chambéry★★

10km/6.2mi S of Lac du Bourget. 24
bd de la Colonne. 04 79 33 42 47.
www.chambery-tourisme.com.

The well-restored old centre is redolent of Chambéry's past splendour as the capital of Savoy. The main shopping street, rue de Boigne is elegantly arcaded and leads to the old ducal château.
Château de Chambéry – This fortress was occupied by the counts of Savoy in 1285, who expanded it during the 14C to serve as their residence and seat of administration.
Musée Savoisien★ – The museum houses interesting exhibits of prehistory, religious art and regional ethnography.

Aix-les-Bains♨♨♨

Aix-les-Bains lies on the eastern shore of Lac du Bourget. Follow A 41 and A 43, 10km/6.25mi from Chambéry.pl. Maurice-Mollard, 73100 Aix-les-Bains. 04 79 88 68 00. www.aixlesbains.com.

Aix-les-Bains is one of the busiest tourist centres in the Alps, with splendid palace hotels near the baths and attractive lake shores.
Taking the waters: a fashionable pastime – Aix's health-giving waters have been famous for almost 2 000 years, ever since the Romans built the ancient baths. Treatment became more sophisticated in the 19C with the introduction of the steam bath and shower-massage, a technique brought back from Egypt by Napoleon's doctors.
The spa town had its heyday during the Belle Époque when luxury hotels attracted the aristocracy and the crowned heads of Europe: Queen Victoria stayed at the "Victoria", three times. After WWII most of these magnificent hotels closed down.
The Spa Town – The spa town is concentrated round the baths, the municipal park with its vast open-air theatre, the Palais de Savoie and casino; along the lake with its beach and marinas. The shopping area centres on Rue de Genève, rue du Casino and adjacent streets.
The Roman Town★ – The remains of the **Roman baths** can only hint at their former splendour (24 kinds of marble were used to decorate them). Other highlights include the **Temple de Diane**.

ÉVIAN-LES-BAINS✝✝✝

Poetically known as the "pearl of Lake Geneva", Évian is remarkably well situated between the lake and the foothills of the Préalpes du Chablais. The resort town, renowned for its old palaces and thermal spas, climbs up from the flat lake area like an amphitheatre, with steep little roads parting in every direction. You can enjoy splendid architecture, walks or simply lazy evenings by the lake, and the town makes a fine base to explore the Chablais.

Practical Information

Getting There

▶TGV: *Évian-les-Bains.* 45min from exit 15 of A 40, or 10km/6.25mi from Thonon-les-Bains.

A BIT OF HISTORY

The medicinal properties of Évian water were discovered in 1789, when a gentleman from Auvergne realised it was dissolving his kidney stones. As well as for drinking, it is prized for its beneficial effects on kidney disorders and rheumatism. You can visit the very modern **bottling factory** (*Guided tour (1hr30) by appointment at the Évian information centre. 04 50 84 86 54*), which produces an average of 5 million litres of water per day, the highest output of any producer.

THE LAKESIDE ★

The most enjoyable walk in Évian. Firstly, because of the rare trees that border the lake, along with lawns and pretty flowerbeds. Next, because it is here that you will find the important buildings of the **palais Lumière**, the **villa Lumière**, today's town hall, and the **casino**. All along the promenade up to the pleasure port Les Mouettes, the water in **musical fountains** plays in time to the music. Behind you, appearing through the chestnut groves of Neuvecelles, are the grand hotels, stacked up on the lower slopes of the Gavot.

Villa Lumière – Once owned by Antoine Lumière, father of the cinema pioneer, this grand 1896 villa now houses the town hall; the ground-floor rooms and the **grand staircase★** are especially elegant, while the next-door **theatre** is a splendid relic of 19C excess. Also on the lakeside, on the same site as the château de Blonay, willed to the town in 1877, are the **casino,** built in 1891, and the **palais Lumière**, a thermal spa until 1984 when it was converted to a cultural centre.

Parc Thermal – The new baths are situated in the **Parc thermal**. The pump room was built in 1956, and the Espace Thermal in 1983. This is partly constructed below ground in order to preserve the appearance of the park.

EXCURSIONS

Amphion-les-Bains – *4km/2.5mi to the west*. The first spa resort of the Chablais region, ever since the 17C, when the Dukes of Savoie regularly took the waters.

Yvoire★★ – *26km/16mi W along the shore from Évian-les-Bains. Place de la Mairie. 04 50 72 80 21.* This picturesque, flowery village, has retained its medieval character. It enjoys a magnificent site on the shores of Lake Geneva (Lac Léman), at the tip of a headland separating the Petit Lac and the Grand Lac.

CHAMONIX-MONT-BLANC★★★

Chamonix lies at the foot of the famous 3 000m/9 842ft Chamonix Needles (Aiguilles de Chamonix). All around are the high mountains of the Mont Blanc Massif. The top of the great White Mountain is just visible from the town.

Practical Information
Getting There

▶**TER**: *Chamonix Mont-Blanc.*
Chamonix is 101km/63mi E of Annecy.

🏔 RESORT

Already a centre of mountaineering thanks to its Compagnie des Guides, Chamonix developed as a skiing destination after it hosted the first Winter Olympic Games in 1924. Today, the Chamonix Valley offers endless outdoor activities, magnificent landscapes, a lively atmosphere and cultural events.

EXCURSIONS
Aiguille du Midi★★★

Cable car: €45.60 round-trip.
www.chamonix.com.

The **panorama★★★**, especially from the central peak (3 842m/12 605ft), is staggering, taking in Mont Blanc, Mont Maudit, the Grandes Jorasses, and the dome of the Goûter whose buttresses are buried in 30m/100ft of ice.

🏔 Mer de Glace★★★

Montenvers train: Runs daily. €26.40.
The view from the upper station of the railway built in1908 takes in the whole of the 7km/4.3mi long "sea of ice" glacier.

Argentière❋❋❋

8km/5mi northeast of Chamonix.

At 1 252m/4 108ft, Argentière is the highest resort in the Chamonix

Valley, offering a wide choice of expeditions to the Massif du Mont Blanc and Massif des Aiguilles Rouges.

Aiguille des Grands-Montets★★ 🚡

Access by the Lognan and Grands-Montets cable cars. 04 50 54 00 71.
www.compagniedumontblanc.
com. About 2hr30min return.

The **panorama★★★** is breath-taking. The view extends to the Argentière Glacier over which tower some of the loftiest peaks in the French Alps.

Col de Balme★★ 🚡

Access by the Col de Balme gondola. 04 50 54 00 58.

The **view★★** extends northeast to the Swiss Alps and southwest to the Chamonix Valley surrounded by the Aiguille Verte, Mont Blanc and the Aiguilles Rouges massif.

VIEWPOINTS
Aiguille du Midi★★★ 🚡 – *Minimum 2hr return.* The ride up to the Aiguille du Midi is the most thrilling in the French Alps.
Le Brévent★★★ 🚡 – *Minimum 1hr30 min return.* **Planpraz★★** relay station offers a splendid view of the Aiguilles de Chamonix and an excellent lunch. From Le Brévent, the **panorama** sweeps over the Mont Blanc massif.

ROUTE DES GRANDES ALPES★★★

Among the many thrilling routes through the French Alps, this high-altitude road is the most famous. The Great Alpine Road links Lake Geneva with the Riviera, crossing mountain passes as it leaps from valley to valley. The route is open from end to end during the summer months only.

Practical Information

Getting There

From Thonon-le-Bains to Menton, across 25 mountain passes.

HIGHLIGHTS
Thonon-les-Bains★★

From the Place du Château the view extends over the great sweep of **Lake Geneva** (**Lac Léman★★★**). Saint Francis of Sales once preached in St Hippolytus' Church (Église St-Hippolyte); Italian craftsmen restored the interior in Rococo style in the 18C. The road rises in steps through the damp beech woodland of the gorges cut by the River Dranse de Morzine to the **Chablais★★** massif, a complex of high ridges and peaks, with rich pastures grazed by Abondance cattle. The most spectacular part of the route is known as the **Gorges du Pont du Diable★★**.

Morzine★★

33km/20.5mi SE of Thonon

The valleys around the resort are dotted with hamlets of chalets with patterned balconies amid sombre forests of spruce. After the pass at Les Gets, the small industrial town of Tanninges marks the beginning of the **Faucigny★★** country, a landscape of pastures and spruce woods.

La Clusaz★★

44km/27.3mi SW of Cluses.

The most important ski resort in the **Massif des Aravis** owes its name to the deep gorge, or cluse, downstream of it. The village huddles around its big onion-domed church, with the jagged outlines of the Aravis mountains in the distance.

Val d'Isère★★★

50km/31mi SE of Cormet de Roselend

In its high valley, 1 000m/3 281ft above Bourg-St-Maurice, the chic resort has an excellent sunshine record. To the south and west are the lofty glaciers and peaks of the Vanoise National Park.
As the road climbs, views open onto the imposing peaks of the Gran Paradiso in Italy to the left and of the Vanoise massif (Grande Motte peak) to the right.

Col du Galibier★★★

52km/32.3mi SW of Modane.

2 642m/8 668ft. From the viewing table there is a superb panorama taking in the Maurienne country (to the north), the Pelvoux region (to the south), and the Massif des Écrins. This is the dividing line between the northern and southern part of the French Alps. At the pass is **Col du Lautaret★★**, with its fine views of the Meije mountains. Turn right in the direction of La Grave, then turn left at the entrance to the second tunnel to le Chazelet.

Oratoire du Chazelet★★★

23km/14.3mi W of Col du Galibier.

From the viewing table, the view extends over the high peaks of the Écrins National Park from the Col des Ruillans on the right to the broken ridges of the pyramid-shaped Meije, girdled by a dazzling white glacier.

Col d'Izoard★★

14km/8.7mi SE of Briançon. 2 361m/7 746ft.

The pass carves through a desolate landscape fringed by dramatic peaks; fine views extend over the Briançonnais to the north and the Queyras country to the south. The road drops in a series of hairpin bends through a strange landscape of screes and jagged rocks known as the **Casse Déserte★★**. The high **Queyras★★** country centres on the valley of the River Guil, where there are fine examples of Alpine houses.

Saint-Véran★★

34km/21mi SE of Col d'Izoard.

At around 2 040m/6 693ft, this is the highest village in France. Its rustic chalets, timber-built on a basement of schist, are a unique window onto the rigours of a high-altitude mountain life. The south-facing dwellings are sited in groups, most with hay-barns and balconies on which cereals are ripened in the strong alpine sun. The village has a strange sculpture showing Christ's Agony. The little town of **Guillestre**, its church characterised by a beautiful **porch★**, lies at the end of the **Combe du Queyras★★** canyon.

Col de la Cayolle★★

30km/18.6mi SE of Barcelonnette.

2 327m/7 635ft. This pass links the Ubaye country and the Upper Verdon to the upper reaches of the Var. From the top, the Grasse Pre-Alps hover in the far distance.

THE UPPER VALLEY OF THE RIVER VAR★★

At **St-Martin-d'Entraunes** the route passes from the High Alps into the Pre-Alps of **Provence**, and the wild **Parc National du Mercantour**.

Gorges de Daluis★★

3.5km/2mi S of Guillaumes.

These deep-cut gorges give striking colour effects. The road from **Guillaumes** to **Beuil** leads to the **Gorges du Cians** in the upper stretch of the River Var. The road climbs steadily to the **Col de Valberg** , then the **Col de Couilloie** (1 678m/5 503ft) descends to the impressive **site★★** of **Roubion**, a village perched 1 300m/4 264ft up on a ridge.

Le Massif de l'Authion★★

32.5km/20.2mi SE of La Bollène-Vésubie.

North of the **Col de Turini**, this massif is a natural fortress standing guard over the roads between the Vésubie and Roya valleys. In April 1945, it was the last sector of France to be liberated. The road goes through **Moulinet**, a charming village in a verdant valley, then passes the **Chapelle de Notre-Dame-La-Menour** with its Renaissance façade. At the **Gorges du Piaon★★** the corniche road overlooks the river Bévéra.

ROUTE DES GRANDES ALPES

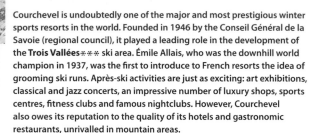

COURCHEVEL★★★

Courchevel is undoubtedly one of the major and most prestigious winter sports resorts in the world. Founded in 1946 by the Conseil Général de la Savoie (regional council), it played a leading role in the development of the **Trois Vallées**✳✳✳ ski area. Émile Allais, who was the downhill world champion in 1937, was the first to introduce to French resorts the idea of grooming ski runs. Après-ski activities are just as exciting: art exhibitions, classical and jazz concerts, an impressive number of luxury shops, sports centres, fitness clubs and famous nightclubs. However, Courchevel also owes its reputation to the quality of its hotels and gastronomic restaurants, unrivalled in mountain areas.

Practical Information
Getting There

▶**TGV**: *Moûtiers*. 50km/31.25mi from Albertville, partly on D 91 with its spectacular panoramic views.

TROIS VALLÉES

Comprising Courchevel, Méribel, Les Menuires, Val Thorens and several smaller resorts, the Three Valleys is the largest linked ski resort in the world, having 200 lifts on a single pass and 600km/375mi of ski runs. At Courchevel, snow cover is guaranteed from early December to May, owing to the north-facing aspect of the slopes and an impressive array of more than 500 snow cannons.
There are excellent runs for beginners along the lower sections of the Courchevel 1850 ski lifts (Verdon, Jardin Alpin). Advanced skiers prefer the great Saulire corridor and the Courchevel 1350 area. Cross-country skiers can explore the network of 130km/81.25mi of trails linked across the Trois Vallées area.
The Courchevel area includes four resorts on the slopes of the Vallée de St-Bon, among pastures and wooded areas, in a vast open landscape framed by impressive mountains.

EXCURSIONS
La Saulire★★★

Access from Courchevel 1850 by the Verdon gondola and the Saulire cable car. The well-equipped summit links the Courchevel and Méribel valleys and is the starting point of a dozen famous runs. Non-skiers can take a gondola to Méribel or Mottaret and a cable car to Courchevel.
From the top platform, the view embraces the Aiguille du Fruit in the foreground, the Vanoise Massif and glaciers further away, the Péclet-Polset Massif to the south, the Sommet de Bellecôte and Mont Pourri to the north with Mont Blanc on the horizon.

Massif de la Vanoise★★★

This famous massif lies between the valleys of the Arc and the Isère. It was proclaimed a national park in 1963. The Vanoise Massif, which is dotted with charming villages and lovely forests, remains nonetheless a high mountain area with over 100 summits in excess of 3 000m/9 842.5ft.
The massif is noted for its diverse fauna (marmots, ibexes, chamois) and flora (around 2 000 species).

GRAND CANYON DU VERDON★★★

The modest-looking River Verdon has cut Europe's most spectacular canyon through a remote, wild landscape.

GEOGRAPHY

The canyon extends 26km/16mi from the meeting point of the Verdon with the Jabron in the east to where it flows into Ste-Croix Lake. The opposite rims of the canyon are between 200–1 500m (656–4 921ft) apart. Its depth varies from 250–600m (820–1 968ft), while the width of its floor ranges from 8–90m (26–295ft).

GRAND CANYON
La Corniche Sublime★★★

South bank scenic route.
The steep and twisting (20km/12.4mi) road was engineered so as to open up the most spectacular views. They include: the **Balcons de la Mescla★★★** overlooking the swirling waters where the Verdon is joined by the Artuby; the bridge, Pont de l'Artuby, linking sheer walls of rock; the Fayet tunnels above the Étroit des Cavaliers (Knights' Narrows), and the **Falaise des Cavaliers★** (Knights' Cliff) 300m/982.2ft high.

La Route des Crêtes★★★

North bank scenic route.
The road (23km/14.3mi long) links a series of viewpoints overlooking the most spectacular section of the canyon. Further eastwards, the viewpoint known as the **Point Sublime★★★** dominates the downstream section of the canyon and the impressive narrows, the **Couloir de Samson★★★**.

🚶WALKING★★★

Sentier Martel★★★ – Between the Chalet de la Maline and the Point Sublime, GR 4, known as the Sentier Martel, offers a tiring day's hike with unforgettably close contact with the Grand Canyon.
Belvédère de Rancoumas★★ – The natural Belvédère de Rancoumas offers a **panorama★★** of the whole Falaise de l'Escalès with the Sentier Martel running below.

Moustiers-Ste-Marie★★

The small town has a dramatic **site★★** at the foot of a cleft in the limestone cliff, across which a knight returning from the Crusades stretched the chain that can still be seen today. The church **tower★** has arcading in Lombard style. Faïence pottery was introduced here in 1679; the most sought-after pieces were fired at high temperatures and are decorated with hunting scenes in blue.

EXCURSION
Sisteron★★

On the Route Napoléon between Gap and Digne. Hôtel de Ville. 04 92 61 36 50. www.sisteron.com.

The lofty citadel of Sisteron, guards a narrow ravine and looks down on the clustered lanes of the 14C town. It still makes an impressive spectacle despite the battering it took from Allied bombing raids during 1944. Sisteron lies on the Route Napoleon and the River Durance and is the main mountain gateway to Provence.

LYON★★★

Two millennia of history, a site at the meeting point of the Rhône and Saône corridors and an exceptionally enterprising population have combined to make Lyon France's second city. Its past periods of greatness, in Roman and Renaissance times, are matched by its present industrial, commercial and cultural dynamism. Truly the heart of the city, la Presqu'île offers great views of the quays of the Saône River and Vieux Lyon. Department stores, boutiques, cinemas and bars line rue de la République, well known for its 19C architecture.

Practical Information

Getting There
▶**TGV**: *Lyon Part-Dieu/ Perrache/ Saint-Exupéry*. Lyon lies 100km/62mi W of Chambéry.

Getting Around
♦ **Maps** – In addition to the maps included in this guide, Michelin town plans 30 and 31 will be useful.
♦ **Access** – By road via motorways A 6, A 7, A 42 and A 43. The city also boasts a regular 2hr link with Paris by TGV. There are flights to and from most major cities via Lyon-St-Exupéry airport, linked to the city centre by a shuttle service.
♦ **Parking** – underground car parks give easy access to the city centre.
♦ **Public transport** – The underground train/subway (métro) is the best way to get around. The best-value ticket is the 1-day **Ticket-liberté**, for unlimited travel on the whole Lyon urban transport network. Details from TCL kiosks and *www.tcl.fr*.
♦ **Cultural Pass** – a 1, 2 or 3 day **Lyon City Card** gives admission to museums, sights and transport, as well as reductions at theatres, on shopping, etc. Adult prices range between 1 day (€21), 2 days (€31) and 3 days (€41). *04 72 77 69 69. www.lyon-france.com*.

Touring the town
♦ **Planning your visit** – If you have only **one day** to spend in Lyon, spend the morning in Old Lyon; see the Fourvière terrace and the Roman theatres (use the funicular). Spend the afternoon touring Presqu'île; visit its Fabric Museum, then either the Fine Arts Museum or a walk around the Gros Caillou in the Croix-Rousse quarter. **Two days** is enough to see Fourvière and its museums and stroll along the River Saône on the first day. Spend day two touring Presqu'île and its museums, and fit in a stroll in the Croix-Rousse.
♦ **Organised tours** – The Lyon tourist office offers tours of the city on foot, or by bus, boat, or taxi. **Lecture tours** are available around Old Lyon, Croix-Rousse and the Tony Garnier district.
♦ **Bateaux-mouches river trips** – *13 bis quai Rambaud. 04 78 42 96 81. www.naviginter.fr*. Discover a different face of Lyon from its rivers: explore the confluence of the Saône and Rhône, or follow the Saône up to and round the Île-Barbe.

Shopping
♦ **Markets** – Top-quality craft markets are held on Sunday mornings on quai Romain-Rolland, and quai Fulchiron. Used-book sellers line the quai de la Pêcherie every afternoon. For food, regional producers set up stall on quai Saint-Antoine; find local products and small taverns at the Halles de Lyon.

A BIT OF HISTORY

Lyon was chosen as a base camp by Julius Caesar for his conquest of Gaul. Under Augustus it became the capital of the Roman Empire's "Three Gauls" (Aquitaine, Belgium and the province around Lyon), complementing the older province centred on Narbonne.

Agrippa chose Lyon as the hub of the road system; it was here that the route coming north from Arles met the other highways from Saintes, Orléans and Rouen, and from Geneva and Aosta.

The Amphitheatre of the Three Gauls on the hill, Colline de la Croix-Rousse, was joined by the Temple of Rome and of Augustus and by the Federal Sanctuary where the noisy annual assembly of the 60 tribes of Gaul was held under Roman supervision. Christianity reached Lyon in the 2C, brought by soldiers, traders and Greek missionaries.

The era of invention

Lyon played a leading role in science and technology in the 19C. Its eminent citizens include: **Marie-Joseph Jaquard** who built a power-loom in 1804; **André Ampère,** inventor of the galvanometer, electromagnetism and electrodynamics; **Barthélemy Thimonnier**, who invented the sewing machine in 1829; **Jean-Baptiste Guimet**, who, in 1834, succeeded in making the dye ultramarine; the **Lumière brothers** (Auguste and Louis), the creators of cinematography; **Hector Guimard**, one of the founders of Art Nouveau architecture, and designer of the entrances to the Paris metro stations.

HIGHLIGHTS
Fourvière Hill

The Roman forum was still here in the reign of King Louis I in the 9C. Its site is now occupied by the pilgrimage chapel (with its Black Virgin) next to the 19C basilica. The heart of Roman Lyon, its public buildings include the imperial palace (the Capitol), the forum, a theatre, baths, and several temples.

Old Lyon★★★

The medieval and Renaissance quarter of Lyon extends along the west bank of the Saône at the foot of the Fourvière hill. The old town hides many passages or alleyways known as "traboules" linking the buildings by means of corridors with vaulted or coffered ceilings leading to inner courtyards.

Quartier St-Jean★★

Lyon was incorporated into the French kingdom at the beginning of the 14C. Charles VII made it a trading centre of European importance when he founded the twice-yearly fair in 1419. Louis XI introduced the weaving of raw silk imported from the Levant and from Italy. Trade flourished, and with it came a period of great prosperity for the city. Lyon seethed with activity and ideas; its streets were lined with elegant Flamboyant Gothic façades; behind them, down narrow alleys, lay courtyards like the ones at 11 and 58 rue St-Jean. Renaissance houses were decorated with Italianate motifs like the figure of the ox at the junction of rue du Bœuf – Hôtel Paterin (4 r. de la Juiverie).

The **Hôtel de Gadagne★** houses the **Musée historique de Lyon★** (*1 pl. du Petit Collège;*

www.museegadagne.com) and the **Musée international de la Marionnette★**, the latter founded by Laurent Mourget creator of the iconic **Guignol** character.

Printing made its first appearance on the banks of the Saône in 1485; by 1548 there were almost 400 printers working in the city, including Étienne Dolet, the publisher of **Rabelais**; the latter served as a doctor at the Pont-du-Rhône hospital for three years, and his great works – *Pantagruel* in 1532 and *Gargantua* in 1534 – were published to coincide with the Lyon fairs.

La Presqu'île

The formation of the "Peninsula" on which the modern centre of the city sits, has shifted the junction of the two rivers 4km/2.5mi southwards since Roman times. The two rivers made it an ideal place for trading and warehousing. Finally it became the very core of the city; its development begun under Henri IV and continued in the 18C and 19C, until the urban area spread outwards to the modern suburbs and beyond. The great city's character comes across not only in the busy Rue de la République, with its fine 19C façades and elegant shops, but also in the pleasantly shaded Place de la République, with its trees and fountains.

Place Bellecour

The original 17C buildings lining the square were razed during the Terror in retribution for the city's resistance to the Convention. "Lyon is no more," it was triumphantly proclaimed at the time, but the square was rebuilt in the 19C.

Hôtel-Dieu

1 pl. de l'Hôpital.
The plans for this, one of the kingdom's most important buildings, were drawn up by Soufflot in 1740. It marks a significant stage in the evolution of French architecture.

Place des Terreaux

This is where the Saône flowed into the Rhône in Roman times. The older inhabitants of the city are particularly fond of the square with its **fountain★**, which has four eager horses representing rivers bounding towards the ocean.

Museums

Musée gallo-romain de Fourvière★★ – *17 r. Cléberg. Open Tue–Sun 10am–6pm. €4-7. 04 72 38 49 30. www.musees-gallo-romains. com.* The most striking exhibit is perhaps formed by the Claudian Tables (**Table Claudienne★★★**) of bronze, discovered in 1528. They record the speech made by Claudius in AD 48 which gave the citizens of Gaul the right to become senators.

Musée des Beaux-Arts★★ – *20 pl. des Terreaux. Open Wed-Sun 10am–6pm. 04 72 10 17 40. www. mba-lyon.fr.* The museum presents a remarkable survey of art through the centuries. Its collections cover painting, sculpture, art objects, antiquities and graphic art.

Musée des Tissus et Musée des Arts Décoratifs★★★ – *34 r. de la Charité. 04 78 38 42 00. Open Tue-Sun 10am-5.30pm. €10. www.musee-des-tissus. com.* A superb collection of Lyon silk and tapestries from the 17C onwards, by masters such as Philippe de Lasalle.

EXCURSIONS

Pérouges★★ – *25km/15.5mi NE of Lyon. Entrance of the Cité. 04 74 46 70 84.* On its hilltop site dominating the Ain valley, this fortified town was originally founded by settlers who came from Perugia in central Italy long before Caesar's invasion of Gaul. It was virtually rebuilt in its entirety after the war of 1468 with Savoy. Tightly contained within the ramparts, the tortuous streets and ancient houses of the old town have formed the perfect setting for many a period film.

Vienne★★ – *38km/24mi S of Lyon.* Vienne sits in a sunny **site★** on the east bank of the Rhône, overlooking a bend in the river. The Romans ruled Vienne 60 years before Caesar's conquest of Gaul. In the 3C and 4C, the city was the centre of the vast province stretching from Lake Geneva to the mouth of the Rhône. Great public buildings were erected at the foot of Mount Pipet, opposite **St-Romain-en-Gal**, the Gallo-Roman city (**cité gallo-romaine★**) with its houses and shops. In the 5C, the Burgundians ruled the east bank of the Rhône before losing it to the Franks in 532. The city later became contested by the Kingdom of France and the Holy Roman Empire, until its final incorporation into France in 1349.

The Classical **Temple d'Auguste et de Livie★★** was first built in the reign of Emperor Augustus shortly before the beginning of the Christian era. It has been well preserved through successive re-use as public buildings (church, Jacobin club, tribunal, museum, library), and through its restoration by Prosper Mérimée in 1850.

Built from the 12–16C, the **Cathédrale St-Maurice★★** combines Romanesque and Gothic elements. Only 35 years after its completion, the cathedral suffered mutilation during the Wars of Religion. It underwent extensive restoration in the 19C, but much remains to be admired.

Beaujolais★ *The Beaujolais region lies around 46km/29mi NW of Lyon. www.beaujolais.com.* The Lyonnais joke that a third river flows with the Rhône and Saône through their city – the River Beaujolais. Ideal opportunities for tasting its fruity red wines await in the scenic vineyards around the pretty villages that give their names to its *crus*. It is an inviting landscape with many hills climbing to over 1 000m. Most of the 10 Beaujolais *cru* wine-producing appelations – Morgon, Brouilly, côte de Brouilly, Chénas, Chiroubles, Fleurie, Juliénas, Morgon, Moulin à Vent, Régnié and Saint-Amour – can be fitted into a day's car touring.

La Dombes★ *The Dombes plateau lies between Lyon and Bourg-en-Bresse and is bordered by the River Ain and the Saône. 3 Place de l'Hôtel de Ville, 01330 Villars les Dombes. 04 74 98 06 29. www.villars-les-dombes.com.* The Dombes plateau owes its unusual appearance and its charm to the presence of over 1 000 lakes dotted across its entire area. Low hills, formed by moraines, were transformed in the Middle Ages into veritable earth fortresses surrounded by moats. Rural housing in the Dombes region is built mainly of cob (pisé), whereas the castles and outer walls are built of rough red bricks known as carrons (terracotta).

LYON

BORDEAUX & DORDOGNE

The Atlantic Coast region of France stretches from the estuary of the Loire in the north to the mighty natural frontier of the Pyrénées to the south. In the north there are great marshy tracts like the Marais Poitevin and dune-fringed sandy beaches. To the south is the broad estuary of the Garonne. Behind the endless sandy beaches rise the highest sand dunes in Europe. In Classical times the Roman province of Aquitania included all the Atlantic Coast region. In the medieval period the region passed to the English Crown as part of Eleanor of Aquitaine's dowry, and did not revert to France until the end of the Hundred Years' War. The taste for Bordeaux wine continues in England to this day.

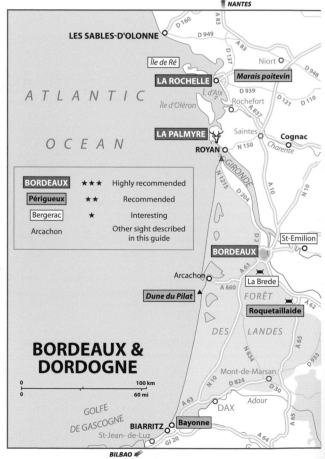

With its hills, fertile agricultural landscapes, deciduous woodlands and mellow stone buildings, the Dordogne (known by the French as Périgord) is not unlike parts of southern England. The Périgord region forms a plateau dissected by the Dordogne River; along the banks grow maize, tobacco, sunflowers and cereals. Poultry farmers ensure that the Périgordian table is never short of duck and goose confit, and the area's celebrated foie-gras. The Dordogne area has been settled since the very earliest times as evidenced by its renowned cave paintings at Lascaux and Font-de-Gaume. There are numerous reminders of Anglo-French struggle, from the planned towns, or bastides, like Monpazier, Domme, Villefranche-du-Périgord and Beaumont, to rugged strongholds such as Beynac and Castelnaud.

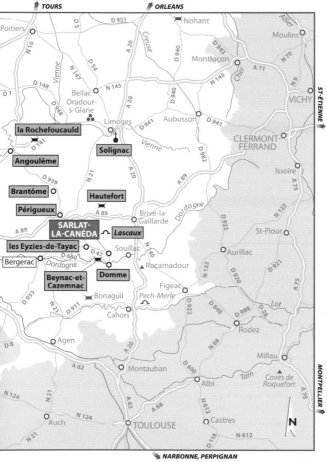

BORDEAUX★★★

"Take Versailles, add Antwerp, and you have Bordeaux" was Victor Hugo's summary, impressed as he was by its 18C grandeur and tidal river. Bordeaux had, however, played an important role in the affairs of France long before Versailles had been envisioned. Capital of the Aquitaine region, and a UNESCO World Heritage Site, Bordeaux is a town full of history.

Practical Information

Getting There

▶**TGV**: *Bordeaux-Saint-Jean.* Bordeaux is not far from the coast, on the south bank of the River Gironde; the town has an airport.

A BIT OF HISTORY

From 7C, Good King Dagobert created the Duchy of Aquitaine. In 1152, when **Eleanor of Aquitaine** married Henry Plantagenet, the bride's dowry consisted of most of southwestern France. Two months later her husband became Henry II of England, and Bordeaux became English for the next three centuries. It was English demand for wine that drove the expansion of the Bordeaux **vineyards**.

During the 18C, medieval Bordeaux acquired the Classical face it wears today, seen in the quaysides, the Place de la Bourse, the great avenues, the Town Hall (Hôtel de Ville) and the Grand Théâtre. During the French Revolution, the Bordeaux *députés* formed the group known as the **Girondins**. Accused of conspiring against the Revolution, 22 of them were tried in May 1793 and executed.

VIEUX BORDEAUX

The old town has undergone extensive restoration in an effort to return the ancient ochre stonework of its 18C buildings to their original splendour. The restored buildings include those along the **quayside**

following the bend of the Garonne for 1km/0.5mi.

Grand-Théâtre★★ – *pl. de la Comédie. 05 56 00 85 95. www. opera-bordeaux.com.* This theatre is one of the finest in France. Its architect was Victor Louis (1731–1802), a proponent of the Louis XVI style; here he succeeded in creating a combined theatre and concert hall which recalls antiquity not only in its sheer scale but also in its restrained use of decoration.

Place du Parlement★ – A good example of the urban planning carried out in the reign of Louis XV, the square has a number of houses with ground-floor arcades, transom windows and decorative masks. The harmony and unity of the square is emphasised by the balcony running the whole length of the façades.

Quartier des Chartrons★ – This old neighbourhood, behind the quayside devoted to the wine trade and ships' chandlers, became fashionable in the 18C when the city's great families built their town houses here. Some of the streets (Rue Notre-Dame, Cours de la Martinique, Cours Xavier Arnozan) have fine dwellings with Classical façades.

Esplanade des Quinconces – The sheer size of this esplanade is impressive. It was laid out on the site of the old Château de la Trompette during the Restoration (early 19C).

OTHER HIGHLIGHTS

Place de la Bourse★★ – The Stock Exchange (La Bourse) and the Hôtel des Fermes (now the **National Customs Museum**) grace this magnificent square.

Basilique St-Michel★ – *pl. Canteloup et Meynard. Open Mon–Sat 8.30am–6pm, Sun 8am–noon. 05 56 94 30 50.* Building of the Basilica began in 1350, and lasted for two centuries. The side chapels were added after 1475.

Cathédrale St-André★ – *pl. Pey Berland. Organ concerts Jul–Aug Tue 6.30pm. No charge. 05 56 52 68 10.* This cathedral, the most impressive in Bordeaux, has superb medieval sculptures on the Porte Royale.

Musée des Beaux-Arts★★ – *20 cours d'Albret. Open Wed–Mon 11am–6pm. No charge, except for temporary exhibitions: €5. 05 56 10 20 56.* The Fine Arts Museum bordering the gardens of City Hall displays a fine collection of 15–20C paintings in its two wings.

Musée d'Aquitaine★★ – *20 cours Pasteur. Open Tue–Sun 11am–6pm. No charge. 05 56 01 51 00.* This excellent museum, housed in the former Literature and Science Faculty traces the life of the Aquitaine region.

Musée d'Art contemporain★ (CAPC) – *7 r. Ferrère. Open Tue–Sun 11am– 6pm (Wed 8pm). No charge. 05 56 00 81 50.* The former **Lainé warehouse**★★is now a Museum of Contemporary Art, majoring on works from the 1960s and 1970s.

Croiseur Colbert★★ – *Open Jun–Aug, daily 10am–6pm; rest of year times vary. €8 (child €5.50). 05 56 44 96 11. http://colbert.croiseur.free.fr.* This anti-aircraft cruiser, launched in 1959, was the Mediterranean Squadron's flagship.

EXCURSIONS
Bordeaux Vineyards★

The Bordeaux wine region in the Gironde *département,* is the world's largest producer of quality wines – Médoc on the west bank of the Gironde, Bourg on the east bank, and St-Émilion and Pomerol north of the Dordogne. White wines include: Entre-Deux-Mers between the Dordogne and the Garonne, and Graves and Sauternes to the south.

Haut Médoc – Famous cellars open to visitors include Château Margaux, **Château Mouton-Rothschild**★ and Château Lafite.

St-Émilion★★ – Famous for its full-bodied and fragrant red wines. The town's sun-baked, pantile-roofed stone houses nestle in an **amphitheatre**★★ on the slope of a limestone plateau. It is also known for its strange underground church.

Sauternes – These vineyards produce renowned sweet white wines, in particular Château Yquem.

Château de Roquetaillade★★

Guided tours (1hr) Jul–Aug, daily 11am–5pm; rest of year times vary . €8. 05 56 76 14 16. http:// chateauroquetaillade.free.fr.

An imposing walled medieval castle built in 1306. Six enormous round towers encircle a courtyard with a powerful square keep.

Château de La Brède★

Guided tours only €7. 05 56 78 47 72. www.chateaulabrede.com.

This moated 15C **château**, was the birthplace of **Charles Montesquieu** (1689–1755), Baron de la Brède.

BORDEAUX

117

ARCACHON★★

A century and a half ago, the site of Arcachon was no more than a pinewood.
Today, it is one of the most popular resorts on the French Atlantic.

Practical Information

Getting There

▶**TGV**: *Arcachon*. The resort fronts the vast Bassin d'Arcachon inlet, 64km/40mi SW of Bordeaux.

A BIT OF HISTORY

Arcachon was born when the **Pereire brothers** laid a railway line to the coast in 1852. It is divided into "seasons" – a winter resort (**ville d'hiver★**), with fine villas among the pines; a summer resort (**ville d'été**), with the seafront and attractive **Boulevard de la Mer★**; and the fashionable autumn and spring districts (**ville d'automne** and **ville de printemps**) with opulent houses near Pereire park.

HIGHLIGHTS

Bassin★ (Bay)

Bordered by the resorts of Arcachon, Andernos and the wooded dunes of the Cap Ferret peninsula, this vast airy bay, with Bird Island (Île aux Oiseaux) at its centre, extends over an area of 250sq km/96.5sq mi, four-fifths of

which is exposed at low tide. With its great stretches of oyster beds, Arcachon is one of the main oyster-farming areas. A trip in a *pinasse*, one of the traditional boats used by the oyster farmers, is a good way to see it. Excursions from Thiers and Eyrac landing stages (Arcachon) and elsewhere around the Bassin (*05 57 72 28 28. www.bateliers-arcachon.com*).

Dune du Pilat★★
7.5km/4.5mi S.

The highest (114m/374ft) and longest (2 800m/3 062yd) sand dune in Europe drops steeply on its landward side to the pine woodland. Its summit offers a thrilling view along the long, straight sands of **Côte d'Argent** (Silver Coast) with its splendid Atlantic rollers.

Every year the ocean deposits vast volumes of sand, continually building up the dune that in 1774 swallowed up the church at Soulac. The **panorama★★** of ocean and forest is especially lovely at dusk.

Dune du Pilat

ANGOULÊME★★

Angoulême has a walled historic Upper Town, which rises high above a more industrial modern Lower Town; narrow streets lace through the lofty Upper Town, lined with beautiful old buildings, and the ramparts give immense views. Angoulême is France's "Cartoon Capital", and everywhere you'll see the influence of its celebrated Festival International de la Bande Dessinée, devoted to the art of the strip cartoon.

Practical Information
Getting There
▶**TGV**: *Angoulême*. Angoulême is 115km/71mi S of Poitiers and 43km/27mi E of Cognac.

A BIT OF HISTORY
Honoré Balzac (1799–1850), the renowned novelist and playwright, made Angoulême his home in the 19C. In 1806, 77-year-old **General Resnier** launched himself from the city's northern ramparts in a **flying-machine** of his own invention. The general broke a leg, and his plan for invading England by this method was shelved. **Bande Dessinée** (strip cartoon, often known simply as BD) are treated as an art form and important entertainment for adults and kids alike in France. Angoulême's cartoon festival owes its origins to an exhibition in 1972, "Dix Millions d'images". In 1974, a regular *Salon de la bande dessinée* was started, which attracted many top cartoonists. Since 1996, a popular international festival has been held in January each year.

CATHÉDRALE ST-PIERRE★★

18 r. Fénélon, Angoulême.

Extensively destroyed by the Calvinists, the much-restored cathedral's elaborate 12C statuary of the west front (**façade★★**) is mostly intact; its themes include the Ascension and the Last Judgement.

EXCURSIONS
Château de La Rochefoucauld★★

The château and village are in the Charente, NE of Angoulême. 05 45 63 07 42. www.chateau-la-rochefoucauld.com.

This elegant Renaissance château is the seat of a noble family that gave the name François to all its first-born sons. **François VI** (1613–80) established his reputation as the greatest of France's maxim-writers in the 17C.

Cognac★

43km/27mi W of Angoulême.

For many years Cognac was a river port on the calm waters of the Charente, exporting salt and, from the 11C, wine. In 1570, it was one of the four strongholds conceded to the Protestants under the Treaty of St-Germain. Place François I, a busy square with an ornamental fountain, links the old part of Cognac, on the slope above the river Charente, with the sprawling modern town. Cognac has been distilled here since the 17C, aided by popularity in Holland, Scandinavia and Britain. In town, the distilleries of **Hennessy** and **Rémy Martin** are worth a visit.

LA ROCHELLE★★★

This lively port is much frequented by artists and tourists. It owes its origin to the fort built in the 11C during the centuries of English rule.

Practical Information

Getting There

▶TGV: *La Rcohelle*. 62km/39mi SW of Niort. The town centre lies around the Vieux Port.

A BIT OF HISTORY

La Rochelle was one of the first places in France where the Reformation took hold. After the St Bartholomew's Day Massacre (1572), La Rochelle became one of the main centres of Protestant resistance. By 1627, however, the town's keen Protestantism had become intolerable to Richelieu, who personally led a siege that took 15 months to starve the populace into submission. By the end, 23 000 citizens had perished. La Rochelle played a large part in opening up the world beyond Europe; in the 15C, the first colonists embarked for Canada and Jean de Béthencourt discovered the Canary Islands; in the 16C, La Rochelle's fishing fleet operated in the rich fishing grounds off Newfoundland.

La Rochelle's shipowners profited from international trade, and above all with the West Indies, where they owned vast plantations; they grew wealthy, too, on the triangular trade involving selling cloth to Africa, transporting African slaves to the Americas, and bringing American products to Europe.

VIEUX PORT★★

The old port was originally laid out by Eleanor of Aquitaine; its entrance is guarded by two towers,

probably built by the English in the 14C and once forming part of the town's ring of fortifications.

VIEUX VILLE★★

The 18C **Porte de la Grosse-Horloge★**leads into the Old Town. As well as timber-framed medieval houses and fine Renaissance residences, there are substantial 18C stone townhouses adorned with astonishing gargoyles. The **Hôtel de Ville★** is splendid.

EXCURSIONS

Île de Ré★ – This upmarket resort has been linked to the mainland by a viaduct since 1988.

Marais Poitevin★ – The vast Poitou marshlands are now a conservation area. The boats of the marshlanders glide over a complex network of waterways.

Les Sables-d'Olonne⌂⌂⌂ – A major seaside resort on the Côte de la Lumière, built on the sands of what was once an offshore bar.

Royan⌂⌂⌂ – The capital of the Côte de Beauté was reduced to rubble by bombing in 1945. It is once again popular thanks to its excellent beaches of fine sand, and a lively ambience.

Zoo de la Palmyre★★★ – 08 92 68 18 48. www.zoo-palmyre.fr. This attractive 14ha/33-acre zoo is one of the most visited in France. The zoo breeds endangered species (such as elephants and cheetahs); more than 1 600 animals from every corner of the globe live among the pine forest's lakes and hills, in areas similar to their natural habitat.

BIARRITZ★★★

With its splendid beaches of fine sand and high-quality facilities, golf courses and luxury hotels, this Basque Coast resort enjoys an international reputation. Biarritz is Europe's 🏄 **surfing** capital and teems with thousands of visitors coming to ride the waves year-round.

Practical Information
Getting There
▶**TGV**: *Biarritz*. Biarritz lies on the Atlantic coast, 32km/20mi N of the Spanish border.

RESORT
Fame came suddenly to Biarritz over a century ago, with visits by Empress Eugénie and Napoleon III. Queen Victoria was here in 1889, and after 1906 Edward VII took a shine to the place.
Biarritz is still going strong thanks to its three beaches, the best surfing in Europe, two casinos, and promenades and gardens on each side of the rocky promontory of the Plateau de l'Atalaye; uninterrupted **views**★★ extend to the mountain peaks of the Basque Country.

EXCURSIONS
Bayonne★★ – Biarritz, Anglet and Bayonne merge to form a single urban area of which Bayonne, with its busy quaysides and old streets, is the commercial centre.

The picturesque Rue du Pont-Neuf is flanked by arcades and tall houses. The Musée Bonnat's art and sculpture, as well as the Musée Basque's ehtnographic displays are worth a visit.
Route Impériale des Cimes★ – *Bayonne to Hasparren 25km/15.5mi.* Napoleon I's scenic highway was intended to link Bayonne with St-Jean-Pied-de-Port for strategic reasons. It snakes its way through fine **views**★ of the Basque coast and countryside.
Bidart⚓ – *6km/3.7mi S.* Bidart perches on a clifftop at the highest point on the Basque coastline. From Chapelle Ste-Madeleine, the clifftop **view**★ looks over the Jaizkibel promontory, the Trois Couronnes and La Rhune.
The charming **place centrale** is framed by the church, the pelota (*jai alai*) fronton and the town hall. Local pelota matches and competitions are always watched by enthusiastic crowds.

Grande Plage, Biarritz

© Y. Kanazawa/MICHELIN

BIARRITZ

PÉRIGUEUX★★

Périgueux is an ancient town built in the fertile valley of the River Isle. Its long history can be traced in its urban architecture and two distinctive districts, each of which is marked by the domes of its sanctuary: the Cité district, overlooked by St Stephen's tiled roof, and the Puy St-Front district, with the Byzantine silhouette of the present cathedral bristling with pinnacles. Périgueux's gastronomic specialities, with truffle and foie gras occupying prize position, have become famous around the world and attract many visitors.

Practical Information

Getting There

▶**TER**: *Périgueux*.
93km/60mi SW of Limoges.

A BIT OF HISTORY

This ancient town began as a Gaulish settlement, which prospered in Roman times under the name of Vesunna; its site, the "Cité", is marked by the amphitheatre gardens and St Stephen's Church (St-Étienne). In the Middle Ages, the quarter known as "Puy St-Front" is where the cathedral was built; in the 13C the area became the heart of Périgueux, absorbing the older Cité. In the 18C, a planned extension of the city linked the two districts by means of broad streets lined with public buildings.

HIGHLIGHTS

Vesunna – Musée Gallo-Romain de Périgueux★★★ – This museum houses the remains of an opulent Gallo-Roman residence.
St-Étienne-de-la-Cité★ – Two of the domes of the original sanctuary have survived. The earlier is thought to have been built in 1117.
Cathédrale St-Front★★ – The church was an important stopping-place for pilgrims on their way to Santiago de Compostela since it was here that the remains of St Front, the apostle of Périgord,

could be seen. His tomb dates from 1077. The cathedral was virtually rebuilt from 1852 onwards.
St-Front District★★★ – The old artisans' and merchants' district has been given a face-lift by a major conservation programme. Renaissance façades, medieval houses, courtyards, staircases and shops are gradually being brought back to life. Place du Coderc and place de l'Hôtel-de-Ville are colourful and busy every morning with their fruit and vegetables; place de la Clautre holds the larger Wednesday and Saturday markets.

EXCURSIONS

Brantôme★★ – *27km/17mi N of Périgueux on D 939.* **Abbaye de Brantôme**. *05 53 05 80 52. www.ville-brantome.fr*. Brantôme lies in lush countryside, in the charming Vallée de la Dronne, north of Périgueux. Its old abbey and picturesque setting make it one of the most delightful little places in Périgord, with its slate-roofed riverside dwellings, and crooked bridge reflected in the water. The 18C abbey has a fine west front and a Romanesque **bell tower★★**.
Château de Hautefort★★ – *The castle is 41km/25.4mi E of Périgueux. €8.50. 05 53 50 51 23. www.chateau-hautefort.com*. The elegant château rises proudly on its hilltop site, above extensive grounds.

SARLAT-LA-CANÉDA★★★

This attractive old Dordogne market town has narrow medieval streets lined with restored Gothic and Renaissance houses.

Practical Information

Getting There

▶TER: *Sarlat-la-Canéda.*
64km/40m SE of Périgueux.

A BIT OF HISTORY

Sarlat is the capital of the Périgord Noir (Black Périgord), a fortunate and abundant region between the Dordogne and Vézère rivers.
The town grew up around the Benedictine abbey founded in the middle of the 9C. The wealth of the surrounding countryside poured into the town, enabling it to support a prosperous population of merchants, clerics and lawyers. Sarlat reached its peak during the 13C and 14C.
The town long played host to fairs and markets, which still take place every Saturday, when the stalls are loaded with seasonal produce, poultry, cereals, horses, nuts, geese, foie gras, truffles and other goods.

OLD SARLAT★★★

Sarlat's old district was cut into two in the 19C by the Traverse (rue de la République). The town houses are quite unique: built with quality ashlar-work in a fine golden-hued limestone, with interior courtyards; the roofing, made of heavy limestone slabs (*lauzes*), necessitated a steeply pitched framework so that the enormous weight (500kg per sq m – about 102lb per sq ft) could be supported on thick walls.
Over the years new floors were added: a medieval ground floor, a High Gothic or Renaissance upper floor and Classical roof cresting and lantern turrets.
This architectural unit escaped modern developments and was chosen as one of the new experimental national restoration projects, the goal of which was to preserve the old quarters of France's towns and cities. The project, begun in 1964, has allowed the charm of this small medieval town to be re-created.
St Sacerdos' Church was built here in the 12C. In 1504 Bishop Armand de Gontaut-Biron had the church razed, in order to build a cathedral. However, the bishop left Sarlat in 1519 and the construction work was not completed for more than a century.

EXCURSIONS

Beynac-et-Cazenac★★

The castle and village are on the N bank of the Dordogne, 12km/7.4mi S of Sarlat. Open daily Jun–Sept 10am–6.30pm; Oct–Feb 10am–dusk; Dec–Feb noon–dusk. €7.50. 05 53 29 50 40.

One of the great castles of Périgord, **Château de Beynac** is famous for its history, its architecture and for its panoramic setting on top of a rugged rock face.
Defended on the north side by double walls, the castle looms over the river from a precipitous height of 150m/492ft. Crouching beneath its cliff is a tiny village, once the home of poet Paul Eluard.
A square keep existed here as early as 1115; it was strengthened

at the time of the great rivalry between the Capetians and the Plantagenets.

Domme★★

The village is S of the River Dordogne, 12km/7.4mi from Sarlat. 05 53 31 71 00. www.ot-domme.com.

One of the many medieval fortified towns (*bastides*) founded in southwest France by both French and English, Domme was founded by Philip the Bold in 1283 in order to keep watch on the Dordogne Valley and check the desire for expansion of the English, already established in Gascony. The normal rectangular plan of such settlements was here distorted in order to fit it to the rocky crag overlooking the Dordogne 145m/475.7ft below.

The king granted the town important privileges including that of minting coins and Domme played an important role during the Hundred Years' War. In the 17C, its wine-growing and river-trading activities were thriving and its markets were renowned throughout the region.

There are splendid views over the alluvial valley of the Dordogne from the Barre belvedere or, better still, from the cliff-top walk (Promenade des Falaises) just below the public gardens.

Les Eyzies-de-Tayac★★

20km/12.4mi from Sarlat.

The village occupies a grandiose setting of steep cliffs crowned with evergreen oak and juniper, at the confluence of two rivers. In the base of the cliffs are caves that were prehistoric habitations, where the art and crafts of our distant ancestors can still be seen.

Grotte du Grand-Roc★★ – *Laugeri-basse, 24620 Les Eyzies de Tayac. Guided tours (30min) Apr–Oct 10am–6pm (Jul–Aug 9.30am–7pm). €7.50. 05 53 06 92 70.* The cave is set in a magnificent cliff overlooking the Vézère, and is renowned for its stalagmites and stalactites which display considerable variety.

Musée National de Préhistoire★ – *Open Jul–Aug daily 9.30am–6.30pm. Rest of year times vary. €5. 05 53 06 45 45. www.musee-prehistoire-eyzies.fr.* Displays of prehistoric artefacts in an old 13C fortress with good views.

Grotte de Font-de-Gaume★ – *Open daily except Sat mid-May to mid-Sep, rest of year closed noon-2pm. €7. 05 53 06 86 00. Advance booking essential; only 200 visitors allowed per day.* Since its discovery in 1901, dozens of polychrome paintings have been found in the Grotte de Font-de-Gaume.

Abri de Laugerie-Haute – *On D 47 where it turns away from the Vézère. Guided tours by appointment; call for other opening times. Closed public holidays.* Representing 7 000 years of civilisation, this rock shelter was used during the Upper Palaeolithic period as a workshop for flints.

Grotte de Lascaux★★★

The cave is situated 2km/1.2mi S of Montignac, and 26km/16mi S of Sarlat. The actual Lascaux cave is closed to the public. However, a replica, known as Lascaux II, is open for visits at Montignac, just 200m away. 05 53 05 65 65. www.lascaux.culture.fr.

The world-famous cave paintings of Lascaux were discovered by accident on 12 September 1940 by a young man looking for his dog, which had disappeared down a hole.

The Paintings – Most of the paintings in the cave appear to date from the end of the Aurignacian period, others from the Magdalenian. They cover the walls and roofs of the cave with a bestiary of bulls, cows, horses, deer and bison, depicted with such skill as to justify Abbot Breuil's epithet "the Sistine Chapel of prehistoric times".

Unfortunately, the damage caused by visitors was such that the caves were closed to the public and a full-size replica was constructed.

Bergerac★

49km/30.5mi S of Périgueux. 05 53 57 03 11. www.ville-bergerac.com.

Spread out on both banks of the Dordogne where the river tends to be calmer, this distinctly southern town is surrounded by prestigious vineyards and fields of tobacco, cereals and maize. A project to restore the old quarter has seen the gentrification of a number of Bergerac's 15C and 16C houses.

Intellectual/commercial crossroads – The town's expansion began as early as the 12C. Benefiting from the town's situation as a port and bridging point, the local merchants profited from successful trade between the Auvergne and the Limousin and Bordeaux on the coast. This flourishing city and capital of the Périgord became one of the bastions of Protestantism as its printing presses published pamphlets that were widely distributed. In August 1577 the Peace of Bergerac was signed between the king of Navarre and the representatives of King Henri III. Despite this, in 1620, Louis XIII's army took over the town and destroyed the ramparts. After the Revocation of the Edict of Nantes (1685), a certain number of Bergerac citizens, faithful to their Calvinist beliefs, emigrated to Holland, a country where they had maintained commercial contacts. Bergerac was the capital of Périgord until the Revolution, when the regional capital was transferred to Périgueux. In the 19C, wine-growing and shipping prospered until the onslaught of phylloxera and arrival of the railway.

Bergerac today – Essentially an agricultural centre, Bergerac is the capital of tobacco in France (complete with **tobacco museum★★**). In addition, extensive vineyards surrounding the town produce wines with an *appellation d'origine contrôlée* including: Bergerac, Côtes de Bergerac, Monbazillac, Montravel and Pécharmant. Find out more at the **Musée Régional du Vin et de la Batellerie★** and tyhe **Maison des Vins – Cloître des Récollets**.

Famous citizens – Oddly enough, the Cyrano of Edmond Rostand's play was inspired by the 17C philosopher **Cyrano de Bergerac** whose name had nothing to do with the Périgord town. Not discouraged in the slightest, the townspeople took it upon themselves to adopt this wayward son and erect a statue in his honour in place de la Myrpe.

SARLAT-LA-CANEDA

LANGUEDOC ROUSSILLON

Languedoc-Roussillon follows the arc of the coastal plain from the mighty Rhône to the massive barrier of the Pyrénées. It is a hugely diverse area, ranging from seaside resorts to mountain villages and rural hamlets, as well as large towns and cities - Montpellier, Toulouse and Perpignan. After the Roman era, the region was ruled by the Counts of Toulouse. Following the persecution of the Cathars in the 13C, French kings took control; the region has been part of France ever since. From the 11–13C, wandering poets (troubadours) sang songs of unrequited love in a Romance language – Langue d'Oc. Today the term

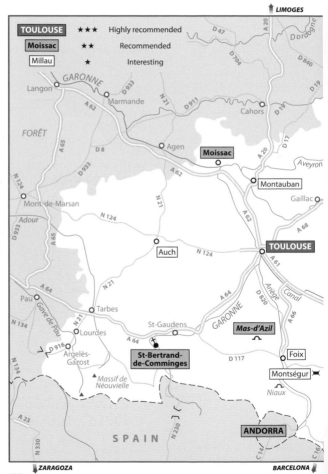

LIMOGES

TOULOUSE	★★★	Highly recommended
Moissac	★★	Recommended
Millau	★	Interesting

Langon

GARONNE

Marmande

Cahors

FORÊT

Agen

Moissac

Montauban

Gaillac

Mont-de-Marsan

Adour

Auch

TOULOUSE

Pau

Tarbes

St-Gaudens

Mas-d'Azil

Lourdes

Argelès-Gazost

St-Bertrand-de-Comminges

Foix

Montségur

Massif de Néouvielle

Niaux

SPAIN

ANDORRA

Occitan is used; street signs in Occitan (similar to the Catalan language of Spain and Andorra) can be seen across the region. In this part of France, you're never far from vineyards, the mainstay of the local economy. Much of the Midi-Pyrénées region is given over to agriculture and tourism. Languedoc-Rousillon Is the fourth most visited tourist area in France. With some 15 million visitors a year, tourism is a huge economic player, with summer beach holidays on Languedoc's "sunshine coast," cultural tourism, spas like d'Amélie-les Bains at Vallespir and ski resorts like Cerdagne et le Capcir.

The economic diversity of the region ranges from the casting of church bells to high-tech wonders of the aerospace industry around Toulouse.

MONTPELLIER★★★

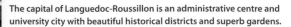

The capital of Languedoc-Roussillon is an administrative centre and university city with beautiful historical districts and superb gardens.

Practical Information

Getting There

▶**TGV**: *Montpellier-Saint-Roch.*
170km/106mi west of Marseille.

A BIT OF HISTORY

Origins – Montpellier had its beginnings with two villages: Montpellieret and Montpellier. In 1204 Montpellier became a Spanish enclave and remained so until 1349 when John III of Majorca sold it to the king of France for 120 000 *écus*. In the 16C, the Reformation arrived in Montpellier, and Protestants and Catholics fought for the town. In 1622 royal armies of Louis XIII laid siege to Montpellier's fortifications and Richelieu built a citadel to keep watch over the rebel city.

Modern Montpellier – After the Revolution the town became the *préfecture* of the Hérault *département*. The high-speed (TGV) rail makes Paris only 4hr away. The city's dynamism is reflected in the **Corum** conference and concert centre, the **Antigone** district that is linked to old Montpellier by the Triangle and Polygone centres, and the **Odysseum** leisure district.

PROMENADE DU PEYROU★★

The upper terrace of the promenade affords a sweeping **view**★ of the Garrigues, Cévennes, Mediterranean and Mont Canigou. The key feature of the Promenade du Peyrou is the ensemble of the *château d'eau* and St-Clément aqueduct. On Saturday, Promenade des Arceaux becomes a flea market.

The late-17C **Arc de Triomphe** depicts the victories of Louis XIV and major events from his reign: the Canal du Midi, revocation of the Edict of Nantes, the capture of Namur in 1692 and the United Provinces of the Netherlands kneeling before Louis XIV.

ANTIGONE DISTRICT★

Starting from place de la Comédie (east side), walk to the Antigone district via the Polygone shopping centre. Catalan architect **Ricardo Bofill** designed the bold new Antigone district. This vast Neoclassical housing project combines prefab technology with harmonious design. Behind a profusion of entablatures, pediments, pilasters and columns are low-income housing, public facilities and local shops, arranged around squares and patios. **Place du Nombre-d'Or** continues with the cypress-lined **place du Millénaire**, place de Thessalie then place du Péloponnèse. The vista stretches from the "Échelles de la Ville" past the crescent-shaped buildings of **esplanade de l'Europe**, to the **Hôtel de Région**, converted into a dock for Port Juvénal.

HISTORIC CENTRE

Ancient buildings and elegant hôtels particuliers; note the **Cathédrale St-Pierre**; the Montpellier Faculty of Medicine; the Jardin des Plantes, the oldest botanical gardens in France (1593); and the **Musée Fabre★★**, which displays Greek and European ceramics, as well as paintings.

EXCURSIONS

🚢 **Sète** – *36km/22.5mi SW of Montpellier*. Sète's town-centre canals are the scene of the famous *joutes nautiques*, jousting tournaments, particularly well attended on the day of St-Louis in August. The **old harbour★**, with its picturesque fishing boats and yachts, is the most interesting part of Sète port. The 12km/7.5mi-long Plage de la Corniche is nearby.

Massif de l'Aigoual★★★ – *At the heart of the Cévennes National Park, the Aigoual summit, 37km/23mi S of Florac, is reached on the steep D 118.* The highest point of the massif is **Mont Aigoual★★★**; it surveys a landscape of long straight ridges cut by deep ravines and arid limestone *causses*.

From 1875 onwards a massive programme of reafforestation has created a forest covering some 140sq km/ 54sq mi.

Grotte des Demoiselles★★★ – *In the upper Hérault Valley near the town of Ganges. Opening times vary. 04 67 73 70 02. www.demoiselles. com.* The cave, discovered in 1770, contains an enthralling underground landscape of extraordinary forms – stalactites, stalagmites and translucent draperies – to the great columns and huge 'organ-case' of this underground cathedral.

Cirque de Navacelles★★★ – *Between Lodève and Ganges, in the Hérault département.* This spectacular 300m/984ft-deep basin, separating the Causses – (high plateaux) – de Larzac and Blandas marks the former course of the River Vis before it cut through the base of the meander. On the valley floor a pretty single-arched bridge leads to the village of Navacelles; the little settlement clings to a rocky outcrop where, thanks to a mild microclimate, figs are grown.

St-Guilhem-le-Désert★★ – *The village is in the Hérault gorge. 04 67 57 70 17. www.saint-guilhem-le-desert.com.* In its remote and dramatic **site★** where the Val de l'Infernet runs into the valley of the Hérault, this 9C **village★** grew up around an abbey founded by William of Aquitaine. It is a timeless place whose narrow streets cluster around the Romanesque abbey church shaded by a huge and ancient plane tree.

Grotte de Clamouse★★★ – *3km/1.8mi S. Opening times vary. €9 (children, 12–18, €7.70. 04 67 57 71 05. www.clamouse.com.* The caves, a UNESCO World Heritage Site, run beneath the Larzac plateau and were carved by an extensive network of underground streams. There are remarkable stalactites and stalagmites, but best of all are the splendid crystallisations in fantastical shapes.

La Couvertoirade★ – *The village stands to one side of the highway, which crosses Larzac. Opening times vary. 05 65 58 55 59. www.lacouvertoirade.com.* High up on the lonely Larzac limestone plateau *(causse)*, this old fortified settlement once belonged to the Knights Templar. Its robustly-built houses date mostly from the 17C. The towers and the sentry-walk of the **ramparts** look over the Renaissance houses of its main street, rue Droite, and the 14C **fortified church**, whose graveyard has unusual disc-shaped gravestones.

GORGES DU TARN★★★

The deep gorges cut by the Tarn through the harsh limestone plateaux (causses) to the south of the Massif Central make up one of France's most spectacular natural landscapes. The source of the Tarn lies high (1 575m/5 167ft) in the granitic uplands of Mount Lozère; tumbling torrent-like down the slopes of the Cévennes, the river then enters the most spectacular section of its course at Florac.

Practical Information

Getting There

The River Tarn has cut through the limestone plateaux of the Cévennes to create a plunging gorge that snakes for 25km/15mi between Florac and Millau. There are small villages, notably Ste-Énimie, along the gorge, but no communities of any great size.

THE AREA

The Tarn River – 381km/237mi long – flows through gorges and canyons, joined by side valleys such as the Jonte and the Dourbie, in Millau. Escape from the valley bottom is by means of roads that twist and turn up the precipitous slopes to join the surface of the Causse Méjean. All along there is a striking contrast between the fertility at the riverside, and the barrenness of the *causse* high above. In high season, the gorges are busy with tourists who come for pursuits such as canoeing, climbing and hiking, and to see the amazing stalactites and stalagmites in the underground realm of chasms and caverns of **Aven Armand★★★**.

EXCURSIONS

Les Détroits (The Straits)★★ – The narrowest part of the valley, hemmed in by plunging cliffs of coloured limestone and slightly to the east of La Malène.

Cirque des Baumes★★★ – Below Les Détroits, the gorge widens, forming a magnificent natural amphitheatre.

Le Point Sublime★★★ – *Just W of Cirque des Baumes.* Splendid viewpoint overlooking both the Tarn Canyon and the Tarn Causse.

Grotte de l'Aven Armand★★★ – *43km/27mi NE of Millau. Open late Mar–early Nov. €8.50. 04 66 45 61 31. www.aven-armand.com.* Deep within the arid limestone of the Causse Méjean, subterranean waters have created a vast cavern, 60m wide and 120m long (197 x 394ft). Four hundred stalagmites, some up to 30m/97.5ft high, make a stunning spectacle.

Millau★ – *116km/72.5mi N of Montpellier. 1 pl. du Beffroi. 05 65 60 02 42. www.ot-millau.fr.* Millau is a lively provincial town, close to a remarkable modern **viaduct★★★** that takes the A75 autoroute soaring over the Tarn Valley.

Chaos de Montpellier-le-Vieux★★★ – *18km/11.2mi NE.* Extraordinary natural rock formations (the Sphinx, the Elephant, the Gates of Mycaenae).

Caves de Roquefort★ – *25km/15.5mi SW. Opening hours vary. €5. 05 65 58 54 38. www. roquefort-societe.com.* A must for cheese aficionados, Roquefort's eponymous blue-veined cheese has its own AOC status and must be matured underground in natural caves in which the temperature and humidity are constant.

LANGUEDOC
ROUSSILLON

MUST SEE

TOULOUSE★★★

A vibrant regional capital with attractive red-brick architecture, Toulouse is a lively university town with a thriving high-tech industrial sector and plenty of attractions for the visitor to enjoy.

Practical Information

Getting There

▶**TGV**: *Toulouse-Matabiau.*
Toulouse lies between Bordeaux (243km/152mi to the W) and Narbonne (150km/94mi to the E).

A BIT OF HISTORY

Toulouse was the capital of the Visigothic kingdom, and enjoyed considerable prosperity between the 9C and 13C under the Raymond dynasty, whose extensive territories were known as the "Langue d'Oc". In the 13C, the whole domain of the Raymonds embraced Catharism, prompting the Capetian kings, with the authority of the pope, to launch the Albigensian Crusade against Catharism. The Crusade ended the power of the Raymonds and broke up their territories, allowing the Capetian kings to push their frontier southwards into Languedoc.

In 1323, Europe's oldest literary society was founded here to further the cause of the language of southern France (Langue d'Oc). In the 16C, the city grew rich on a boom in the deep blue-black plant dye, known as woad.

From 1917, strategic industries like aircraft manufacturing were set up away from the country's vulnerable eastern border, and Toulouse has since remained the focus of France's aeronautics industry.

HIGHLIGHTS

Basilique St-Sernin★★★ – *pl. Saint-Sernin. Open daily Jul-Sept 8.30am–6.30pm; rest of year 8.30-* noon, 2pm-6pm. 05 61 21 70 18. *www.basilique-st-sernin-toulouse.fr.*
The great church was a major Romanesque pilgrimage church on the route to Compostela. Its octagonal bell tower is typical of the area.

Église des Jacobins★★ – *69 r. Pargaminières.Open daily 9am–7pm. 05 61 22 21 92. www.jacobins.mairie-toulouse.fr.* Built from the 13–15C to help fight against Catharism, the church is a masterpiece of Gothic palm-tree vaulting.

Musée des Augustins★★ – *Open daily 10am–6pm (Wed 9pm). €3. 05 61 22 21 82. www.augustins.org.* The museum is housed in the former convent, with a famous **Pietà** and superb collection of **Romanesque sculpture★★★**.

Hôtel d'Assezat★★ – This splendid Renaissance mansion houses the **Fondation Bemberg** (*open daily except Mon 10am–12.30pm, 1.30–6pm (Thu 9pm); €6; 05 61 12 06 89; www.fondation-bemberg.fr*), an impressive collection of painting, sculpture and *objets d'art* from the Renaissance to the 20C.

Muséum d'Histoire Naturelle★★ – *Open daily except Mon 10am–6pm. €6. 05 67 73 84 84. www.museum.toulouse.fr.* Extensive collections of prehistoric and ethnographical exhibits, plus lovely gardens for a pleasant stroll.

Musée St-Raymond★★ – *Open Jun–Aug 10am–7pm; Sept–May 10am–6pm. €3. 05 61 22 31 44.* The old 13C Collège St-Raymond, restored by Viollet-le-Duc, houses collections of archaeology and antique art.

Canal du Midi★★★ – *The Canal runs from Sète on the Languedoc coast to Toulouse, then joins the Canal Lateral to the Garonne and then on to Bordeaux.* It is hard to believe that this beautiful waterway, now so popular for leisurely boating holidays, was a daunting engineering achievement enabling the transport of industrial goods directly between the Mediterranean and the Atlantic. The notion of a canal between the Atlantic and the Mediterranean enabling shipping to avoid the long route via Gibraltar had preoccupied not only the Romans but also François I, Henri IV and Richelieu. The natural obstacles, however, seemed insurmountable. Then in 1662, Pierre-Paul Riquet (1604–80) succeeded in interesting Colbert in overcoming them. The canal was to prove his ruin; all the work was carried out at his own expense and he died six months before the opening. The completed Canal du Midi is 240km/149mi long and has 103 locks; it proved a huge commercial success – too late for the great man.

Becoming obsolete in the late 19C, it is used mainly by leisure craft today. In 1996 it was named as a World Heritage Site by UNESCO.

Auch★ – *Auch lies 76.4km/47.4mi W of Toulouse. 1 r. Dessoles. 05 62 05 22 89. www.auch-tourisme.com.* Auch is an attractive, bustling local capital in the heart of Gascony, beside the River Gers. It owes some fame to the story of *The Three Musketeers* – the real d'Artagnan, Charles de Batz, was from this area. The **Cathédrale Ste-Marie★★** contains a masterly series of Renaissance **stained-glass windows★★**, completed in 1517.

The **choir stalls★★★** are an inspired work of woodcarving.

Montauban★ – *55.3km/34.3mi N of Toulouse (autoroute A 62). 4 r. du Collège. 05 63 63 60 60. www. montauban-tourisme.com.* The old bastide of Montauban, built with a geometric street layout, is a good point of departure for excursions into the Aveyron gorges. Warm-hued pink brick lends the buildings here a distinctive character, which is also found in most of the towns and villages in Bas Quercy and the Toulouse area. The **Place Nationale★**, formerly the Place Royale, dates from the foundation of the town in the 12C.

Devoted to the eponymous artist's works, the **Musée Ingres★** is housed in a former bishop's palace.

Moissac★★ – *70km/44mi NW of Toulouse, via A 62. 6 pl. Durand de Bredon. 05 63 04 01 85. www. moissac.fr.* Moissac's highlight is the former Benedictine abbey church, **Église St-Pierre★**. Founded in the 7C and consecrated in 1063, the **cloisters★★** were completed 35 years later. The church's **south doorway★★★** is a triumph of Romanesque sculpture.

St-Bertrand-de-Comminges★★ – *St-Bertrand lies 112km/70mi SW of Toulouse, S of A 64, junction 17. 22 pl. Valentin-Abeille, Montréjeau. 05 61 95 80 22.* This is one of the most picturesque and charming villages in the Pyrénéan foothills, perched on an isolated hilltop, encircled by ancient ramparts and dominated by an imposing cathedral.

After the Burgundians laid waste to the town in AD 585, the site lay abandoned for centuries, until in 1073 St Bernard saw its potential for the building of a cathedral and monastery.

CARCASSONNE★★★

A visit to fortified Carcassonne, a UNESCO World Heritage Site, is a return to the Middle Ages. Its immaculately restored outline of ramparts and turrets make a fairy-tale vision. On Bastille Day (14 July) a dramatic fireworks display makes the stunning citadel seem to go up in flames.

Practical Information

Getting There

▶**TGV**: *Carcassonne. 93km/58mi SE of Toulouse and 59km/37mi W of Narbonne.*

A BIT OF HISTORY

First fortified by the Gauls, then occupied by Romans, Visigoths and Franks in turn, Carcassonne became subject to the County of Toulouse in the 9C. Its long period of prosperity was brought to an end by the Crusade against the "Albigensians" – Cathars. On 1 August 1209 the army under Simon de Montfort besieged the city, which put up a feeble defence, capitulating within a fortnight.

LA CITÉ★★★

The "Cité" of Carcassonne on the Aude's east bank is the largest fortress in Europe. It consists of a fortified nucleus, the Château Comtal, and a double curtain wall: the outer ramparts, with 14 towers, separated from the inner ramparts (24 towers) by the outer bailey, or lists (*lices*). It owes its survival to huge restoration works in the 19C led by Viollet-le-Duc. Nowadays, huge numbers of tourists descend on Carcassonne year-round; the cité is totally pedestrianised; tours of the ramparts are available by tourist train or horse-drawn carriage (*calèche, 04 68 71 54 57; www.carcassonne-caleches.com*).

EXCURSIONS

Castres★ – *70km/43.5mi F of Toulouse. 2 pl. de la République. 05 63 62 63 62. www.tourisme-castres.fr.* This industrial town on the Agout River has fine 16–17C mansions, and the **Musée Goya**★, with outstanding works by Goya.

Foix★ – *90km/56mi SW of Carcassonne. 29 r. Delcassé. 05 61 65 12 12. www.tourisme-foix-varilhes.fr.* Ruggedly set against a skyline of jagged peaks and three castle towers, its old narrow streets radiate from Rue de Labistour and Rue des Marchands.

The **Parc Pyrénéen de l'Art Préhistorique**★★ at Lacombe, on the road to Banat via the N 20, is devoted to cave paintings.

Grotte du Mas-d'Azil★★ – *31km/19mi NW of Foix. Call or see website for opening hours. €6.30. 05 61 69 97 / 1. www.grotte-masdazil.com.* This cave is one of the outstanding natural phenomena of southwestern France, as well as a very important prehistoric site.

Château de Montségur★ – *56.6km/35mi N of Ax-les-Thermes. 05 61 03 03 03. www.montsegur. org.* The last episode of the Albigensian Crusade took place on this fearsome peak. The stronghold was occupied by 400 adherents to the Cathar faith, whose austerity contrasted sharply with the venality of the Catholic clergy. They were massacred when they refused to retract; the last 200 faithful were brought down from the mountain to be burnt on a huge pyre.

NARBONNE★★

Narbonne, which in its time has been the ancient capital of Gallia Narbonensis, the residence of the Visigoth monarchy and an archiepiscopal seat, is now a lively Mediterranean city with an important role as a wine-producing centre.

Practical Information

Getting There

▶**TGV**: *Narbonne*. 61km/38mi E of Carcassonne and 96km/60mi SW of Montpelier.

A BIT OF HISTORY

The long history of this ancient Mediterranean city reaches back many centuries BC. The Roman Empire chose Narbonne to be the commercial centre of the Celtic province, with an artificial port created by diverting an arm of the River Aude. Finally it was made the flourishing capital of Gallia Narbonensis (today's Languedoc and Provence regions) After the end of the Roman Empire, the Visigoths made it their capital. Trading activity continued (Muslim raiders found the city still worth looting in 793), and medieval shipping made use of the extensive shallow lagoons lining the coast behind the rampart of sand bars. However, in the 14C, the city's large and long-established Jewish community was expelled; the famous port silted up, and the town's prosperity came to an abrupt end. The construction of the Canal du Midi in the 17C, the coming of the railway in the 19C, and the development of tourism on the Languedoc coast in the 20C halted the process of decline.

HIGHLIGHTS

Cathédrale St-Just-et-St-Pasteur★★ – *Open daily 9am–noon, 2–6pm. 04 68 32 09 52.* The present building was begun in 1272. The cathedral **treasury** has a wonderful late-15C **Flemish Tapestry★★** in silk and gold thread, a 10C ivory missal plaque and a rare marriage casket in rock crystal.

Palais des Archevêques – *Open daily Jun–Sept 10am–6pm; Oct–May daily except Tue 10am–noon, 2–5pm. €6. 04 68 90 30 30.* The huge palace and cathedral complex is split between the 12C **Old Palace** (Palais Vieux), and the **New Palace** (Palais Neuf), which houses the museums.

Archaeological Museum★★ – *Palais Neuf. Open daily Jun–Sept 10am–6pm; Oct–May daily except Tue 10am–noon, 2–5pm. €6. (Museum Pass €9). 04 68 90 30 54.* Narbonne undoubtedly possesses one of the finest collections of **Roman paintings★★** in France.
Museum of Art and History★ In the old archbishops' apartments.
Lapidary Museum★ – housed in the deconsecrated 13C church of Notre-Dame-de-la-Mourguié.
Basilique St-Paul – This basilica was built on the site of a 4–5C necropolis near the tomb of the city's first archbishop.

EXCURSIONS

Abbaye de Fontfroide★★ – *15km/9.3mi SW.* This beautiful old Cistercian abbey nestling among the Corbières vineyards is a particularly serene spot at sunset.
Réserve Africaine de Sigean★ – *18km/11m S of Narbonne and 54km/34m N of Perpignan by the N 9.* This **safari park** owes much of its unique character to the wild landscape of coastal Languedoc.

PERPIGNAN★★

Perpignan, once the capital city of the counts of Roussillon and the kings of Majorca, is an outpost of Catalan culture north of the Pyrénées, and a lively commercial city, with shaded walks lined with pavement cafés.

Practical Information

Getting There

▶**TGV**: *Perpignan*. 64km/40mi S of Narbonne, Perpignan, the most southerly city in mainland France, lies on the banks of the River Têt and its tributary the Basse.

A BIT OF HISTORY

In the 13C, the city prospered from growing trade with the eastern Mediterranean and became capital of Roussillon, part of the Catalan kingdom of Majorca, and later, part of the principality of Catalonia. From 1463, the French Crown tried to take possession of Roussillon, and in 1640 Richelieu offered Roussillon a degree of autonomy if it would become part of France, which it agreed to do, leading to the Siege of Perpignan as the Spanish tried to retain the city. The French victory was ratified by the Treaty of the Pyrénées.

HIGHLIGHTS

Palais des Rois de Majorque★ The restored Catalan palace lies within a citadel constructed later by Vauban.
Rue de la Loge★ – Sumptuous Renaissance buildings grace the bustling Rue de la Loge.
Le Castillet★ – This pink brick citadel, dating from the reign of Peter IV of Aragon, houses the **Musée Catalan**.

EXCURSIONS

La Côte Vermeille★★ – Towards the Spanish border lie small ports such as picturesque **Collioure★★**, which attracted artists of the Fauve School in the early 20C; **Banyuls** is famous for its sweet wine.
Fort de Salses★★ – *20km/12.4mi N of Perpignan*. This huge brick 15C and 17C fortress rises from the vine-covered plain north of Perpignan.
Les Corbières★★ – *04 68 45 69 40. www.corbières-sauvages.com*. Ruined castles, fruity, full-bodied wines, and a luminous, sweet-smelling *garrigue* landscape make the **Corbières** a special region.
Principat d'Andorra★★ – *26 ave de l'Opéra 75001 Paris. 01 42 61 50 55. www.tourisme-andorre.net*. No mere tax-free shopping haven, this tiny Catalan-speaking nation is also a wild, scenic land of lofty plateaux and precipitous valleys.
Château de Peyrepertuse★★★ – *47km/29mi NW of Perpignan. Open daily Jul–Aug 9am–8pm; rest of year times vary. €6. 04 82 53 24 07. www.chateau-peyrepertuse.com*. The Château de Peyrepertuse is the only Cathar fortress that was never taken by force.
Abbaye de St-Martin-du-Canigou★★ – *2.5km/1.5mi S of Vernet-les-Bains. €6. 04 68 05 50 03. http://stmartinducanigou.org*. This Romanesque abbey, built on a rocky pinnacle grew up around a monastic community founded in the 11C.
Prieuré de Serrabone★★ – *Open daily 10am–6pm. €3. 04 68 84 09 30*. Among wild mountains, this former priory contains superb Romanesque sculpture. The chapel gallery (**tribune★★**) boasts wonderful 11C carved capitals.

PROVENCE

The name Provence evokes an image of a magical land in the Midi, or south, of France where the sun always shines and Mediterranean influences are supreme: from the extensive remains of six centuries of Roman occupation to the traditional triumvirate of wheat, vine and olive, alternating with the remnants of the natural forest and the infertile but wonderfully aromatic *garrigues* (arid scrubland). Among the fertile Provençal plains stand the **mas**, shallow-roofed pantiled farmsteads protected from the fierce sun by stone walls with few window openings. Crops and buildings are shielded from the effects of the mistral, the strong regional wind, by serried ranks of cypresses.

Beautiful Provence is synonymous with serene landscapes. Ranges of limestone hills run east–west including the Alpilles, the rugged Luberon range and the Vaucluse plateau with its chasms and gorges. The River Rhône brings down 20 million cu m/706 293cu ft of silt annually, creating the huge delta of the Camargue.

Further north the Gorges of the Ardèche form one of the most impressive natural sights in France. The Romans founded a settlement at Aix in 122 BC. The collapse of the Roman Empire led to incursions by Visigoths and later by the Franks. Provence was annexed by the Holy Roman Empire in 1032, then incorporated into France in 1486.

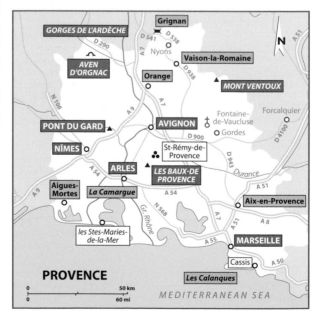

MARSEILLE★★★

The 19C Romano-Byzantine Basilica of Notre-Dame-de-la-Garde stands in a commanding position overlooking this great Mediterranean seaport. The view★★★ from the church is immense, taking in the islands standing guard in the bay, the harbour, and the background of limestone hills as well as the sprawling city itself.

A BIT OF HISTORY

Marseille began life as a trading post set up by Greeks from Asia Minor around 600 BC. Its inhabitants soon established other commercial bases both in the interior and on the coast, at Nice, Antibes, the Lérins Islands, Agde, Glanum (St-Rémy) and Arles. By the 3–2C BC the city they called Massilia covered an area of some 50ha/123.5 acres to the north of the Old Port, and the knolls rising above the busy streets were crowned with temples.

In 123 BC Massilia found it prudent to conclude an alliance with Rome. The Senate took the opportunity to begin its programme of expansion into Provence and Gaul.

Seventy years later, when Caesar and Pompey were engaged in civil war, Marseille had the ill fortune of siding with the loser. The victorious Caesar besieged the city and sacked it in 49 BC. Narbonne, Arles and Fréjus grew rich on the spoils, and Marseille went into decline. Even after its sack by Caesar, Marseille remained a free city. Its life as a port carried on, with many ups and downs, based on the "Horn" (corne), the original basin sited to the northeast of today's Old Port, which itself came more and more into use as an outer harbour. Nevertheless, the decline of the city as a whole made it difficult to maintain the installations, and the original harbour gradually silted up, finally becoming completely blocked in the 11C.

The Crusades led to a revival of the city's fortunes in the 12C. Further expansion followed, with the incorporation of Provence into the French kingdom in 1481 and even more with the construction of new quays under Louis XIII (a blow to its old rival Arles). In the 19C,

---

Practical Information

Getting There and Getting Around

▶**TGV**: *Marseille-Saint-Charles.* On the Mediterranean coast, 32km/20mi S of Aix-en-Provence.

◆ **Metro** – The RTM is the most convenient mode of transport; the two lines operate from 5am–9pm (12.30am Fri–Sun). From 10.30pm–12.35am during the week, the metro is substituted by the "fluobus". 04 91 36 58 11. www.le-tram.fr.

Magnetic card tickets are valid for a single trip (€*1.50*), 1 day (*carte journée:* €5) or for several journeys (*carte liberté:* €*6.30 for 5 journeys, €12.60 for 10*). Network maps are given out at ticket offices. *04 91 91 92 10. www.rtm.fr.*

◆ **Ferry boat** – Trips from one side of the Vieux Port to the other (saving you about 800 paces!): place aux Huiles to the town hall. Journeys daily 9am–7pm. No charge.

the city's fortunes revived further with the expansion of French (and European) colonial activity in the Orient as well as in Africa.

HIGHLIGHTS

Basilique St-Victor★ – A Christian quarter grew up opposite the old Greco-Roman city. It was here that St Victor is supposed to have met a martyr's death at the very beginning of the 4C, and here too that a fortified abbey is said to have been built in his memory around AD 420. The basilica was rebuilt in 1040. Its crypt and nave were altered in the early Gothic period.

Old Port★★ – On the south side of the Old Port is the bust of Vincent Scotto (1876–1952), the composer of much-loved popular melodies, surveying what is almost always a highly animated scene. To the east is the **Canebière**, the city's busy main artery, whose fame has been spread around the world by the mariners of Marseille.

For a glimpse into the long history of the port, visit **Musée des Docks romains★** (*4 pl. Vivaux; open Tue–Sun Oct–May 10am–5pm; Jun–Sept 11am–6pm. Closed public holidays; €2; 04 91 91 24 62*), part of the **Musée d'Histoire de Marseille★**, known as the Garden of Ruins (Jardin des Vestiges).

The "horn" formed by the first harbour is dramatically visible, and inside there is a 3C boat excavated from the mud.

Centre de la Vieille Charité★★ – *Opening times vary with each exhibition. €2–5. 04 91 14 58 38. www.vieille-charite-marseille. org.* The old workhouse and hospice (1671–1749) has been carefully restored. The **chapel★** is a masterpiece by Pierre Puget, a Marseille man; it has a little ambulatory and recessed steps allowing the different categories of inmates to make their separate ways to the chapels and galleries, and a central, oval-shaped cupola resting on a drum and supported by Ionic columns and pilasters. The second-floor gallery affords unusual views of the oblong chapel dome. The rich and varied collections of the **Musée d'Archéologie de Marseille**, has some 900 artefacts from the Near East, Greece, Etruria and Rome.

Corniche Président J. F. Kennedy★★ – This Corniche runs for nearly 5km/3mi – almost entirely along the sea-front. It is dominated by elegant villas built at the end of the 19C. Level with the **Monument aux morts de l'armée d'Orient** (*60 Corniche Kennedy*), attractive views open out towards the coast and the islands.

Musée de la Faïence★ – *157 ave de Montredon. Open daily except Mon: Jun–Sept 11am–6pm; Oct–May 10am–5pm. 04 91 72 43 47.* Set up in the Château Pastré, a fine 19C mansion built at the foot of the Marseilleveyre massif, this museum is devoted to the art of ceramics, from the early Neolithic Era up to the present day.

Musée Grobet Labadié★★ – *140 Longchamp. Open daily except Mon: Jun–Sept 11am–6pm; Oct–May 10am–5pm. €3. 04 91 62 21 82.* The bourgeois interior of this town house has been preserved, with its Flemish and French (16–18C) tapestries, furniture, faïence ware, religious plate work, wrought-iron work and musical instruments.

Musée Cantini★ – *19 r. Grignan. Open daily except Mon: Jun–Sept 11am–6pm; Oct–May 10am–5pm. €3. 04 91 54 77 75.* This museum specialises in 20C art after WWII until 1960, with particular attention to Fauvist, early Cubist, Expressionist and Abstract art.

EXCURSIONS

Îles du Frioul

Boats leave from quai des Belges, Vieux Port. €10 return to If or Frioul, and €15 to both. For times, see website. 04 91 46 54 65. www.frioul-if-express.com.

Château d'If★★ – *By boat from Embarcadère Frioul If Express, 1 quai de la Fraternité. Open mid-May–mid-Sept, daily 9.30am–6.15pm; rest of year times vary. €5. 04 91 59 02 30. http://if.monuments-nationaux.fr.*
Alexandre Dumas (1802–70), the 19C author of *The Three Musketeers*, imprisoned three of his characters here: the Man in the Iron Mask, the Count of Monte Cristo and Abbé Faria. After falling into disuse, it became a state prison for Huguenots and political prisoners. The **panorama**★★★ from the old chapel terrace is remarkable.

🚶 Massif des Calanques★★

The Massif des Calanques, with Mont Puget (565m/1 854ft) its highest peak, stretches almost 20km/12.4mi between Marseille and Cassis. The wild beauty of the famous *calanques*, which have been chiselled out along its coastline, have long attracted nature lovers.

👁 *There are no direct approach roads by car to the calanques with the exception of the less attractive coves of Goudes, Callelongue and Port-Miou. The only way to reach the others is on foot. Footpaths are often steep and rocky: it is advisable to get yourself the IGN map Les Calanques de Marseille à Cassis (www.ign.fr).*
👁 *Make sure to wear walking boots; carry water with you as there is none available.*

👁 *No access either on foot or by car to the calanques between 1 July and the second Sunday in September, or on days when the mistral is blowing fiercely.*
Goudes – An old fishing village, nestled amid grandiose rocky scenery. A sunny lunch in one of the small restaurants is a delight.
Sormiou★ – Considered by the local Marseillais to be the best of all the *calanques*, there are numerous *cabanons*, a small port, a beach, and several fish restaurants. Sormiou is separated from Morgiou by the viewpoint at **Cap Morgiou**.
Morgiou★★ – A wild setting with tiny creeks for swimming, crystal-clear water, *cabanons* clustered at the far end of the valley, restaurant, small port. Not to be missed!
Sugiton★★ – A small *calanque* with turquoise water, sheltered by cliffs, and popular with naturists.
En-Vau★★ – The best known *calanque* with its white cliffs, emerald water and stony beach. It is encircled by a forest of rock pinnacles overlooked by the "Doigt de Dieu" (Finger of God).
Cassis – *25km/15.5mi E of Marseille. Quai des Moulins, Cassis. 08 92 25 98 92. www.cassis.fr.* Cassis, a bustling fishing port, lies in an attractive **setting**★ at the end of a bay between the Puget heights and Cap Canaille. It is a popular summer resort with three beaches. Boat trips to the *calanques* are a popular excursion.
Corniche des Crêtes★★ – *From Cassis to La Ciotat 19km/12mi.* The highlight of the coast road between Cassis and La Ciotat is the **Cap de Canaille**★★★ and the outstanding **view**★★★ of the cliff face, Massif de Puget and the *calanques* and Massif de Marseilleveyre.

MARSEILLE

AIX-EN-PROVENCE★★★

The old capital of Provence has kept much of its 17C and 18C character: the elegance of its mansions, the charm of its squares, the majesty of its avenues and the loveliness of its fountains. It is also a lively city whose large student population keeps the café terraces busy. The new part of town is rapidly expanding and attracting more residents; it has established itself as a city of the arts, a thermal spa and an important centre for industry and the tourist trade.

Practical Information
Getting There

▶**TGV**: *Aix-en-Provence.*
32km/20mi N of Marseille, 35km/ 22mi SE of Salon-de-Provence.

A BIT OF HISTORY

The Aix of today is the legacy of Good King René (1409–80). The ruined Roman city Aquae Sextiae rose again in the 12C thanks to the Counts of Provence who made it their place of residence.
The last and most illustrious of the line was René, Duke of Anjou, Lorraine and Bar, King of Naples, Count of Provence and Piedmont; he supported literature and the arts and completed Aix cathedral. After his death, Louis XI incorporated Provence into France (1486). Leading the long roll-call of great men who were born or who lived in Aix is Paul Cézanne (1839–1906), one of the founders of modern painting; his many studies of Mount Ste-Victoire are justly renowned.

HIGHLIGHTS

Vieux Aix★★ – Elegant 17–19C mansions with corner statues, pleasant squares and charming fountains give the old town its distinctive character.
Cours Mirabeau★★ – Fountains splash under the canopy of plane trees and grand 17C and 18C

mansions line the south side of the Cours, opposite busy cafes and shops selling *calissons*, the local marzipan sweets.
Musee Granet★ – *Open Tue–Sun Jun–Sept 10am–7pm; Oct–May noon–6pm. €4. 04 42 52 88 32. www.museegranet-aixenprovence.fr.* Works by Cézanne are the highlight of the town's principal art museum.
Cathédrale St-Sauveur★ – *Open daily 7.30am–noon, 2–6pm. 04 42 43 45 65. www.cathedrale-aix.net.* The Merovingian **baptistery★** dates to the 4C. In the nave is the **Triptych of the Burning Bush★★**, painted around 1475 by Nicolas Froment.
Musée des Tapisseries★ – *Open mid-Apr–mid-Oct 10am–6pm; rest of year times vary. €3.50. 04 42 23 09 91.* The former bishop's palace, houses 19 magnificent tapestries made in Beauvais in the 17C and 18C.
Fondation Vasarely★ – *Open Tue–Sun 10am–1pm, 2–6pm. €9. 04 42 20 01 09. www.fondationvasarely.fr.* This vast museum complex consisting of 16 hexagonal structures is dedicated to Hungarian geometric artist Victor Vasarely (1906–97).
Atelier Paul Cézanne (Cézanne's Studio) – *Open Jul–Aug 10am–6pm; rest of year times vary. €2. 04 42 21 06 53. www.atelier-cezanne.com.* The studio, called the *Lauves*, where he painted *The Bathers*, among other works, has been left as it was at his death in 1906.

ARLES★★★

Arles is one of the most important centres of Provençal culture, proud of its past and famed for an exceptional Roman and medieval heritage. Van Gogh produced many of his greatest works here; what he loved was not the culture or history, but the brilliance of the light. The town continues to play a role in artistic life, hosting a renowned annual summer photography festival, Les Rencontres d'Arles.

Practical Information

Getting There

▶**TGV**: *Arles.*
On the edge of the Camargue wetlands and the Rhône delta, 80km/50mi W of Aix-en-Provence and 45km/28mi S of Avignon.

A BIT OF HISTORY

The ancient Celtic-Ligurian town was colonised by the Greeks of Marseille as early as the 6C BC and was already a thriving town when the Romans conquered the region. They built a canal linking it to the sea so that it could be supplied directly from Rome.

Growing into a prosperous port town, and well placed on the major Roman highways, it became an administrative and political capital of Roman Gaul.

HIGHLIGHTS

Théâtre Antique★★ – This is among the most important surviving Roman theatres, and dates from the end of the 1C BC. All that remains of its stage wall are two elegant columns. The theatre was broken up for its stone as early as the 5C, and disappeared under houses and gardens. It was excavated in the 19C.

Amphithéâtre★★ – Up to 20 000 spectators enjoyed games pitting men against wild animals, and gladiatorial combat. Dating from about AD 75, the sturdy structure was later filled in with as many as 200 houses and two chapels.

Église St-Trophime★ – Its **porch★★** is one of the masterpieces of late 12C Provençal Romanesque architecture; fine sculpture in the **cloisters★★**.

Musée d'Arles et de la Provence antique★★ – The town's extensive collection of ancient art.

Musée Réattu★ – Small museum of contemporary art, showing paintings by Pablo Picasso, including **Picasso Bequest★**.

Thermes de Constantin★ – The largest baths in Provence.

Alyscamps★ – A famous Roman necropolis, located just outside the town walls of Old Arles.

EXCURSIONS

Les Alpilles★★ – The jagged, white peaks of the Alpilles standing out against the blue sky above almond and olive trees and dark lines of cypresses evoke Van Gogh's shimmering landscapes.

La Camargue★★ – The Rhône delta forms an immense wetland plain, a remarkable area with a culture and history all its own, as well as distinctive flora and fauna. It is divided into three distinct regions: a cultivated region north of the delta, salt marshes west of the Petit Rhône, and the watery nature reserve to the south. The main town in the Camargue is Les Saintes-Maries-de-la-Mer on the coast. Try to catch sight of the three creatures that symbolise the Camargue – white horses, black bulls and pink flamingos.

LES BAUX-DE-PROVENCE★★★

With its ruined castle and deserted houses capping an arid rocky spur plunging abruptly to steep ravines on either side, the old village of Baux has the most spectacular of sites. Baux has also given its name to bauxite, a mineral first discovered here in 1822 that led to the development of aluminium.

Practical Information

Getting There

▶**TGV**: *Avignon, then local bus.*
30km/18.6mi S of Avignon; 9.5km/
6mi SW of St-Rémy-de-Provence.

A BIT OF HISTORY

The lords of Baux were renowned in the Middle Ages, described by Mistral as "warriors all – vassals never". They traced their ancestry back to the Magi king Balthazar and boldly placed the Star of Bethlehem on their coat of arms.

HIGHLIGHTS

Town – The original entrance into the town is guarded by a gate (Porte Eyguières). Go through the fortified gateway into the town, and simply wander in the old streets. The **Place St-Vincent★**, pleasantly shaded by elms and lotus-trees, has a terrace giving views of the small Fontaine Valley and Val d'Enfer. The 17C former Town Hall (Hôtel de Ville) has rooms with ribbed vaulting.
The church (Église St-Vincent) dates from the 12C; dressed in their long capes, the shepherds from the Alpilles hills come here for their **Christmas festival★★**, celebrated at Midnight Mass. The **Rue du Trencat★** was carved into the solid rock that has subsequently been pitted and eroded by wind and rain.
Château des Baux – *Open daily, summer 9am–8.15pm; rest of year*

times vary. €8–9 . 04 90 54 55 56.
www.chateau-baux-provence.com.
The powerful lords of Baux were a great irritant to Louis XIII who in 1632 ordered the castle and ramparts to be dismantled. From the remains of the 13C keep a fine **panorama★★** unfolds over the Alpilles with the windmills of Fontvieille to the west. One of them is Daudet's Mill (Moulin de Daudet), where **Alphonse Daudet**, the Nîmes-born author is supposed to have written his delightful *Letters from My Mill*.
Musée Yves-Brayer★ – *pl. François -de-Hénain. Open Apr–Sept daily 10am–12.30pm, 2–6.30pm; rest of year times vary. €5. 04 90 54 36 99. www.yvesbrayer.com.* Museum housing works by figurative painter Yves Brayer (1907–90).

EXCURSION

St-Rémy-de-Provence★ – *9km/6mi north of Les-Baux-de-Provence. 04 90 92 38 52. www.saintremy-de-provence.com.*
St-Rémy is the essence of inland Provence; plane trees shade its boulevards and charming old alleyways wind around the Renaissance Place de la République.
1km/0.6mi south of the town, **Les Antiques★★** are the fascinating remains of the Roman city of Glanum. The 1C BC **mausoleum★★** is the best preserved of its kind in the Roman world.

NÎMES★★★

Nîmes lies between the limestone hills of the Garrigue to the north and the alluvial plain of the Costière du Gard to the south. Its elegant and bustling boulevards are shaded by lotus-trees. The quality of its Roman remains is outstanding.

Practical Information

Getting There

▶**TGV:** *Nîmes*. Nîmes is 32km/19.8mi NW of Arles.

A BIT OF HISTORY

Emperor Augustus heaped privileges on Nîmes and allowed the building of fortifications. The town, situated on the Domitian Way, then proceeded to erect splendid buildings: the Maison Carrée along the south side of the forum, an amphitheatre able to hold 24 000 people, a circus, baths fed by an imposing aqueduct, the Pont du Gard. In the 2C the town won favour with Emperors Hadrian and Antoninus Pius (whose wife's family came from Nîmes); it continued to flourish and build and reached the peak of its glory.

In 1873, a Bavarian emigrant to the United States named Lévy-Strauss called his new trousers, made from locally manufactured blue serge, "Denims", meaning "from Nîmes".

HIGHLIGHTS

Arènes★★★ – *Open daily Jul–Aug 9am–8pm, rest of year times vary. Closed to visitors during events. €7.90 (The Pass Nîmes Romaine €10 gives entry to the Arènes, Maison carrée and Tour Magne). 04 66 21 82 56. www.arenes-nimes.com.* This superb structure was built in the reign of Augustus, possibly some 80 years before the amphitheatre at Arles. The scale of the great structure is extraordinarily impressive, as is the achievement

in cutting, transporting and placing stonework of such dimensions with such precision. The big, crowded bullfights still held here give a flavour of the original arena.

Maison Carrée★★★ – *Open daily Jul–Aug 10am–8pm, rest of year times vary. Closed to visitors during events. €4.60. 04 66 58 38 00. www.arenes-nimes.com.* Heading northwest along boulevard Victor-Hugo, the Maison Carrée sits in the centre of an elegant paved square separated from the Carré d'art by the boulevard. This house, built in the reign of Augustus (1C BC), is the purest and best preserved of all Roman temples; it is not known which cult was observed here.

Jardin de la Fontaine★★ – In Roman times this site was occupied by a spring, a theatre, a temple and baths. Today's shady gardens exemplify the subtle use of water in the landscapes of Languedoc: laid out in characteristic 18C manner, with pools leading into a canal, balustraded walks and porticoes.

Musée Archéologique★ – *Open Tue–Sun 10am–6pm. No charge for permanent exhibitions; otherwise €5. 04 66 76 74 80.* In the ground-floor gallery, pre-Roman carvings and Roman inscriptions are displayed. Upstairs are Gallo-Roman coins, utensils, headdresses, funerary stelae, oil lamps, glassware and pottery (Archaic Greek, Etruscan and Punic). There is also a collection of cork models of the city's ancient monuments.

Musée des Beaux-Arts★ – *r. Cité-Foulc. Open Tue–Sun 10am–6pm. No charge for permanent exhibitions. 04 66 28 18 32. www.nimes.fr.* On the ground floor there is a large Roman mosaic depicting the marriage of Admetus; it was discovered in Nîmes in the 19C. The museum displays works from the French, Italian, Flemish and Dutch Schools (15–19C), including paintings by Bassano, Rubens, and Andrea della Robia. Local works are represented by the portraits of Xavier Sigalon (1787–1837) from Uzès, a seascape by Joseph Vernet, historical paintings by Natoire, a native of Nîmes, and *Landscape near Nîmes*, by J. B. Lavastre.

Carré d'Art★ – *pl. de la Maison Carrée. Open Tue–Sun 10am–6pm. No charge for permanent exhibitions; 04 66 76 35 70.* Designed by the British architect **Norman Foster** to house both the city's Museum of Contemporary Art and its media library, the Carré d'Art stands opposite the Maison Carrée, from which it has copied several of its architectural features. Its collection includes paintings, sculptures and drawings from 1960 onwards.

EXCURSION

Aigues-Mortes★★ – *Aigues-Mortes is 46.6km/29mi SW of Arles. 04 66 53 73 00. www.ot-aiguesmortes.fr. Parking is available outside the ramparts. Climb to the the Tour de Constance (53 steps) for an impressive panorama over the town and surrounding flatlands.*

Few places evoke the spirit of the Middle Ages as vividly as Aigues-Mortes sheltering behind its ramparts in a landscape of marshland, lakes and saltpans. A tourist train runs around Aigues-Mortes, offering an overview of the main attractions and entertainment options. Shops, restaurants and hotels lie within the city walls, and a traditional market can be found on Avenue Frédéric-Mistral.

A Bit of History – In 1240, Louis IX (St Louis), then 26 years old, wanted France to be involved in the kind of commerce undertaken by the merchant fleets of Pisa and Genoa. He was also taken by the idea of a Crusade, but lacked a Mediterranean port – at this time Provence was part of the Holy Roman Empire, Sète did not exist, and Narbonne was silting up. Louis' solution was to buy a site from a priory and grant a charter to the township that began to develop on what had up to then been virtually an island. The new settlement was laid out on the geometrical lines of a bastide and linked to the sea by an artificial channel.

On 28 August 1248, Louis IX set sail from here on the 7th Crusade, which was a failure. On 1 July 1270 he left from here again, on the 8th Crusade, which only reached Tunis, where Louis died.

By the 14C Aigues-Mortes' population totalled 15 000, but its waterways had begun to silt up; the Tour de Constance lost its military significance and instead became a prison.

For more than a century after the revocation of the Edict of Nantes in 1665, Protestant rebels were held here, from 1715–68 the Tour de Constance being reserved for women prisoners.

The silting up of the port and the incorporation of Marseille into the French kingdom in 1481 pushed Aigues-Mortes into decline and the coup de grâce was the founding (17C) and subsequent development of Sète.

AVIGNON★★★

Protected by a ring of imposing ramparts, the historic core of Avignon is a lively centre of art and culture. For 68 years it was the residence first of seven French popes, then of three others once Pope Gregory XI had returned to Rome in 1377; the Papal Legates remained until the city was united with France in 1791.

Practical Information
Getting There

▶TGV: *Avignon.* Avignon is located 37km/23mi N of Arles.

A BIT OF HISTORY

At the beginning of the 14C the popes felt the need to escape from the turbulent political life of Rome. Avignon formed part of the papal territories, and occupied a central position in the Europe of the time. The case for moving there was put by Philippe le Bel (the Fair), possibly with a view to involving the papacy in his own political manoeuvring. In 1309 Pope Clement V took the plunge, and Avignon became for most of a century the capital of Western Christendom. When Pope Clement VI succeeded him in 1342, he greatly enlarged the Papal Palace, and brought to Avignon his love of the arts.

Avignon remains an influential cultural centre. It owes much to Jean Vilar, who in 1947 founded the prestigious annual event, **Festival d'Avignon**.

HIGHLIGHTS

Palais des Papes★★★ – *Open daily; Jul 9am–8pm; Aug 9am–9pm; rest of year times vary. €10.50 (€13 combined ticket with pont St-Bénézet). 04 32 74 32 74. www.palais-des-papes.com.* The huge feudal structure, fortress as well as palace, conveys an overwhelming impression of defensive strength with its high bare walls, its massive corbelled crenellations and stalwart buttresses. Inside, a maze of galleries, chambers, chapels and passages contains almost no furnishings. While the popes were in residence the palace was extremely luxuriously equipped.

Pont St-Bénézet★★ – *Accessed via ramparts. r. Ferruce. Open daily Jul 9am–8pm; Aug 9am–9pm; rest of year times vary. €4.50 (€13 combined ticket with Palais des Papes). 04 32 74 32 74.* Stepping out into the swirling Rhône, and coming to an abrupt end in mid-stream, this beautiful bridge was first built in 1177, according to legend, by a shepherd-boy called Bénézet. Until the Bridge Brotherhood (Frères Pontifes) built Pont-St-Esprit more than a century later, this was the only stone bridge over the Rhône. It helped the economic development of Avignon long before becoming a useful link with Villeneuve when the Cardinals built their villas. Eighteen of its arches were carried away by the floodwaters of the river in the 17C.

Rocher des Doms★★ – There is a well laid-out garden planted with different species on this bluff. From the terraces you will encounter superb **views★★** of the Rhône and Pont St-Bénézet, Villeneuve-lez-Avignon with Tour Phillipe-le Bel and Fort St-André, the Dentelles de Montmirail, Mont Ventoux, Vaucluse plateau, the Luberon hills and the Alpilles.

EXCURSIONS
Le Pont du Gard★★★

Pont du Gard site, rte du Pont du Gard. 0820 90 33 30. www.pontdugard.fr. Both banks of the river have a large car park, open 7–1am (€5).

This superb aqueduct and road bridge was built between AD 40 and 60. It formed part of a water-supply system 49km/30mi long, stretching from its source near Uzès via a series of cuttings, trenches, bridges and tunnels to supply the Roman Nîmes with fresh water. The three great rows of arches of the aqueduct rise 49m/160.7ft above the valley of the Gardon: imagine the effect such a structure must have had on the imagination of the local Gauls, impressing with the power and prestige of Roman achievement.

Careful calculation of the dimensions of the huge blocks of stone meant that they could be put in place without mortar. The channel on the topmost level was faced with stone in order to maintain water quality and alongside it ran the carriageway of a Roman road. The Pont du Gard fulfilled its function until the 9C, when lack of maintenance and blocking by deposits of lime finally put it out of use.

Le Luberon★★★

La Maison du Parc, 60 pl. Jean Jaurès, Apt. 04 90 04 42 00. www.parcduluberon.fr.

The mountainous Luberon region is full of charm: striking solitary woods and rocky countryside plus picturesque hilltop villages and dry-stone huts. The villages of most interest to visitors are Ménerbes, Bonnieux, Gordes and Roussillon. Oak forests, Atlas cedar, Scots pine, moors of broom and boxwood, *garrigues*, and an extraordinary variety of aromatic plants (herbs of Provence) clinging to the rocky slopes are a delight for nature lovers.

Gorges de l'Ardèche★★★

The Ardèche gorge runs from Vallon Pont d'Arc to St Martin-d'Ardèche. 🛈 *Vallon-Pont d'Arc. 04 75 88 04 01. www.vallon-pont-darc-07.com.*

The Ardèche rises in hills to the north of the Col de la Chavade and flows 119km/74mi to the Rhône. Notorious spring floods and sudden spates can increase its flow by as much as 3 000 percent, causing immense damage. Vertical cliffs, dramatic meanders and rapids mean that canoeing and rafting are popular sports here.

Aven d'Orgnac★★★

Open daily guided tours (1hr): Jul–Aug 9.30am–6pm; rest of year times vary. €10 (includes museum). 04 75 38 65 10. www.orgnac.com.

This extraordinary chasm, Aven d'Orgnac, lies among the woods covering the Ardèche plateau. It was first explored by Robert de Joly (1887–1968) on 19 August 1935. Of the four caverns at Orgnac, only **Orgnac I** has so far been opened up to the public. Orgnac III is known to have been inhabited 300 000 years ago; the **museum** has displays on the cultures which flourished in the region before the Bronze Age.

ORANGE ★★

Gateway to the Midi, Orange is famous for its remarkable Roman remains, including the triumphal arch and the Roman Theatre, as well as for its prestigious international music festival, Chorégies d'Orange.

Practical Information
Getting There

▶**TGV**: *Orange.* Sited at the meeting of *autoroutes* and other highways, 32km/20mi N of Avignon.

A BIT OF HISTORY

Orange flourished in the days of the Pax Romana as an important staging post on the great highway between Arles and Lyon. In the 16C, it came into the possession of William the Silent, who took the title of Prince of Orange and founded the Orange-Nassau line. Orange is still proud of its association with the royal house of the Netherlands, whose preferred title is Prince (or Princess) of Orange. In 1678 under the Treaty of Nijmegen, the town became French territory.

HIGHLIGHTS

Théâtre Antique★★★ – Dating from the reign of Roman **Emperor Augustus**, this theatre is the best-preserved structure of its type in the whole of the Roman world.
Arc de Triomphe★★ – A UNESCO World Heritage Site, Orange's Arc de Triomphe was built between the years AD 21 and 26 as a tribute to Emperor Augustus. It is a remarkable piece of architecture covered with beautiful sculptures. On its north and east sides are reliefs depicting the exploits of the Second Legion in Gaul (weapons both of Gauls and of Amazons).

EXCURSIONS

Vaison-la-Romaine★★ – *The town is on the N slopes of the Dentelles de Montmirail hills, some 30km/18.6mi E of Orange. 04 90 36 02 11. www.vaison-la-romaine.com.* This picturesque old market town in the hills near Mont Ventoux has outstanding and extensive ruins of the original Gallo-Roman town, as well as a Romanesque cathedral and cloisters.

The layout of modern Vaison has allowed two parts of the Roman city to be excavated. The La Villasse quarter (**quartier de la Villasse**) lies to the southwest of the Avenue Général-de-Gaulle on either side of a paved central street; there are shops, houses and a basilica. The **quartier de Puymin** lies to the east of the avenue.

The **Musée Archéologique Théo-Desplans★** displays the finds excavated at Vaison, covering Gallo-Roman religion, living quarters, pottery, glassware, arms, tools, ornaments, and coins.

Château de Grignan★★ – *Grignan is SE of Montélimar, E of the Rhône. Open daily 9.30am–noon, 2–6pm. €5.50. 04 75 91 83 50. Place Sévigné, Grignan. 04 75 46 56 75. www.ville-grignan.fr.* The old town of Grignan is dominated by its medieval château, which owes its fame to the delightful letters written over a twenty-year period in the 17C by Mme de **Sévigné** to her daughter Mme de Grignan.

Mont Ventoux★★★ – *The massif is served by a scenic route 67km/41.6mi long between Vaison and Carpentras.* Isolated Mount Ventoux is a commanding presence in northwestern Provence, visible over vast distances especially when snow-topped in winter.

CÔTE D'AZUR

The Riviera's abundant sunshine, exotic vegetation and dramatic combination of sea and mountains have made it a fashionable place of pleasure since its "discovery" in the 19C. The coast is densely built up, the resorts linked by triple 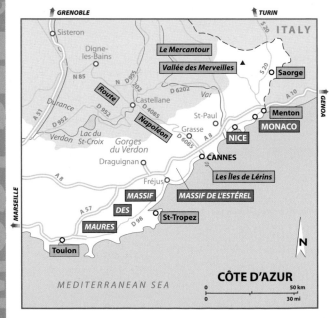 corniche roads. Further north are the Maritime Alps, dissected by the upper valleys of the Var, Tinée, Vésubie and Roya. To the west of Nice the coast flattens out, forming wide bays with fine beaches, before again rising beyond Cannes to higher ground.

The bustle of the coast is in contrast to the quieter charm of the interior, with its olive groves, spectacular gorges and hill villages. There is no defined boundary for the Riviera, but it is widely accepted as extending from the border with Italy, west to St-Tropez. Between Nice and Menton, the Pre-Alps plunge into the sea while the limestone plâteaux of the Provence tableland are separated from the sea by two massifs, Estérel and Maures. Its coastline has great promontories extending into the sea defining wide bays like that of the Gulf of St-Tropez. The Toulon coast is characterised by vertical cliffs, and attractive beaches. The Romans' presence in the region can be seen today at Fréjus and Cimiez (Nice). In the Middle Ages Provence changed hands several times and did not become part of France until the late 15C. Nice remained part of Savoy until 1860.

MUST SEE CÔTE D'AZUR

CÔTE D'AZUR

NICE★★★

Enclosed by an amphitheatre of hills, extending around a beautiful blue bay, the capital of the Riviera has artistic treasures, countless attractions, distinctive cuisine, a wonderful climate and a magnificent setting that has long attracted visitors.

Practical Information

Getting There

▶**TGV**: *Nice-Ville.* Nice is 27km/17mi W along the coast from the border with Italy.

A BIT OF HISTORY

Some 400 000 years ago, bands of elephant hunters made their encampments on the fossil beach at Terra Amata, 26m/85.3ft above the present level of the sea. In the 6C BC, Celto-Ligurians settled on the castle hill; a little later it was the turn of merchants and sailors from Marseille, who established themselves around the harbour. These were followed by the Romans, who favoured the Cimiez district. In 1388, aided and abetted by the **Grimaldi** family, Count Amadeus VII of Savoy (1360–91) incorporated Provence into his domain and made a triumphal entry into Nice.

As a result of the alliance of 1859 between France and Sardinia, Napoleon III helped drive out the Austrians from the Lombardy and Veneto regions; in return, France received from the House of Savoy the lands to the west of the Alps and around Nice, which had once been hers. A plebiscite produced an overwhelming vote in favour of a return to France (25 743 for, 260 against) and the ceremony of annexation took place on 14 June 1860.

SIGHTS
Le Vieux Nice★

The core of the city, huddling at the foot of the castle hill, has a lively, utterly Mediterranean character.

Château – The landscaped slopes of the castle hill, with their umbrella pines shading pleasant walks, reach a height of 92m/301.8ft. The summit provided a place of refuge for the denizens of Cimiez at the time of the fall of the Roman Empire. In the 12C, the Counts of Provence built a castle here which was subsequently strengthened by the Angevin princes and the Dukes of Savoy but was demolished by Louis XIV in 1706. From the top there is a fine **view★★** over the city, the Pre-Alps and the bay (Baie des Anges).

Place Garibaldi – The square is named after the great fighter for Italian unity who was born in Nice. The ochre walls and arcading of the buildings along its sides recall the urbane elegance characteristic of 18C Piedmontese town planning.

Place Masséna – The linear park laid out on what was once the bed of the River Paillon is interrupted by this square, begun in 1015. Its buildings, with their façades rendered in reddish ochre and their arcades, recall the planned urban spaces of Turin.

Site archéologique gallo-romain★ – *Open Wed–Mon 10am–6pm. No charge. Guided tours (1-2hr) €5. 04 93 81 59 57. www.musee-archeologique-nice.org.* The Cimiez district originated in the Roman settlement whose growth soon eclipsed that of the older town laid out around the harbour. The archaeological site consists of

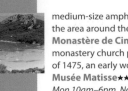

medium-size amphitheatres and the area around the baths.

Monastère de Cimiez★ – The monastery church possesses a Pietà of 1475, an early work of Louis Bréa.

Musée Matisse★★ – *Open Wed–Mon 10am–6pm. No charge. Guided tours €3. 04 93 81 08 08. www.musee-matisse-nice.org.* Housed in the Villa des Arènes, the museum traces the artist's evolution, from *1890 through to 1952.*

Musée Marc-Chagall★★ – *Open daily except Tue: 10am–6pm (Nov–Apr 5pm). €7.50 (free 1st Sun in the month). 04 93 53 87 31. www.musee-chagall.fr.* The museum was designed to display the 17 great paintings making up the artist's Biblical Message.

Promenade des Anglais★★ – Until 1820 access to the shore was difficult, but the English colony constructed the seafront promenade, which now carries its name, and provides wonderful views of the Baie des Anges.

Musée des Beaux-Arts★★ – *Open daily except Mon 10am–6pm. No charge. 04 92 15 28 28. www.musee-beaux-arts-nice.org.* Housed in an 1878 Renaissance-style residence, the Fine Arts Museum displays a rich collection of art.

Musée d'Art Moderne et d'Art Contemporain★★ – *Open daily except Mon 10am–6pm. No charge. 04 93 62 61 62. www.mamac-nice. org.* The Museum of Modern and Contemporary Art is made up of four striking square towers linked by glass passageways.

Musée Masséna★ – *Open daily except Tue 10am–6pm. No charge. 04 93 91 19 10.* This museum in a delightful 19C Italianate villa reopened in 2008 after complete renovation. Its exhibits evoke old Nice from Napoleonic times.

EXCURSIONS

Corniches de la Riviera★★★ – *Circular tour of 41km/25.4mi.* The Grande Corniche road gives spectacular views over Villefranche-sur-Mer and its bay. Both **Cap Ferrat★★** and the nearby headland, Pointe St-Hospice, offer splendid views of the Riviera; the village of Èze-Bord-de-Mer, the jetset resort of Beaulieu, Cap d'Ail can all be identified; rising out of the sea in the distance is Cap Martin. Clinging like an eagle's nest to its inaccessible rock spike, **Èze★★** seems the very archetype of a hill village. In 1706 it was demolished on the orders of Louis XIV, but rebuilt after 1760.

Vallée des Merveilles★★ – At the foot of **Mont Bégo** lies a region of glacial lakes, valleys and rocky cirques formed during the Quaternary Era, cut off by the scarce roads and harsh mountain climate. In this dramatic landscape is the Vallée des Merveilles, famous for the thousands of prehistoric rock engravings found there.

The Engravings – The name Bégo is Indo-European in origin, meaning the sacred mountain (*Be*) inhabited by the bull-god (*Go*). The region of Mont Bégo is an **open-air museum** comprising over 40 000 engravings. Cut into the rock face, the engravings date from the early Bronze Age, through the Middle Ages to the present.

The Mercantour National Park – *04 93 16 78 88. www.parc-mercantour.eu.* Created in 1979, and once part of the hunting grounds of the kings of Italy, Mercantour is now twinned with the Parco Naturale delle Alpi Marittime across the border in Italy.

PRINCIPAUTÉ DE MONACO★★★

World-famous haunt of the super-rich, the Principality of Monaco's history really began when the Grimaldi family bought it from the Republic of Genoa in 1308. Prince Rainier III ruled the principality from 1949–2005. His only son Prince Albert then took power, but unless he produces a legitimate heir, the line of succession will pass to Rainier's daughter, Princess Caroline. The districts of the town of most interest to visitors are Monaco-Ville, the historic seat of the Principality, and Monte-Carlo, the district surrounding the casino.

Practical Information

Getting There

▶**TGV**: *Monaco-Monte-Carlo.*

LE ROCHER (THE ROCK)★★

The miniature city of Monaco is built on a rocky peninsula 60m/196.8ft above the sea.
Musée Océanographique★★ – *ave St-Martin. Open daily Jul–Aug 9.30am- 7.30pm, rest of year times vary. €14 (children, €7). 00 377 93 15 36 00. www.oceano.mc.*
Founded by Prince Albert I, the museum displays the skeletons of whales and sea-cows, as well as stuffed specimens. A splendid **aquarium★★** teems with rare species of marine life.
Cathédrale – *ave St-Martin. Open daily 8am–7pm (6pm in winter). 00 377 93 30 87 70. www.cathedrale.mc*
The white stone neo-Romanesque building, contains early paintings of the **Nice School★★**.
Palais Princier (Prince's Palace)★ – The oldest parts of the Palace are 13C although the buildings on the south side are in 15–16C Italian Renaissance style. Its medieval battlements and walls were strengthened by Vauban. The palace overlooks a square, the **Place du Palais★**, ornamented with cannon presented by Louis XIV. The imposing gateway leads into the arcaded Court of Honour; the Throne Room and state apartments, hung with signed portraits by Old Masters.
One wing of the Palace is devoted to a **museum★** on Napoleon; genealogical charts show how the Bonapartes are related to the Grimaldi princes, alongside many of the Emperor's personal effects.

MONTE-CARLO★★★

Europe's gambling capital was launched in the 19C and its success has led to high density building. But Monte-Carlo remains attractive with its luxurious casino, villas, shops and its pretty gardens. From the fine **terrace★★** of the Casino, the view sweeps across the Bordighera headland in Italy.
Jardin Exotique★★ – *bd du Jardin-Exotique. Open mid May–mid-Sept 9am–7pm (rest of year 6pm). €7. 00 377 93 15 29 80.* 900 varieties of cacti cling to the cliffs above Monaco, cascading down a steep rock face with huge candelabra-like euphorbia, and giant aloes.
Nouveau Musée National de Monaco★ – *bd du Jardin Exotique. Open daily 10am–6pm. €6.00 377 98 98 48 60. www.nmnm.mc.* The new history and culture museum, housed in the lovely Villa Paloma.

MENTON★★

Between mountain and Mediterranean, Menton stretches out agreeably on its **sunny site★★** on the lower slopes of a picturesque natural amphitheatre of mountains. The town is known for its citrus groves and its dazzling annual Lemon Festival (during Carnival).

Practical Information
Getting There
▶**TGV**: *Menton.* Menton is the last town on the Riviera before the Italian border, 29km/18mi E of Nice.

A BIT OF HISTORY
The town was bought by the Grimaldi family of Monaco in the 14C, then incorporated into the French kingdom when the county of Nice was annexed.

OLD TOWN★★
The old town nestles underneath the hill just above r. Longue and r. St-Michel and is fragrant with orange trees. **Parvis St-Michel★★** is a charming square in the Italian style, laid out by the Grimaldis, whose monogram can be seen in the pebble mosaic forming the paving. It is bordered by a number of houses in the local style, by a pink-walled chapel (Chapelle de la Conception), and by the **Basilique St-Michel ★** (*open Mon–Fri 10am–noon 3–5.15pm; Sat–Sun 3–5.15pm*), a fine 17C Baroque building.

SEAFRONT AND BEACHES★★
The wide **Promenade du Soleil★★** follows the shore beneath the old town. The **harbour**, used by local fishermen and tourists alike, is flanked by the **Jetée Impératrice-Eugénie** and **Quai Napoléon-III** and its lighthouse. The far end of the port, home to Volti's sculpture of St Michael, commands pleasant **views★** of old Menton.

The gravel beach of **Plage des Sablettes** is dominated by Promenade de la Mer and **Quai Bonaparte**. From the top, there is a nice view of the old quarter. A huge flight of steps leads up to the church of St-Michel. The luxurious residential suburb of **Garavan**, running between Promenade de la Mer and Boulevard de Garavan, has many examples of the eclectic architecture of the Belle Époque (like the Fondation Barriquand-Alphand, d'Abel Gléna on Boulevard de Garavan). The pretty 17C Baroque **Chapelle St-Jacques** houses a contemporary art gallery.

EXCURSIONS
Roquebrune-Cap Martin★★ – *2km/1.2mi SW.* Roquebrune is a most picturesque hill-top village (**village perché★★**), where you can stroll the small streets towards the **keep★** From the top, wonderful **panorama★★** of the sea, Cap Martin, the Principality of Monaco and the Mont Agel.
Saorge★★ – *ave Docteur Joseph Davéo. 04 93 04 51 23. www.saorge.fr.* The **gorges★★** of the Upper Roya form a spectacular **setting★★** for the village clinging to the steep, south-facing slopes. Rising abruptly from the river far below, Saorge is a maze of stepped and tunnelled streets dominated by the belfries of its churches and monasteries, overlooking terraces and balconies, old houses with open-fronted drying lofts and roofs tiled with heavy stone slabs.

CÔTE D'AZUR

MUST SEE

CANNES★★★

A charming old quarter, chic town centre and glamorous beachside promenade make Cannes one of the most enjoyable places on the Riviera. Spread out between the Suquet Heights and La Croisette Point on the shore of La Napoule Bay, Cannes became known as early as 1834 for its mild climate, making it the preferred winter salon of the world's aristocracy. Framed to the west by the red rocks of the Esterel and across the bay by the forested Îles de Lérins, this beautiful setting forms the backdrop to the palm-lined beaches of La Croisette and the world-famous Cannes Film Festival.

Practical Information

Getting There

▶**TGV**: *Cannes. 34.4km/21.3mi along the coast SW of Nice.*

TOURS AND TRANSPORTATION

TAM – *0800 06 01 06.* Buses operate between Cannes and Nice, including a direct service to the airport. **Train Station** – *SNCF Gare de Cannes. 0 800 11 40 23. www.ter-sncf.com/paca.* Cannes is served by national TGV and regional TER trains. The Carte Isabelle day rail pass offers excellent value along the Côte d'Azur between Fréjus and Vintimille (*1 Jun–30 Sept; €14, family passes also available*). **Boats** – *Trans Côte d'Azur, Quai Laubeuf. 04 92 98 71 30. www.trans-cote-azur.com.* Regular service to the Île Ste-Marguerite (15min), plus seasonal tours to l'Île de Porquerolles, Monaco, Saint-Tropez, San Remo, la Corniche d'Or, etc.

A BIT OF HISTORY

In 1834, Lord Henry Brougham, was on his way to Italy when he was prevented from entering the County of Nice, then part of Italy, due to a cholera epidemic. Forced to wait, he made an overnight stop at a fishing village called Cannes. Enchanted by the place, he built a villa here and returned to it every winter, establishing a trend among the English aristocracy that led ultimately to Cannes' establishment as a holiday resort.

SIGHTS
Boulevard de la Croisette★★

This broad seafront road has lovely gardens along its centre. To one side extends the splendid sandy beach and broad promenade; along the other are the impeccably maintained façades of palatial hotels and exclusive boutiques. At the eastern end of La Croisette is a busy marina; at its western end is the Festival and Conference Centre (Palais des Festivals et des Congrès) where the **Cannes International Film Festival** is held every May.

Le Suquet

The old town area of Cannes climbs a hill beside the Old Port. The lower streets are the centre for nightlife and restaurants. From a terrace in front of the Tour du Mont Chevalier, there is a fine **view★** over the beach and bay to the Lérins Islands The 11C Cannes castle today houses the remarkable **Musée de la Castre★★** (*Le Suquet; 04 93 38 55 26; guided tours (1hr) available*), an eclectic 19C private collection of exceptional ethnographic artefacts taken from around the world.

EXCURSIONS
Les Îles de Lérins★★

The peaceful **islands** (*boat service from Cannes*) are clad in pines, cypresses and eucalyptus and have a fascinating historic and archaeological heritage. The fine view back to the coast of the mainland stretches from Cap Roux to Cap d'Antibes.

Île Ste-Marguerite★★ – There are fine **forest walks** as well as through the botanical collection and along the avenue, Allée des eucalyptus géants. **Fort Royal** was built for coastal defence by Richelieu. The fort served as a prison for the mysterious Man in the Iron Mask (1687–98).

Massif de l'Esterel★★★ – 40km/24.8mi W by N 98. The Esterel between St-Raphaël and La Napoule is an area of breathtaking natural beauty. One of the loveliest parts of Provence, it was opened up by the Touring Club's creation in 1903 of the scenic Corniche d'Or, where the fiery red rocks contrast with the deep blue of the sea.

The Massif – The massif's jagged relief of eroded volcanic rock dips vertically into the deep blue sea between La Napoule and St-Raphaël. The rugged coastline is fringed with rocks, islets and reefs. From **Mont Vinaigre★★★**, its highest peak (alt 618m/2 027ft), a vast panorama sweeps over the pine and cork-oak forests clothing the wild and lonely massif.

Via Aurelia – The Esterel was bordered to the north by the Via Aurelia (Aurelian Way), one of the most important routes of the Roman Empire, connecting Rome and Arles via Genoa, Cimiez, Antibes, Fréjus and Aix. The 2.5m/8ftwide paved road made use of many bridges and other civil engineering works to create the shortest route possible.

Esterel Gap – The road skirting the north side of the Esterel, once the only land route to Italy, was rife with highwaymen; "to survive the Esterel Gap" became a local saying. Until the end of the 19C the massif remained the refuge of convicts escaping from Toulon.

RESORTS

Stretching more than 30km/18.6mi between St-Raphaël and La Napoule, the striking landscape of the Corniche de l'Esterel is punctuated by inviting resorts.

Boulouris, has several little beaches and a harbour.

Agay borders a deep port, which was used in earlier times by the Ligurians, the Greeks and the Romans. The scenic bay of the **Rastel d'Agay** is lined by a large, sunny beach.

The resort of **Anthéor** is dominated by the three peaks of the Cap Roux range. Just before the Pointe de l'Observatoire is a **view** of the red rocks of St-Barthélemy and Cap Roux.

Le Trayas is divided into two parts: one terraced on wooded slopes, the other by the seashore. The largest beach lies at the end of Figueirette Bay.

Miramar is an elegant resort with a private harbour in Figueirette Bay.

La Galere is built on wooded terraces on the slopes of the Esterel where it forms the western limit of La Napoule Bay. Below the road is the seaside development of **Port-la-Galère** (*private port*).

Théoule-sur-Mer, sheltered by the Théoule promontory, has three small beaches.

ST-TROPEZ★★

After half a century of fame, the little town of St-Trop' (as the locals call it) is still in fashion, thanks to an exquisitely picturesque harbour, a stunning location, and a constant stream of artists, journalists and photographers.

Practical Information

Getting There

▶**TGV**: *Saint-Raphaël-Valescure, then local bus.* 86km/54mi from Cannes; congested roads around the peninsula mean that the easiest way in is by passenger ferry from Port Grimaud across the bay.

VISIT

Celebrities can often be spotted in St-Tropez and the atmosphere is created by an impressive array of luxury charter yachts moored in the picturesque harbour, which teems with life. The old fishing village was discovered by writer **Guy de Maupassant** and his friend painter **Paul Signac**, and went on to attract Matisse and major post-Impressionist artists as well as the writer **Colette**. It remains a fashionable resort frequented by writers, artists and celebrities from the entertainment world.

Two *Bravades*, or "acts of defiance", take place each year in May. The first is a religious procession in honour of St-Tropez, while the second commemorates an event of local history which took place in 1637.

Musée de l'Annonciade★★ – *pl. Georges Grammont. Open Wed–Mon 10am–noon, 2–6pm. €5. 04 94 17 84 10.* The quayside museum has an impressive collection of post-Impressionist pictures of St-Tropez.

EXCURSIONS

St-Tropez Peninsula★★ – Its east coast is fringed with popular sandy beaches, notably the famous **Plage de Pampelonne**. The south coast has some scenic rocky headlands. The interior is hilly with small vineyards, pine copses and two charming old villages commanding wide views, **Ramatuelle** and smaller **Gassin**. A **footpath** extends around the coast of the whole peninsula.

Massif des Maures★★★ – The vast forests of pine, cork oak and chestnut trees from Fréjus to Hyères have often been devastated by fire. Chapels, monasteries and villages dot the hinterland, while the coast is fringed by coves, bays and small beach resorts.

Abbaye du Thoronet★★ – *Reached from autoroute A 8, junction 13. Open daily: hours vary. €7.50. 04 94 60 43 90 98. http:// thoronet.monuments-nationaux.fr.* Of the "Three Cistercian Sisters of Provence" (the others are Silvacane and Sénanque), Le Thoronet is the earliest; founded in 1136, when St Bernard was still alive, it is a typically austere Cistercian abbey. The plain architecture of the abbey is unrelieved by decoration, save in the chapter-house, where just two roughly sculpted capitals relieve the prevailing rigour. The abbey **church★** has a simple beauty. Built from 1160 onwards, it has remarkable stonework that was cut and assembled without the use of mortar (notably in the oven-vaulted apse). The **cloisters★** of about 1175 have kept their four barrel-vaulted walks.

TOULON★★

Backed by high hills whose summits are crowned by forts, Toulon is France's second most important naval base, set in one of the Mediterranean's most beautiful harbours. The pedestrianised Old Town of Toulon is located on the Old Port, or Vieille Darse, bounded to the east by Cours Lafayette, to the west by Rue Anatole-France and to the north by Rue Landrin.

Practical Information
Getting There
▶TGV: *Toulon*. 64km/39.7mi E of Marseille.

LA RADE★★
Construction of Toulon's Old Port (Darse Vieille) began under Henri IV. Richelieu oversaw the building of the first naval installations. In the reign of Louis XIV, the base was extended and the New Port (Darse Neuve) laid out by Vauban. In the 19C, the naval base – the home port of the French Mediterranean Fleet – was completed.
To the west of the Quai Cronstedt (landing-stage for boat trips) is the **Navy Museum** (Musée de la Marine). Once the entrance to the old Arsenal, its doorway is a Louis XV masterpiece, flanked by sculptures of Mars and Bellona. The balcony of the former **Town Hall** is supported by two muscular **Atlantes★** by Pierre Puget.

MONT FARON★★★
A telepherique travels over pine-clad slopes to the summit for thrilling views of Toulon, the inner and outer anchorages, the St-Mandrier and Cap Sicié peninsulas and Bandol. (*bd Amiral Vence*. €6.80. *04 94 92 68 25*).

EXCURSIONS
Hyères★
Magnificent villas and Belle Époque palace hotels reveal the faded glory of the 19C town once populated by wealthy aristocrats.

Beaches – The long sandy beach of **L'Almanarre** is used by surfing schools. The Route du Sel leads past a vast salt marsh to the Étang des Pesquiers, home to many aquatic birds. Boats leave from the **port** for the Îles d'Hyères. The old port of Hyères, **Ayguade-le-Ceinturon**, is a pleasant resort area with two sandy beaches.
Jardins Olbius-Riquier – *Open daily 7.30am–5pm* (*summer until 8pm*). *No charge*. Rich variety of tropical plants, palms and cacti.
Villa de Noailles – *04 94 01 84 40. www.villanoailles-hyeres.com*. In 1923 the Noailles, a rich couple of art patrons, commissioned one of the first modern homes on the Riviera; it became a favourite rendez-vous for avant-garde artists of the 1920s (Picasso, Giacometti, Man Ray, Dalí).

Îles d'Hyères★★★
These popular islands off Hyères harbour offer many beautiful scenic walking trails and sandy beaches.
Île de Porquerolles★★★ – The best way to discover the island's sandy beaches bordered by pine trees, heather and scented myrtle is by bicycle (hired in the village).
Île-de Port-Cros★★★ – Hilly and rugged Port-Cros is designated a **Parc National**.
Île du Levant – Ninety percent of the island is occupied by the Marine Nationale (access is forbidden).

ROUTE NAPOLÉON★★

This scenic highway follows the route taken by Napoleon on his return from Elba in 1815. It leads from the Riviera northwest through the Pre-Alps and is marked along its length by the flying eagle symbol inspired by Napoleon's remark: "The eagle will fly from steeple to steeple until he reaches the towers of Notre-Dame".

Practical Information
Getting There

The route runs for 336km/209mi, from Golfe-Juan to Grenoble, via Grasse, Digne and Gap, mainly following the N85.

A BIT OF HISTORY

The Emperor escaped from Elba on 26 February 1815, landing on the beach at Golfe-Juan on 1 March.
2 March: After a brief overnight stop at Cannes, Napoleon and his band halted outside Grasse and took to the mule tracks.
3 March: Midday halt at Castellane and overnight in Barrème.
4 March: The party rejoined the highway at Digne, and passed the night at the Château de Malijai.
5 March: The Emperor lunched at Sisteron, then continued to Gap.
6 March: At Les Barraques, Napoleon declined the offer of the local peasants to join his force.
7 March: Near Laffrey, the way was barred by troops. Ordered to fire, they broke ranks to shouts of "Vive l'Empereur!" Escorted by the men of the 7th Regiment, Napoleon made a triumphal entry into Grenoble at 7pm.

HIGHLIGHTS

Antibes★★ – Inside, the 12C and 16C **Château Grimaldi**, is the **Musée Picasso★** *4 r. des Cordiers. 04 92 90 54 20)*, which has a superb selection of the master's works. To the west of the **Cap d'Antibes★★**

stretches the fine sandy beach of Golfe-Juan.
Grasse★★ – The Old Town's (**Vieille Ville★**) picturesque streets are the centre of the world's perfume industry, with perfume manufacturers open to the public and the **Musée international de la Parfumerie** (*www.musees degrasse.com*).
To the north of the **Pas de la Faye** with its **view★★** over mountains and Mediterranean, the road enters Haute Provence.
Castellane★ – The sheep-grazed valley in which the town is situated is overlooked by the "Roc", a limestone cliff.
Digne-les-Bains★ – Digne spreads out beneath the rise on which its old town is situated.
At **Malijai**, the route enters the **Durance basin**, between the Valensole plateau to the east and the Vaucluse to the west.
Sisteron★★ – The massively imposing citadel looms above the old town and the River Durance.
Gap★ – Gap is pleasantly sited in the valley carved out by the glacier that was the ancestor of the Durance. The **Col Bayard** links the southern and northern Alps. by way of the Drac Valley.
Laffrey★ – Just south of the village lies the spot known as "Prairie de la Rencontrea", where the vain attempt was made to bar Napoleon's progress. The road now descends towards Grenoble.

ENTERTAINMENT

PARIS
Entertainment

Consult *L'Officiel des Spectacles*, *Une Semaine à Paris* and *Pariscope*, and the daily press for details of exhibitions. The monthly booklet *Paris Selection* lists exhibitions, shows and other events.

With 100 theatres and performing arts venues, Paris is one huge "living stage". Most are near the Opéra and the Madeleine, but from Montmartre to Montparnasse, from the Bastille to the Latin Quarter and from Boulevard Haussmann to the Porte Maillot, state-funded theatres (Opéra-Garnier, Opéra-Bastille, Comédie Française, Odéon, Chaillot, La Colline) stand alongside local and private theatres, singing cabarets and café-théâtres.

Paris has over 400 cinemas, with particular concentrations in the same areas as the theatres and on the Champs-Élysées. There are also two open-air cinema festivals in the summer: one at Parc de la Villette; the other, Cinéma au Clair de Lune, in parks and squares across Paris. Music-hall, variety shows and reviews can be enjoyed at such places as the Alcazar de Paris, the Crazy Horse, the Lido, the Paradis Latin, the Casino de Paris, the Folies Bergère and the Moulin Rouge. As well as the Opéra-Garnier, the Opéra-Bastille and the Comic Opera (Opéra-Comique), there are a number of concert halls with resident orchestras like the Orchestre de Paris at the Salle Pleyel, the Ensemble Orchestral de Paris at the Salle Gaveau, and the orchestras of the French Radio at the Maison de Radio-France. There are also nightclubs, cabarets,

dens where chansonniers can be heard, café-théâtres, television shows open to the public, concerts and recitals in churches, circuses, and other entertainment.

Fairs and Exhibitions

Paris hosts a number of trade fairs and exhibitions, including:

Paris – Expo, *pl. de la Porte de Versailles. www.viparis.com.* Over 200 exhibitions, conventions and events per year including the Paris Nautical Trade Show.

Parc International d'Expositions, *Paris-Nord Villepinte. www.viparis. com.* Trade Show for Crafts (SMAC) in March, the Maison & Objet home style expo, the International food industry exhibition (SIAL).

Parc des Expositions, *Le Bourget aerodrome. www.paris-air-show.com.* Paris Air Show (odd years: next, the 50th, is in 2013).

Versailles

Fenêtres sur cour – *pas. de la Geôle, Quartier des Antiquaires. 01 39 51 97 77. Closed 3 weeks Aug.* A glass-roofed restaurant-salon de thé. The bric-a-brac décor – tile floor, carpets, lamps, chandeliers, plaster statues and paintings – is in perfect harmony with the neighbourhood antique shops.

Fontainebleau

Le Franklin-Roosevelt – *20 r. Grande. 01 64 22 28 73.* Wine bar with mahogany furniture and red leatherette wall seats, a library dedicated to the period between 1890 and 1920, and intimate ambience with jazz in the background and some fine vintages on offer. Heated terrace.

MUST DO

Lille

L'Échiquier (*Bar of the Alliance Hotel*), *17 quai de Wault. 03 20 30 62 62*. This bar is installed in a former convent, part of the Alliance Hotel.

Les 3 Brasseurs – *22 pl. de la Gare. 03 20 06 46 25. www.les3brasseurs.com.* Sample the four kinds of beer on draught drawn directly from the tuns behind the counter.

Le Grand Bleu – *36 ave Max-Dormoy. 03 20 09 88 44. www.legrandbleu.com. Closed Aug. €12 (children, 6–18, €9–11).* This performance hall caters to a young audience. Dance, circus, theatre, story-telling, hip-hop and other nice surprises.

Orchestre National de Lille – *pl. Mendès-France. 03 20 12 82 40. www.onlille.com. Closed mid-Jul–mid-Aug.* Since 1976, The Orchestre National de Lille has given an average of 120 concerts per season. Performances are held around Lille, the Nord-Pas-de-Calais and internationally.

Théâtre de Marionnettes du Jardin Vauban – *1 ave Léon-Jouhaux, Chalet des Chèvres in the Jardin Vauban, Armentières. 03 20 42 09 95. www.lepetitjacques.fr. Closed Nov–Mar, Sat, Mon. €4.50.* An outdoors Guignol-style puppet show starring characters of local repute, such as Jacques de Lille.

NORMANDY & BRITTANY
Rouen
Nightlife

Le Bateau Ivre – *17 r. des Sapins. 02 35 70 09 05. http://bateauivre.rouen.free.fr. Open Tue-Sun; closed Aug.* Ever on the lookout for new talents, this bar has been livening up Rouen nightlife for the past 20 years. Concerts Fridays and Saturdays, ballads and poetry Thursdays, café-theatre or French songs Tuesday evenings.

Bar de la Crosse – *53 r. de l'Hôpital. 02 35 70 16 68. Closed Sun, Mon, fortnight in Aug and public holidays.* When in Rouen, pay a visit to this small, unpretentious bar. Renowned for its friendly and chatty atmosphere; between concerts and exhibits, laughter abounds.

La Taverne St-Amand – *11 r. St-Amand. 02 35 88 51 34. Closed 3 weeks in Aug & Sun.* Transformed into a bar 30 years ago, this 17C house attracts painters, writers and actors.

Showtime

Théâtre de l'Écharde – *16 r. Flahaut. 02 35 89 42 13.* Theatre with 100 seats where the troupe's creations and shows for young theatregoers are performed.

Théâtre des Deux Rives – *48 r. Louis Ricard. 02 35 70 22 82. www.cdr2 rives.com. Ticket office open Tue–Sat 2–7pm. Closed mid-Jul–end of Aug.* Classical and modern theatre.

Bayeux

Café Inn – *67 r. St-Martin. 02 31 21 11 37.* Coffee beans are roasted on the spot and 75 sorts of tea are served in a bustling ambience. Light meals of salads, omelettes and quiches are offered as prelude to the delicious *Tarte Tatin*, an upside-down apple pie.

ALSACE LORRAINE CHAMPAGNE
Nancy
Nightlife

L'Arquebuse – *13 r. Héré. 03 83 32 11 99. www.larq.fr.* A high-class bar with refined décor and a wide choice of cocktails with atmospheric music and disco, attracting a mixed clientele of smart students and businessmen. The place to go after 2am.

L'Échanson – *9 r. de la Primatiale. 03 83 35 51 58. Closed Sun, Mon.* A pleasant little wine merchant-cum-local bistro. A dozen or so wines are available by the glass, accompanied by a savoury snack.

BAB-Bar Mojito – *29 r. de la Visitation 03 83 32 71 97. Tue–Sat 4pm–2am. http://bab-nancy.fr.* The centre-piece of Nancy cultural life, this cocktail bar doubles up as a restaurant and venue for café-theatre evenings and concerts.

Entertainment
Get hold of a programme! The magazine *Spectacles à Nancy* will keep you informed. *www.spectacles-publications.com.*

Nancy Jazz Pulsations *100 Grande Rue. 03 83 35 40 86. www.nancyjazz pulsations.com.* Ten days of jazz at venues across the city in Oct.

Concerts and Stage Performances
The Opéra de Nancy et de Lorraine, Ballet de Nancy, Théâtre de la Manufacture, Centre dramatique national Nancy-Lorraine, Association de musique ancienne de Nancy, Ensemble Poirel, Orchestre symphonique et lyrique de Nancy, Association Lorraine de musique de chambre, Gradus Ad Musicam and La Psalette de Lorraine all put on concerts and shows throughout the year.

Gastronomie en Musique – Ask the tourist office about these summer evening musical performances (*Thu–Sun in different areas of the city*).

Strasbourg
Au Brasseur – *22 r. des Veaux. 03 88 36 12 13. www.aubrasseur.fr. Daily 11am–1am.* This micro-brasserie offers a variety of beers brewed on the premises. Locals come here to dine and for jazz, rock and blues concerts at weekends.

Bar à Champagne – *5 r. des Moulins. 03 88 76 43 43. www.regent-petite-france.com. 5pm–1am.* This is the hotel bar of the luxurious Regent Petite France, which was a mill for 800 years. Relaxing ambience, chic contemporary décor, riverside terrace, discreet background jazz, a good choice of cocktails and the best champagnes.

Colmar
Théâtre de la Manufacture – *6 rte d'Ingersheim. 03 89 24 31 78. Performances Mon–Wed and Fri 8.30pm, Thu 7pm, Sat 6pm.* Theatre, music, dance.

Alsation Folk Evenings – *pl. de l'Ancienne Douane. Mid-May–mid-Sept Tue 8.30pm.* **Théâtre Municipal** – *3 r. Unterlinden. 03 89 20 29 01/02.* Theatre and opera.

Reims
Nightlife
Place Drouet-d'Erlon – This square is where all of Reims starts before going out on the town. There is something for everyone, whether you are looking for a bar, pub, restaurant, tearoom or brasserie.

La Chaise au Plafond – *190 ave d'Épernay. 03 26 06 09 61.* Founded in 1910, this bar and tobacconist's is famous for the chair that has remained stuck to the ceiling ever since a shell hit the establishment on 12 September 1914. 150 cigars on offer from the Caribbean.

Calendar

Fêtes Johanniques – *2nd weekend in June.* 2 000 walk-ons in period costume accompany Joan of Arc and Charles VII during a massive street festival.

Flâneries musicales d'été – *Jun–Jul.* Over 150 street concerts throughout the town, including shows by major international stars in some of the town's most prestigious and unlikely venues.

Troyes
Nightlife

Le Bougnat des Pouilles – *29 r. Paillot-de-Montabert. 03 25 73 59 85.* The high-quality vintages in this wine bar are sought out by the young proprietor himself, from among the smaller producers in the region.

Le Tricasse – *16 r. Paillot-de-Montabert. 03 25 73 14 80. Closed Sun.* This most famous of Troyes' nightspots is in a smart area and offers a glorious mix of music, from jazz to salsa to house.

Le Chihuahua – *8 r. Charbonnet. 03 25 73 33 53.* This fashionable cellar bar also has dancing.

La Chope – *64 ave du Gén.-de-Gaulle. 03 25 73 11 99.* Wide selection of beers, whiskies and cocktails.

La Cocktaileraie – *56 r. Jaillant-Deschainets, BP 4102. 03 25 73 77 04.* A hundred or so cocktails are on offer, around 45 whiskies and many prestigious champagnes.

Entertainment

Théâtre de Champagne – *r. Louis-Mary. 03 25 76 27 60 / 61. Closed Jul–Aug.* Opera, comedy, art-house theatre, variety shows.

Théâtre de la Madeleine – *r. Jules-Lebocey. 03 25 43 32 10.*

Performances Mon–Sat 10am–12.30pm, 2–6pm. Arthouse theatre, comedy, variety shows.

BURGUNDY
Dijon
Theatres and Opera

Full programme of plays and comedy at the Théâtre du Sablier (R. Berbisey), the Théâtre du Parvis-St-Jean (Pl. Bossuet), the Bistrot de la Scène (R. D'Auxonne). In May the city hosts the Rencontres Internationales du Théâtre.

Nightlife

L'Agora Café – *10 pl. de la Libération. 03 80 30 99 42. Open Tue–Sat 11.30am–2am.* Bistro and piano-bar in a former 16C convent chapel with a laid-back vibe.

ALPS RHÔNE VALLEY
Lyon

Le Guignol de Lyon – *Compagnie des Zonzons, 2 r. Louis-Carrand. 04 78 28 92 57. www.guignol-lyon.com. Reservations essential.* Children's performances combine burlesque and fantasy. The shows for adults are more malicious.

Auditorium-Orchestre national de Lyon – *149 r. Garibaldi. 04 78 95 95 95. www.auditoriumlyon.com.* The Auditorium regularly hosts l'Orchestre National de Lyon.

Maison de la Danse – *8 av. Jean-Mermoz. 04 72 78 18 10. www.maisondeladanse.com.* From flamenco and tap dancing to ballet and the traditional dances of East and West.

Opéra National de Lyon – *1 pl. de la Comédie. 0826 305 325. www.opera-lyon.org.*

Halle Tony-Garnier – *20 pl. Antonin-Perrin. 04 72 76 85 85. www.halle-tony-garnier.com.* This huge

Tram in front of the Grand Théâtre, Place de la Comédie, Languedoc Roussillon

© Gérard Labriet/Photononstop

metallic structure presents eclectic events from circus to Lionel Richie and Johnny Hallyday.

BORDEAUX & DORDOGNE
Bordeaux

L'Onyx – *11 r. Fernand-Philippart, Quartier St-Pierre. 05 56 44 26 12. www.theatre-onyx.net.* The city's oldest café-theatre, L'Onyx is an essential stop for local culture.

La Boîte à Jouer – *50 r. Lombard. 05 56 50 37 37. Performances 8.30pm. Closed Jul–Sept.* Two small rooms (60 and 45 seats) where regional, national or international troupes perform contemporary or musical theatre.

Opéra de Bordeaux-Grand-Théâtre – *pl. de la Comédie. 05 56 00 85 95. www.opera-bordeaux.com.* The Grand Théâtre de Bordeaux is one of the most handsome of France. Symphonies, operas and ballets are performed here under excellent acoustic conditions.

Théâtre Fémina – *20 r. de Grassi. 05 56 79 06 69.* With 1100 seats, this handsome edifice sets the stage for plays, comedies, operettas, dance and concerts.

Biarritz

Gare du Midi – *21 bis av. du Mar.-Foch. 05 59 22 44 66. www.entractes-organisations.com.* The city's main theatre (home of the Biarritz ballet company) seats 1 400 for a range of plays, music concerts and ballets.

Casino Barrière de Biarritz – *1 av. Édouard-VII. 05 59 22 77 77. www.lucienbarriere.com.* This enormous casino on the Grande Plage has a table games room (roulette, blackjack) and 180 slot machines as well as Le Café de la Plage brasserie, Le Baccara restaurant, a show room (theatre, dance) and a ballroom.

LANGUEDOC ROUSSILLON
Toulouse
Nightlife

The bimonthly magazine *Toulouse Culture* lists all upcoming events.

Place du Capitole – The famous central square of the city is a pedestrianised meeting place surrounded by brasserie terraces.

Le Bibent – *5 pl. du Capitole, Toulouse. 05 61 23 89 03.* Classified historic Belle Époque café has a great terrace on Place du Capitole.

Au Père Louis – *45 r. des Tourneurs, Toulouse. 05 61 21 33 45.* First opened in 1889 and now a registered historical building, this wine bar is a local institution.

Events
Fête de la Violette – *mid-Feb. 05 61 11 02 22.* Growing, selling, exhibiting… the ideal opportunity to learn all about the flower that is the city's emblem.

Le Marathon des mots – *Jun/Jul 05 61 99 64 01. www.lemarathondes mots.com.* Literary festival.

Piano aux Jacobins – *Sept. 05 61 22 40 05. www.pianojacobins.com.* International piano solo festival.

Le Printemps de Septembre – *Sept–Oct 05 61 14 23 51. www. printempsdeseptembre.com.* Festival of photography and visual arts.

Festival Occitania – *Sep–Oct. 05 61 11 24 87. http://festival occitania.com.* Regional culture celebrated through various media (cinema, poetry, song).

Le Marché de Noël – *Dec. 05 61 87 55 06.* Toulouse Christmas market.

PROVENCE
Marseille
Nightlife
Bar de la Marine – *15 quai Rive-Neuve. Vieux Port. 04 91 54 95 42.* The setting for Marcel Pagnol's *Marius et Fanny* trilogy, now a haunt of the beautiful people.

Café Parisien – *1 pl. Sadi-Carnot. Colbert. 04 91 90 05 77. Closed Sun.* At weekends this Baroque-style café hosts musical events based on the themes presented in the monthly art exhibitions.

Events
Programmes - see tourist office's monthly magazine, *In Situ*.

Festival de Marseille – *Jun–Jul. 04 91 99 02 50. www.festivalde marseille.com.* Theatre, music and dance events.

Fiesta des Suds – *www.dock-des-suds.org. late-Oct.* World music festival brings 50 000 fans to Marseille.

Folklore – International Folklore Festival at Château-Gombert. (*Jul, www.roudelet-felibren.com*).

Pétanque World Championships – A very popular event - after a few throws by celebs, the champions take over. First week in July (*http://mediterranee.france3.fr/ mondial-petanque*).

Arles
On the town
Bar de l'Hôtel Nord Pinus – *pl. du Forum. 04 90 93 44 44. www.nord-pinus.com.* An unmissable Arles institution, the small bar of the 17C Hotel Nord Pinus has entertained artists, writers, film stars, and bullfighters, including Picasso, Jean Cocteau and Yves Montand.

Café Van Gogh – *11 pl. du Forum. 04 90 96 44 56.* This popular café with its large terrace was the subject of Vincent Van Gogh's *The Cafe Terrace on the Place du Forum*.

L'Entrevue – *pl. Nina Berberova. 04 90 93 37 28.* The arlesien Actes Sud publishing house run this arty café-restaurant, a cultural hub of the town.

Le Méjan – *23 quai Marx-Dormoy. 04 90 93 33 56.* Enjoy evening and afternoon musical performances, jazz concerts, lectures, conferences, and exhibitions in the chapel Saint-Martin-du-Méjan.

Events
Festival Les Suds – *mid-Jul. www. suds-arles.com.* World music festival.

163

Fête des Gardians – *1 May. 04 90 18 41 20.* Mass is held in Provençal dialect, with the blessing of horses, typical Camargue games, local folk music and dances.

Les Rencontres d'Arles – *10 rond-point-des Arènes. 04 90 96 76 06. www.rencontres-arles.com.* Photography festival in locations such as the Roman Theatre.

Nîmes
Nightlife
Nîmes has a huge number and variety of cafés, including café-concerts, and great fin-de-siècle establishments.

La Grand Bourse – *2 bd des Arènes. 04 66 67 68 69. www.la-grande-bourse.com.* Nîmes' most prestigious cafe boasts Napoleon III-style coffered ceiling, a terrace facing the amphitheatre and deep, comfortable rattan armchairs.

Entertainment
Programmes – See newspapers *Midi-Libre, La Semaine de Nîmes,* the *Gazette de Nîmes,* or *Le César* (from the tourist office).

Ferias and bullfighting – There are three major annual ferias: the "spring" feria in Feb, the Pentecost feria across the Whitsun long weekend, and the harvest feria in mid-September.

Le Printemps du jazz – (3rd week in March) Jazz concerts in a variety of venues around town.

Avignon
Nightlife
La Cave Breysse – *41 r. des Teinturiers. 04 32 74 25 86. Closed Sun.* A very popular wine bar, this is a nice place to enjoy a well-priced glass of wine or an apéritif, the ambience and the festivities.

Café In et Off – *pl. du Palais-des-Papes. 04 90 85 48 95. Closed mid-Nov–late Feb.* Don't miss the only café that enjoys unbeatable views of the Palais des Papes.

Cloître des Arts – *83 r. Joseph-Vernet. 04 90 85 99 04. Open Mon–Sat 7am–1.30am (during the festival 7am–3am). Closed the first fortnight of Jan.* Sixty varieties of beer from all over the world and a relaxed atmosphere attract beer enthusiasts of all ages, whether among friends or with family.

Showtime
Le Rouge Gorge – *10 bis, r. Peyrolerie. 04 90 14 02 54. Closed Sun, Jul–Aug.* The only cabaret in Avignon, the Rouge Gorge, modestly sheltered by the Palais des Papes, unveils the sensual charms of its show every Friday and Saturday, while two Sundays a month there is an operetta lunch.

Events
Festival d'Avignon – Every July. It promotes France's cultural life through theatre, dance, lectures, exhibitions and concerts in and around Avignon. *Information: 04 90 27 66 50. Reservations 04 90 14 14 14. www.festival-avignon.com.*

Booking "Festival Off" – The programme for Avignon's Fringe Festival, on at the same time, is available mid-June. *04 90 85 13 08. www.avignonleoff.com.*

Hivernales d'Avignon – This contemporary dance festival takes place during July. *04 90 82 33 12. www.hivernales-avignon.com.*

Animo Nature – *Early Oct at Parc des Expositions d'Avignon. 04 90 84 02 04. www.animo-nature.com.* The largest animal show in France.

CÔTE D'AZUR
Nice
Nightlife

Casino Ruhl – 1 prom. des Anglais. 04 97 03 12 22. www.lucienbarriere.com. 300 slot machines plus French and English roulette, blackjack, stud poker, etc. American bar.

Le Relais – Hôtel Negresco, 37 prom. des Anglais. 04 93 16 64 00. The sumptuous decoration of the legendary Negresco Hotel's bar has remained the same since 1913. Piano bar every evening.

La Trappa – 2 r. Jules Gilly. 04 93 80 33 69. Open since 1886, this lively tapas bar greets you with deep, comfy settees and red walls. Sip a Cuban cocktail and listen to Latin-American music. Friendly atmosphere and local wine list.

Le Livingstone at Grand Hotel Aston – 12 ave Félix Faure. 04 92 17 53 00. A chic rooftop bar providing panoramic vistas over the city.

Events

Nice Carnival – 08 92 70 74 07. www.nicecarnaval.com; mid-Mar for 3 weeks. Colourful themed parades with spectacular floats take place day and night during the Riviera's biggest winter event.

Fête de la Mer et de la St-Pierre Celebrating the sea and St-Peter on the port and Quai des Etats-Unis the last weekend in June.

Nice Jazz Festival – The Roman amphitheatre is the venue for the July jazz festival. 08 92 68 36 22. www.nicejazzfestival.fr.

Monaco
Nightlife

Casino de Monte-Carlo – pl. du Casino. 00 377 98 06 21 21. www.montecarlocasinos.com. Open daily from 2pm.€10. This is Europe's leading casino, with over a million euros in annual profits - from gambling, not slot machines as is the case in other casinos. The gambling salons and lavish dining hall, Le Train Bleu, decorated in the style of the Orient Express, are truly impressive.

Crystal Bar – Hôtel Hermitage, Square Beaumarchais. 00 377 98 06 98 98. www.hotelhermitagemonte carlo.com. A celebrity haunt for many years, its superb terrace overlooks Monaco harbour. Champagne cocktails are the house speciality!

Sass Café – 11 ave Princesse-Grace. 00 377 93 25 52 00. www.sasscafe.com. Exclusive bar-restaurant with a cosy atmosphere where members of the local jet set drop in for a fancy vodka or champagne cocktail before meeting up at Jimmy'z.

Le Jimmy'z – 26 ave Princesse-Grâce. 00 377 92 16 20 00. Reservations recommended. Formal evening wear is expected in this legendary small but select club where the wealthy love to congregate. A unique experience.

Stars'N'Bars – 6 quai Antoine 1er. 00 377 97 97 95 95. www.starsn bars.com. This is the great American bar-of-the-moment, more relaxed than the Principality's other establishments, and catering to a younger clientele eager to drink beer, eat a hamburger or two, play billiards, surf on the internet and dance the night away. The decoration features the paraphernalia of stars. Rock concerts are organised on a regular basis. Terrace with a view of Monaco harbour.

Grimaldi Forum – 10 ave Princesse-Grâce. 00 377 99 99 20 00. www.grimaldiforum.com. This 1 800-seat

ENTERTAINMENT

auditorium plays host to headlining events throughout the year, including performances by the Monte Carlo Ballet and the Monte Carlo Philharmonic Orchestra.

Entertainment

Le Cabaret – *pl. du Casino. 00 377 92 16 36 36. www.montecarloresort.com. Shows mid-Sept–mid-Jun Wed–Sat from 10.30pm; bar/restaurant open from 8.30pm.* This cabaret, run by the Monte-Carlo Casino, presents nightly flamenco, jazz or pop concerts.

Events

Highlights of a packed calendar are:
Monte-Carlo Rally – *Held every year since 1911 (late Jan).*
Feast of Ste-Dévote – *Feast day of Monaco's Patron Saint (27 Jan).*
Sciaratù Carnival – *Monégasque festival (week of Mardi Gras).*
Spring Arts Festival – *Art, music, theatre and dance festival (Apr).*
Formula 1 Monaco Grand Prix – *Race in the Principality's winding streets (late May): 78 laps of a 3.34km/2.08mi circuit.*
National Day – *Picturesque procession and cultural displays (19 Nov).*

Cannes
Nightlife

The best way to get to know this glamorous city is to check out its luxury hotel bars: order a cocktail on the terrace of the Carlton Hotel, on the beach of the Majestic or in the piano bar of the Martinez.
L'Amiral – *73 la Croisette. 04 92 98 73 00. www.hotel-martinez.com.* Attached to the Martinez Hotel, this bar is by far the most popular meeting place along the coast. It owes its reputation to the head barman and to Jimmy, the American piano player. Live music every evening from 8pm.

Events

Cannes International Film Festival – *11 days in May; free open-air cinema on the beach. 01 53 59 61 00. www.festival-cannes.com.*
Nuits Musicales du Suquet – *Mid- to late Jul; classical concerts on the esplanade in front of the Église du Suquet. 04 92 99 33 83. www.nuitsdusuquet-cannes.com.*

St Tropez
Nightlife

Bar du Château de la Messardière – *rte de Tahiti. 04 94 56 76 00.* This bar belongs to one of the Riviera's most prestigious hotels. Cosy ambience in the piano bar of this former 18C private residence.
Le Bar du Sube – *15 quai Suffren sur le Port. 04 94 97 30 04.* Right on the quayside, one of the most beautiful bars in town.
Sénéquier – *quai Jean-Jaurès. 04 94 97 20 20.* The pavement terrace and crimson chairs of this tea room are famous throughout the world – or so say the locals! Renowned personalities such as Jean Marais, Errol Flynn and Colette would come here for the many delights on offer.

Route Napoleon
Events

Fête de la Poterie – This pottery festival takes place on the second Sunday in August.
Biennial International Festival of Ceramic Art – *04 93 64 34 67, http://biennale.vallauris.free.fr.* Even-numbered years Jul–mid Oct.

MUST DO

SHOPPING

PARIS
Shopping districts

Most major stores are concentrated in a few districts, whose names alone are suggestive of Parisian opulence.

Champs-Élysées – All along this celebrated avenue and in the surrounding streets (avenue Montaigne, avenue Marceau), visitors can admire dazzling window displays and covered shopping malls (Galerie Élysée Rond-Point, Galerie Point-Show, Galerie Élysée 26, Galerie du Claridge, Arcades du Lido) devoted to fashion, cosmetics and luxury cars.

Rue du Faubourg-St-Honoré – Here haute couture and ready-to-wear clothing are displayed alongside perfume, fine leather goods and furs.

Place Vendôme – Some of the most prestigious jewellery shops (Cartier, Van Cleef & Arpels, Boucheron, Chaumet) stand facing the Ritz Hotel and the Ministry of Justice.

Place de la Madeleine and r. Tronchet – An impressive showcase for shoes, ready-to-wear clothing, luggage, leather goods and fine tableware.

Department stores

For locals and visitors alike, the city's great department stores are the ideal way to find a vast choice of high-quality fashions and other goods under one roof.

Most leading names are represented. Some have free fashion shows.

Department stores are usually open Monday–Saturday 9.30am–7pm. **Bazar de l'Hôtel de Ville** (52 r. de Rivoli); **Galeries Lafayette** (40 bd Haussmann); **Printemps** (64 bd Haussmann); **Le Bon Marché** (r. de Sèvres).

Versailles

Shops – The principal shopping areas are: Rue de la Paroisse, Rue Royale, Rue du Général-Leclerc, Place du Marché and Les Manèges, opposite the Rive-Gauche station. You'll find many antique dealers in the Passage de la Geôle, near La Place du Marché.

Place Vendôme, Paris

© Jose Ignacio Soto/iStockphoto.com

SHOPPING

Major stores – From the FNAC (books, CDs, cameras, etc.) to Printemps or BHV (department stores), the shopping complex Le Centre Commercial de Parly II, on your way out of Versailles towards St-Germain, has it all.

Chartres

Marché aux légumes et volailles – *pl. Billard.* Each Saturday morning, the covered Vegetable and Poultry Market displays colourful stands featuring authentic Beauce produce. This carrousel of sights, tastes and fragrances is one of the most popular markets in the area.

Atelier Loire – *16 r. d'Ouarville, 28300 Léves. Just N of Chartres on the way to Dreux. 02 37 21 20 71. http:// vitrail-vitraux-chartres.ateliers-loire.fr Closed Aug and public holidays.* A century-old, stately residence set amidst a park and adorned with stained-glass creations is the home of this atelier founded in 1946 by Gabriel Loire, and continued today by his grandchildren.

Brûlerie les Rois Mages – *6 r. des Changes. 02 37 36 30 52. Closed Mon for lunch.* Enter this "retro" coffee-roasting shop and choose among the wide variety roasted on site and the dozens of teas to enjoy in the *brûlerie* or to take home.

Lille

Marché de Wazemmes – *59000 Armentières.* Tue, Thu and especially Sun mornings, the Wazemmes market takes over the Place de la Nouvelle-Aventure.

Rue de Gand – Paved, animated and highly colourful, La Rue de Gand is well worth a visit. Butcher's shops, taverns, bars and especially restaurants serving various types of cuisine line the pavements.

NORMANDY
Rouen

Markets – pl. Saint-Marc (*Tue, Fri and Sat all day*); Place des Emmurés (*Tue and Sat all day*); Place du Vieux-Marché (*daily except Mon, mornings*).

Faïencerie Augy-Carpentier – *26 r. St-Romain. 02 35 88 77 47.* The last handmade earthenware workshop in Rouen. They offer copies of many traditional motifs on white and pink backgrounds, from blue monochrome to multicoloured, and from lambrequin to cornucopia.

Maison Hardy –*22 pl. du Vieux-Marché. 02 35 71 81 55.* In this alluring delicatessen, the Hardys offer Rouen specialities such as terrine de canard, duck being a highly prized fowl in this city (also known for its mutton). Mr Hardy's andouilles de Vire and his Caen tripe cooked in calvados and cider, specialities from Normandy, have clinched his reputation.

Caen

Charcuterie Poupinet – *8 r. St-Jean. 02 31 86 07 25.* For authentic *tripes à la mode de Caen*, visit Poupinet, where you can buy this speciality in jars.

Stiffler – *72 r. St-Jean. 02 31 86 08 94. www.stifflertraiteur.com. Closed Mon, Tue.* At the deli counter, find delicious, prepared dishes and salads for a quick lunch.

Markets – Marché St-Pierre (Sun) r. de Bayeux (Tue), bd Leroy (Wed, Sat), bd de la Guérinière (Thu), Marché St-Sauveur (Fri), Christmas Market (Dec).

Bayeux

Markets – *r. St-Jean. Open Wed 7.30am – 2.30pm; and pl. St-Patrice*

Sat 6.30am–2.30pm. Bayeux's two markets are quite different, each with its own charm. St-Jean pedestrian street *Wednesday* market features some 25 stalls including greengrocers, butchers, fishmongers, cheesemakers and honey-sellers. On the Pl. St-Patrice, every Saturday, some 120 merchants offer their wares, about half of them foodstuffs.

Naphtaline – *14, 16 parvis de la Cathédrale. 02 31 21 50 03. www.naphtaline-bayeux.com. Closed Jan–Feb & Sun.* Three boutiques housed in a fine 18C building offer antique and modern lace, Bayeux porcelain and reproductions of traditional tapestries woven on Jacquard looms.

CHATEAUX OF THE LOIRE
Angers

Maison du Vin de l'Anjou – *5 bis, pl. Kennedy, Angers. 02 41 88 81 13. www.vinsdeloire.fr.* In the centre of town, near the château, this wine shop offers a good selection of Anjou and Saumur wines, which you can taste.

La Petite Marquise – *22 r. des Lices, Angers. 02 41 87 43 01.* Does *Quernons d'Ardoise* mean anything to you? If you don't know about this delicious local speciality of nougatine and chocolate made to look like roof slates, then head to this little shop where they were first created.

Tours

Markets – **Second-hand goods:** 1st and 3rd Fri of the month, *r. de Bordeaux*; 4th Sun in the month, *bd Bérange*; Wed and Sat mornings, *pl. de la Victoire.*

Flowers – Wed and Sat, all day, *bd Béranger.*

Au Vieux Four – *7 pl. des Petites-Boucheries. 02 47 66 62 33. www.auvieuxfour-mahou.com. Closed Sun and Mon.* This boulangerie and museum reveals the secrets of traditional bread-making.

La Chocolatière – *6 r. de la Scellerie. 02 47 05 66 75. www.la-chocolatiere.com. Closed Mon.* "Le pavé de Tours" is one of the great specialities of this exceptional maker of pâtisseries, confectionery and top-of-the-range chocolates.

Colmar

Domaine viticole de la Ville de Colmar. *2 r. Stauffen. 03 89 79 11 87. www.domaineviticolecolmar.com.* Founded in 1895, this estate grows seven *cépages* and boasts a host of *grands crus* in addition to sparkling wines. Wide range of wines, brandies and liquors on sale.

Caveau Robert-Karcher – *11 r. de l'Ours. 03 89 41 14 42. www.vins-karcher.com.* The vineyards of this family business are northwest of Colmar, but the cellar, dating from 1602, is in the town centre.

Fortwenger – *32 r. des Marchands. 03 89 41 06 93. www.fortwenger.fr* It was in Gertwiller in 1768 that Charles Fortwenger founded his gingerbread factory, but this Colmar shop sells a wide range of delicious sweet products.

Maison des Vins d'Alsace – *Civa, 12 ave de la Foire-aux-Vins, BP1217. 03 89 20 16 20. www.vinsalsace.com.* Five local organisations concerned with Alsace wines are based in this centre. Visitors can study a map showing all the wine-making villages and *grands crus*, learn about wine making and see a film.

Reims
Chocolatiers
Deléans – *20 r. Cérés. 03 26 47 56 35. Closed Aug.* Cocoa-based specialities have been made here in the old-fashioned way since 1874. Try Néluskos (chocolate-coated cherries in cognac), and *petits bouchons de champagne,* enclosed in a giant champagne cork made of chocolate.

Fossier – *25 cours JB Langlet. 03 26 47 59 84.* Founded in 1756, the biscuit- and chocolate-maker Fossier creates the ultimate in Reims confectionery.
Pay a visit to the shop and factory and learn how to *piouler* (stir) your glass of champagne correctly!

La Petite Friande – *15 cours JB Langlet. 03 26 47 50 44.* For over 170 years, the establishment has prided itself on being the specialists in authentic *bouchons de champagne*, made with *marc de champagne*. Another of their delicious creations is *bulles à la vieille fine de la Marne*.

Champagne Houses
Several of the world's most renowned champagne-makers have their cellars in Reims, and offer guided tours, tastings and discount purchases.

Mumm *34 r. du Champ-de-Mars. www.mumm.com*

Piper-Heidsieck *51 bd Henry-Vasnier. www.piper-heidsieck.com*

Pommery *5 pl. du Gén.-Gouraud. www.pommery.com.*

Ruinart *4 r. des Crayères. www.ruinart.com.*

Taittinger *9 pl. St-Nicaise. www.taittinger.fr.*

Veuve Clicquot-Ponsardin *1 pl. des Droits-de-l'Homme. www.veuve-clicquot.fr.*

Troyes
Specialities – *Andouillettes* (chitterling sausages): grilled, unaccompanied or drizzled with olive oil flavoured with *fines herbes* and garlic. Other specialities include Chaource cheese, cider or champagne *choucroute*.

Market – Daily market in the Place St-Remy halls. The main market is held on Saturdays. There is another in the Chartreux area on Wed and on Sun morning. Country market every 3rd Wed on Boulevard Jules-Guesde.

Jean-Pierre-Ozérée – *Halles de l'Hôtel-de-Ville.03 25 73 72 25.* Maturing of cheeses, including Chaource, Mussy and Langres. A useful alternative if you don't have time to go to the production site yourself.

Le Palais du Chocolat – *2 r. de la Monnaie. 03 25 73 35 73. www.pascal-caffet.com. Closed Sun afternoon.* An emporium of chocolate, as well as ice cream, sorbets and pastries.

Marques Avenue – *114 bd de Dijon, 03 25 82 00 72. Closed Sun.* With 120 boutiques, Marques Avenue is the biggest centre for discount fashion stores in Europe. Here you will find all the big brand names, French and foreign.

Marques City – *Pont-Ste-Marie. www.marquescity.com. Closed Sun.* Stores offering almost 200 labels at discount prices, ranging across sportswear, formal wear and quality accessories. Three restaurants on site.

McArthur Glen – *Voie des Bois - 10150 Pont-Ste-Marie. 03 25 70 47 10. Closed Sun and 1 May.* Opened in 1995, the village includes 84 end-of-line shops along an outside covered gallery.

BURGUNDY
Dijon

Gastronomic specialities include: mustard that can be flavoured with blackcurrants, raspberries, walnuts and Cognac, pain d'épice (gingerbread), crème de cassis (blackcurrant liqueur) and jambon persillé (ham cooked in white wine, chopped and set in jelly with garlic and parsley).

Mulot & Petitjean, *13 place Bossuet.* Has an interior as deliciously extravagant as its celebrated pain d'épices, bejewelled with crystallised fruit.

Boutique Maille - *32 rue de la Liberté, 03 80 30 41 02. www.maille. com.* Ancient drawers and mustard jars give Maille the feel of an apothecary's dispensary.

BORDEAUX

Librairie Mollat – *15 r. Vital-Carles. 05 56 56 40 40. www.mollat.com.* France's first independent bookshop is still a veritable regional institution.

Baillardran Canelés – *Galerie des Grands-Hommes. 05 56 79 05 89.* Located in the Grands-Hommes market, this boutique makes delicious *canelés*, the small brown Bordelais cakes.

Confiserie Cadio-Badie – *26 allées de Tourny. 05 56 44 24 22. Closed 2 weeks in Aug, Sun and public holidays except Christmas and Easter.* You can't help but be charmed by the old-fashioned style of this appealing boutique founded in 1826. Their truffes and Armagnac-flavoured *bouchons bordelais* are worth a special trip.

Chocolaterie Saunion *56 cours Georges-Clemenceau. 05 56 48 05 75. Closed Sun and Mon morning, public holidays except Christmas, New Year and Easter.* One of the most illustrious chocolate confectioners of Bordeaux – a must.

Conseil Interprofessionnel des Vins de Bordeaux – *1 cours du XXX Juillet. 05 56 00 22 66. www. vins-bordeaux.fr. Closed weekends and public holidays.* This is where you'll find ample information about Bordeaux wines and vineyards. Several different wine cellars are found around this centre.

Darricau – *7 pl. Gambetta. 05 56 44 21 49. www.darricau.com.* Since the turn of the 20C, this chocolatier pampers the city with the irresistible *pavé Gambetta* (praline with raisins soaked in wine), Bordeaux bottle-shaped chocolates (*confits de sauterne* or *de médoc*), la *cadichonne* (crunchy vanilla) and *niniches* (soft caramel with dark chocolate).

Biarritz

Cazaux et fils – *10 r. Broquedis. 05 59 22 36 03.* The Cazaux family has been involved in making ceramic pottery since the 18C. Jean-Marie Cazaux is happy to talk about his profession, describing it as "austere and solitary".

Fabrique de chistéras Gonzalez – *6 allée des Liserons, Anglet. 05 59 03 85 04.* Founded in 1887, the Gonzalez company produces hand-made *cestas* (wicker scoops that extend from the protective pelota glove). In one hour you will learn everything about the history and manufacture of pelotas and *cestas*.

Chocolats Henriet – *pl. Clemenceau. 05 59 24 24 15.* Established after WWII, Henriet is the local guiding light in chocolates and confectionery, featuring *calichous* (Échiré butter and fresh cream caramels) and *rochers de*

SHOPPING

Biarritz (bitter chocolate, orange rinds and almonds).
Maison Arostéguy –
5 av. Victor Hugo. 05 59 24 00 52. www.epicerie-fine.net. Founded in 1875, this famous Biarritz grocery store (formerly the "Epicerie du Progrès") has kept its original walls, shelves and façade.

Perigueux
Le Relais des Caves – *44 r. du Prés.-Wilson. 05 53 09 75 00.* The friendly proprietor sells a wide selection of wines from across France, including a few very special vintages.
Stéphane Malard – *8 r. de la Sagesse. 05 53 08 75 10.* Behind the window arcades of his shop, Stéphane sells the region's finest delicacies, including confits, foies gras, duck magret and wines.
Markets – *pl. de Clautre: Wed and Sat morning; pl. de la Clautre* (food), *pl. Bugeaud and pl. Franche-Ville* (clothing)*; pl. du Coderc* (food); duck and goose products *from Dec–Feb.*

LANGUEDOC ROUSSILLON
Toulouse
Toulouse markets – **Saturday mornings:** organic farmers' market in Place du Capitole.
Sunday morning: farmers' market around Eglise St-Aubin; L'Inquet, a renowned flea market around the Basilique St-Sernin. **Wednesday and Friday** (Nov–Mar): geese, ducks and foie gras are sold in Place du Salin. **Shopping streets** – The main shopping streets are Rue d'Alsace-Lorraine, Rue Croix-Baragnon, Rue St-Antoine-du-T., Rue Boulbonne, Rue des Arts and the pedestrian sections of Rue St-Rome, Rue des Filatiers, Rue Baronie and Rue de la Pomme.

PROVENCE
Marseille
Books
Librairie-galerie-restaurant des Arcenaulx– *25 cours d'Estienne d'Orves. Vieux-Port. 04 91 59 80 40. www.les-arcenaulx.com.* Specialises in books on Marseille, Provence and food; old and rare books. Quality gifts; restaurant.

Clothes
The main shopping street is rue St-Ferréol, which has many individual and chain boutiques plus Galeries Lafayette. Adventurous dressers might like to visit Marseille's well-known designer, **Madame Zaza** (*73 cours Julien. Notre Dame du Mont. 04 91 48 05 57. www.madamezazaofmarseille.com*), for colourful, daring outfits.

Markets
Fish market every morning on *quai des Belges. Food* markets are open Mon–Sat mornings in *cours Pierre Puget, place Jean-Jaurès* (la Plaine), *place du Marché-des-Capucins* and *avenue du Prado. Boulevard La Canebière* has a *flower* market every Tuesday and Saturday morning; this market is also set up on *avenue du Prado* every Friday morning.

Olive oil
Lei Moulins – *4–6 bd Tellène. Estrangin Préfecture. 04 91 59 49 78. www.leimoulins.com. Closed Sun, Mon.* Cave-like shop in the St-Victor quarter. You'll find an interesting selection of olive oil from the Med and also a selection of jams made on the premises.

Santons

Santons Marcel Carbonel – *47–49 r. Neuve-Ste-Catherine. Vieux Port. 04 91 13 61 36. www.santonsmarcelcarbonel.com. Closed Sun.* Visit the workshop where the famous *santons* are made. Take a browse through the little museum before hitting the shop to buy some of the traditional clay figurines – great souvenirs.

Soap

La Compagnie de Provence – *18 r. Francis Davso. Vieux Port. 04 91 33 04 17. www.lcdpmarseille.com. Closed Sun.* Marseille soap and natural products make this shop smell wonderful.

Savonnerie de la Licorne – *34 cours Julien. Notre Dame du Mont. 04 96 12 00 91. www.savon-de-marseille-licorne.com. Mon–Fri 8am–5pm, Sat 10am–6pm.* The only artisan-made soap in the centre of town. Perfumes include rose, violet and pastis.

Markets

Browse traditional markets every Wed in *bd Émile-Combes* and every Sat in *bds des Lices* and *boulevard Clemenceau*. **Antique market** first Wed of the month in *bd des Lices.*

Les Étoffes de Romane – *10 bd des Lices. 04 90 93 53 70.* Choose from wonderful **Provençal fabrics** in an array of colours.

Olive Oil – Best quality Provençal olive oil is found (together with other olive specialities) at **Fad'ola** (*46 r. des Arènes; 04 90 49 70 73*).

Nîmes

Maison Villaret – *13 r. de la Madeleine. 04 66 67 41 79.* Crunchy almond biscuits known as *croquants.*

Wine – *La Vinothèque, 18 r. Jean-Reboul. 04 66 67 20 44.* Local wines.

Markets – *Large market* on Mon on *bd Gambetta. Organic* market Fri mornings on *avc Jean-Jaurès. Flea* market Sun mornings in the *Costières* stadium car park. *Evening market* Jul–Aug Thu 6–10pm (*les jeudis de Nîmes*).

Avignon

Markets – **Les Halles Centrales**, *pl. Pie*, traditional covered market Tue–Sun. **Flower market** Sat in *pl. des Carmes*. **Fair** Sat and Sun, *rempart St-Michel*. **Flea market** Sun in *pl. des Carmes.*

Honey – **Miellerie des Butineuses**, *189 r. de la Source, St-Saturnin-lès-Avignon. 04 90 22 47 52. www.miellerie.fr.* Honey, pollen, and royal jelly, as well as honey-based products.

CÔTE D'AZUR
Nice

Markets – There are street markets all over town, including: **Fish market** – *pl. St-François; Tue–Sun 6am–1pm;* **Flower market** – *Cours Saleya; Tue–Sun 6am–5.30pm;* **Marché aux Puces** (Flea market) *pl. Robilante Tue–Sun 10am–6pm;* **Marché de la Brocante** (Antiques) – *Cours Saleya Mon 7.30am–6pm.*

Alziari – *14 r. St-François-de-Paule. 04 93 85 76 92. www.alziari.com.fr.* One of the best addresses in town for olive oil and regional specialities.

La Maison de l'Olive – *18 r. Pairolière. 04 93 80 01 61.* Marseille soaps made from pure olive oil, lotions and scents for the body and home, and regional products.

À l'Olivier *7 r. St-François-de-Paule. 04 93 13 44 97.* Every brand of French olive oil with the AOC label is sold in this boutique, originally opened in 1822, in Nice since 2004. **Confiserie Auer** – *7 r. St-François-de-Paule. 04 93 85 77 98. www.maison-auer.com.* A gorgeous vintage boutique selling candied fruit and crystallised flowers from the Nice region, as well as chocolates, and calissons from Aix. **Confiserie Florian** – *14 quai Papacino. 04 93 55 43 50. www. confiserieflorian.com. Guided tours of the factory 9am–noon, 2–6.30pm.* Candied fruit, lemon, orange and grapefruit preserve, chocolates and sweets, crystallised petals and delicious jams made with rose, violet and jasmine blossom. **Maison Poilpot – Aux Parfums de Grasse** – *10 r. St-Gaétan. 04 93 85 60 77.* This traditional perfumery produces more than 80 different fragrances, including popular Mediterranean scents such as mimosa, rose, violet and lemon. **L'Art Gourmand** – *21 r. du Marché. 04 93 62 51 79.* This Old Nice boutique has nougats, calisson, candied fruit, cookies, pastries, ice cream and northern France specialities.

Monaco

All the famous fashion brands have boutiques in Monte-Carlo. Find shops specialising in traditional goods in the narrow streets of the Rock (*Le Rocher*) opposite the palace. Boutique du Rocher in Avenue de la Madone is the official shop for local crafts.

Cannes

Market – *Marché de Forville; Tue–Sun 7am–1pm.* Fine stalls displaying fresh regional produce. **Allées de la Liberté** – Flower market every morning. Popular flea market on Saturdays. **Shopping streets** – *r. Meynadie.* Tempting window displays of food and craftwork in lively pedestrian area. Rue d'Antibes: luxury clothes and luggage. **Cannolive** – *16 r. Vénizelos. 04 93 39 08 19.* This shop boasts an incredible choice of Provençal products: household linen, *tapenades*, crockery, *santons*, soap, and even Lérina liqueur from the nearby islands.

St Tropez

Markets – *Tue and Sat, pl. des Lices.* **Shopping streets** – *r. Clemenceau, r. Gambetta and r. Allard* offer an impressive selection of local arts and crafts: pottery, glassware, etc. **Les Sandales Tropéziennes** – *16 r. Georges Clemenceau. 04 94 97 19 55.* The Rondini house has been crafting St-Tropez sandals since 1927. The distinctive, namesake model in natural leather is the most popular, but the snakeskin version sells well, too! **Le Petit Village** – *at La Foux roundabout, follow signs to Grimaud/Cogolin. 04 94 56 32 04.* This showroom brings together wines from eight prestigious vineyards on the St-Tropez peninsula, just off the busy La Foux intersection.

Route Napoléon
Ceramics

Tour of traditional pottery workshops – *Closed Sat–Sun. No charge. Information at the tourist office 04 93 63 82 58.* **Pottery classes** – *Espace Grandjean, bd des Deux-Vallons. Closed winter, Sat–Sun in summer. 04 93 63 07 61.* Pottery classes for kids and adults at the fine arts school (10, 20 or 30 hours).

SPORT & LEISURE

PARIS

Among the most popular sporting events held in and around Paris are the International Roland Garros Tennis Championships, the Paris Marathon, the legendary *Tour de France* with its triumphant arrival along the Champs-Élysées, and several prestigious horse races (Prix du Président de la République in Auteuil, Prix d'Amérique in Vincennes, Prix de l'Arc de Triomphe in Longchamp). The *Parc des Princes stadium* (*24 r. Claude Farrère; www.leparc desprinces.fr*) is host to the great football and rugby finals, attended by an enthusiastic crowd, and the *Palais Omnisport de Paris-Bercy* (*8 bd Bercy; www.bercy.fr*) organises the most unusual indoor competitions: indoor surfing, North American rodeos, ice figure-skating, tennis championships (Open de Paris), moto-cross races, martial arts, Six-day Paris Cycling Event, and also pop concerts by international stars.

Le Mans viewed from the Sarthe

© Chris Rose/iStockphoto.com

Fontainebleu

Jeu de Paume de Fontainebleau – *Château de Fontainebleau. 01 60 71 5070. www.musee-chateau-fontainebleau.fr*. The *jeu de paume*, a sport whose descendants include tennis and squash, has been played since 1601 in this indoor court of the Château de Fontainebleau. Visitors can watch a match or try a game themselves.

NORMANDY & BRITTANY
Caen

Festyland – *bd Péripherique 50 N, exit for Carpiquet, 14650 Carpiquet. 02 31 75 04 04. www.festyland.com. Closed Oct–Mar.* €16 (children, €14). This family leisure park has some 30 attractions. Three daily shows (including a circus show) for young children.

CHATEAUX OF THE LOIRE
Angers

Les Croisières au Mans – *101 quai de l'Amiral-Lalande, Le Mans – 02 43 80 56 62.* Make your reservation through the tourist office for a boat trip or cruise (with a meal) on the Sarthe. A different way of discovering Le Mans and its surroundings.
Maison de l'Environnement – *Parc de loisirs du Lac de Maine, ave du Lac de Maine, Angers – 02 41 22 32 30.* This nature information centre organises various activities including environment-awareness courses.
Public Gardens and Parks – Anger's Jardin des Plantes, Jardin du Mail, Jardin Médiéval, French-style gardens in the moat and

Canal du Midi, Toulouse

© Thieury/Fotolia.com

Parcs de l'étang St-Nicolas on the outskirts of town. *Open daily.*
Boat Trips – Possibilities include a combined tourist-train ride and mini boat trip on the River Maine and a candlelit dinner/cruise. *Batellerie promenade l'Union, cale de la Savatte. 49100 Angers. 02 41 42 12 12.*

BORDEAUX & DORDOGNE
Biarritz

Hippodrome des Fleurs – *av. du Lac Marion. 05 59 41 27 34. www.hippodrome-biarritz.com.* Horse races have been held in this trotter's hippodrome on July and August evenings for over fifty years.
Piscine municipale – *bd du Gén.-de-Gaulle.05 59 22 52 52.* Located on the shore, this municipal complex features sea-water pools as well as a jacuzzi, hammam and sauna.
Thermes Marins – *80 r. de Madrid. 05 59 23 01 22. www.biarritz-thalasso.com.* This spa features a leisure pool and jacuzzi and offers various treatments, such as affusion or underwater showers, seaweed treatment booths, massages and sea-air bath booths.

LANGUEDOC ROUSSILLON
Toulouse

Bateau Mouche Le Capitole – *quai de la Daurade, Toulouse. 05 61 25 72 57. www.toulouse-croisieres.com.* Embark upon this pleasure steamer for a cruise on the Garonne.
Péniche Baladine – *quai de la Daurade, Toulouse. 05 61 80 22 26. www.bateaux-toulousains.com.* Canal du Midi cruises depart at 10.50am and 4pm; Garonne cruises at 2.30pm, 5.30pm and 7pm.
Parc Toulousain – On an island in the River Garonne, Parc Toulousain has four pools (three outdoors); the Stadium; the Parc des Expositions and the Palais des Congrès.

PROVENCE
Marseille
Boat trips

From Marseille – *ICARD Maritime, quai des Belges. 04 91 33 03 29. www.visite-des-calanques.com.* Trips in catamarans to Cassis along the coast. *€10–25.*
From Cassis – *Les Bateliers de Cassis. 04 42 01 03 31. www.calanques-cassis.com.* Departure from the port of Cassis visiting Port-Miou,

Port-Pin and En-Vau, without landing. *€14–23.*

From La Ciotat – *Les Amis des Calanques, quai Ganteaume. 06 09 35 25 68. www.visite-calanques.fr.*

Tours

Guided Tours – *By reservation at the tourist office. €6.50.* Guided tours (2hr) take place on various themes, in several languages, most days.

Le Grand Tour (**bus**) – *Leaves from quai du Port daily, on the hour from 10am. 1€8 (€20 2 days). 04 91 91 05 82. www.marseillelegrandtour.com.* Hop on-hop off bus tour (1hr 30min circuit) with audio commentary in several languages that takes you around all the major sights.

Tourist train – *Leaves from quai du Port. €7 (children, €4). 04 91 25 24 69. www.petit-train-marseille.com.* There are two itineraries: to Notre-Dame de la Garde going past the Basilica of St-Victor, and Le Panier, the old town.

Avignon

© Philip Lange/iStockphoto.com
Pont du Gard, Avignon

Avignon by boat – *Croisi-Europe. 03 88 76 44 44. www.croisi europe.com.* Audio tours of Avignon and along the Rhône.

Coach excursion – Provence Vision (**Cars Lieutaud**) – *36 bd St-Roch. 04 90 86 36 75. www.cars-lieutaud.fr.* Offers half-and full-day excursions from Avignon to the Camargue, Pont du Gard, Fontaine-de-Vaucluse, the Alpilles, a lavender tour and a wine tour to Châteauneuf-du-Pape.

Trips on the Rhône – "Grands Bateaux de Provence" *(04 90 85 62 25. www.avignon-et-provence.com/ mireio)* organises several full day round-trip boat outings from Avignon along the Rhône.

CÔTE D'AZUR
Monaco

Aquavision – *quai des Etats-Unis, Port Hercule. 00 377 92 16 15 15. Departures several times daily throughout the season. €12 (child €8).* Views of the sea depths, and marine fauna and flora, with commentary in four languages.

Cannes

Watersports Plongée Club de Cannes (*46 r. Clémenceau; 04 9338 6757*).

Beaches – Not all the beaches on La Croisette charge a fee (details of prices are listed at the top of the steps), or belong to a hotel (located opposite). There are also three free beaches, one of which is located behind the Palais du Festival. The other public beaches lie west of the old port, on Boulevard Jean-Hibert and Boulevard du Midi, at Port Canto and on Boulevard Gazagnaire beyond La Pointe.

Ponton Majestic Ski Nautique – *10 bd de la Croisette. 04 92 98 77 47. http://majesticskiclub.online.fr.* Water-skiing and parasailing.

SPORT AND LEISURE

177

RESTAURANTS

MICHELIN GUIDE

We've selected a few restaurants from the Michelin red guide. Look for listings in red:

☺ – Best-value

❀ | ❀❀ | ❀❀❀ – Michelin-starred

✗ | ✗✗ | ✗✗✗ | ✗✗✗✗ | ✗✗✗✗✗ – Charming

WHERE TO EAT
Prices and hours

	Provinces	Cities
⊜	<14€	<16€
⊜⊜	14–25€	16–30€
⊜⊜⊜	25–40€	30–50€
⊜⊜⊜⊜	>40€	>50€

PARIS

⊜⊜**Pharamond** – 24 r. de la Grande-Truanderie, 75001. ⊜Châtelet-Les-Halles. 01 40 28 45 18. www.pharamond.fr. An institution dating back to the heyday of Les Halles. The Pharamond still serves traditional dishes.

⊜⊜**Vaudeville** ✗✗ – 29, r. Vivienne, 75002. ⊜Bourse. 01 40 20 04 62. www.vaudevilleparis.com. This large brasserie with its sparkling Art Deco details in pure Parisian style is especially lively after theatre performances.

⊜⊜**Le Carré des Vosges** ✗ – 15 r. St-Gilles, 75003. ⊜Chemin Vert. 01 42 71 22 21. www.lecarredesvosges.fr. Friendly bistro a stone's throw from the Rue des Francs-Bourgeois and its trendy boutiques.

⊜⊜**Bofinger** ✗✗ – 5 r. Bastille, 75004. ⊜Bastille. 01 42 72 87 82. www.bofingerparis.com. The famous clients and remarkable décor have bestowed enduring renown on this brasserie created in 1864.

⊜⊜**Atelier Maître Albert** ✗✗ – 1 r. Maître Albert, 75005. ⊜Maubert Mutualité. 01 56 81 30 01. www.

ateliermaitrealbert.com. A huge medieval fireplace and spits for roast meat take pride of place in this handsome interior. Guy Savoy is responsible for the mouth-watering menu.

⊜⊜**Florimond** ✗ – 19 av. La Motte-Picquet, 75007. ⊜Ecole Militaire. 01 45 55 40 38. http://leflorimond.com. Pocket-sized restaurant named after Monet's gardener in Giverny.

⊜⊜⊜**La Maison de l'Aubrac** – 37 r. Marbeuf, 75008. ⊜Franklin D. Roosevelt. 01 43 59 05 14. www.maison-aubrac.com. Aveyron farmhouse-style décor, generous portions of rustic cuisine (with an emphasis on Aubrac beef) and an excellent wine list. Close to Champs-Élysées.

⊜⊜**Chardenoux** ✗✗ – 1 r. Jules Vallès, 75011. ⊜Charonne. 01 43 71 49 52. www.restaurantlechardenoux.com. Reopened under the chef Cyril Lignac on its 100th anniversary, this bistro is bringing back traditional cuisine.

🍴⊜⊜⊜**La Coupole** – 102 bd Montparnasse, 75014. ⊜Vavin. 01 43 20 14 20. www.flobrasseries.com. The spirit of Montparnasse lives on in this huge Art Deco brasserie opened in 1927. The 24 pillars were decorated by artists of the period, while the cupola sports a contemporary fresco.

⊜⊜**Le Troquet** ✗ – 21 r. François Bonvin, 75015. ⊜Cambronne. 01 45 66 89 00. An authentic Parisian bar: single set menu shown on the blackboard, retro-style dining room, and tasty market-based cuisine.

⊜⊜**Bistro de la Muette** – 10 chaussée de la Muette, 75016. ⊜Mo La Muette. 01 45 03 14 84.

www.bistrocie.fr. The very attractive, all-inclusive formula of this elegant bistro explains part of its appeal in the neighbourhood.

Versailles

😊😊 **La Brasserie du Théâtre** – *15 r. des Réservoirs. 01 39 50 03 21. www.flobrasseries.com. Reservations advisable evenings.* The walls of this 1895 brasserie situated next to the theatre are covered with photos of artists who have frequented it over the years. 1930s-style décor, covered terrace and traditional cuisine.

😊😊 **Le Bœuf à la Mode** – *pl. du Marché, 4 r. au Pain. 01 39 50 31 99. www.leboeufalamode-versailles. com.* A typical 1930s bistro with a convivial, relaxed atmosphere. The décor – red wall-seats, knick-knacks, posters, mirrors – is a hit and the regional specialities are delicious. Very busy on market days.

😊😊😊 **Le Potager du Roy** – *1 Mar.-Joffre. 01 39 50 35 34. Closed Sun–Mon.* Delightfully retro setting and meat and fish dishes with vegetables in pride of place.

😊😊😊 **Au Chapeau Gris** – *7 r. Hoche. 01 39 50 10 81. www.auchapeaugris.com. Closed Tue eve and Wed. Reservations required.* This restaurant, said to date back to the 18C, is a veritable institution hereabouts. Quintessential Versailles ambience and décor are the setting for appetising, traditional cuisine. Nothing too wild, just a reliable, very much sought-after establishment.

😊😊😊😊 **Valmont** ✕✕ – *20 r. au Pain. 01 39 51 39 00. www.levalmont. com. Closed Sun eve and Mon.* This old house on the Place des Halles is bound to catch your eye. Venture inside and appreciate the first-rate reception, charming decoration, elegant tables and succulent cookery.

Fontainebleau

😊😊😊 **Croquembouche** – *43 r. de France. 01 64 22 01 57. www. restaurant-croquembouche.com. Closed Sat & Mon for lunch, Sun.* A plain and simple restaurant in the city centre frequented by regulars who appreciate the warm reception, the inviting dining room decorated in soothing colours, and the traditional food prepared from fresh produce.

😊😊😊 **L'Île aux Truites** – *6 chemin Basse-Varenne, Vulaines-sur-Seine. 7km/4.3mi E of Fontainebleau dir. Samoreau. 01 64 23 71 87. Closed Thu lunch and Wed. Reservations required.* A pretty thatched-roof country house on the banks of the Seine. Diners can savour trout and salmon from the restaurant's fish tank while enjoying an incomparable view of the river and forest. Summertime, meals are served outdoors.

Chartres

😊😊 **Le Café Serpente** – *2 r. du Cloître Notre-Dame. 02 37 21 68 81.* A bicycle on the ceiling, posters on the walls and enamelled plaques in the stairwell comprise the décor of this thoroughly genial old café opposite the cathedral.

😊😊😊 **Le Pichet** – *19 r. du Cheval-Blanc. 02 37 21 08 35.* Just down the street from the cathedral, a very friendly little bistro that suits our tastes. Inside, there is a pleasant jumble of bric-a brac: wooden chairs, a collection of coffeepots, pitchers, old street signs and other good stuff. The food is traditional French cuisine.

⊜⊜ **Le Tripot** – *11 pl. Jean-Moulin. 02 37 36 60 11. Closed Sun–Mon & public holidays.* This house built in 1553 used to accommodate a *jeu de paume* (real tennis court) called "Le Tripot" whose Latin motto meaning "Belligerents: stay away" may still be seen above the front door.

Compiègne

⊜⊜ **Le Bistrot des Arts** – *33 cours Guynemer. 03 44 20 10 10. Closed Sat lunch and Sun.* Located on the ground floor of the Hôtel des Beaux-Arts, an appealing, authentic bistro decorated with various objects and etchings. In the kitchen, the chef concocts appetising dishes using market-fresh produce.

⊜⊜ **Brasserie du Nord** – *pl. de la Gare. 03 44 83 58 84. www.brasseriedunord.sitew.com. Closed Sun & public holidays.* This has become quite an institution locally for its seafood dishes. The dining room is modern and bright.

⊜⊜⊜ **Auberge du Buissonnet** ✗✗ – *825 r. Vineux, Choisy-au-Bac. 5km/3mi NE of Compiègne via N 31 and D 66. 03 44 40 17 41. Closed Sun eve, Tue eve and Mon. Reservations recommended.* Ask for a table near the bay windows of the dining room or on the terrace, weather permitting, and watch ducks and swans glide peacefully over the pond, then shake themselves off and waddle proudly toward the garden.

⊜⊜⊜ **Le Palais Gourmand** – *8 r. du Dahomey. 03 44 40 13 13. http://le-palaisgourmand.com. Closed Sun eve and Mon.* This spruce-timbered house (1890)

has a string of rooms and an attractive verandah where heaters, Moorish pictures and mosaics create an agreeable atmosphere. Traditional cuisine.

Lille

⊜⊜ **Le Domaine de Lintillac** – *43 r. de Gand. 03 20 06 53 51. Closed Sun, Mon.* The red façade of the building will lead you directly to this rustic restaurant in old Lille. The plentiful cuisine of the Périgord region is honoured here.

⊜⊜ **Aux Moules** – *34 r. de Béthune. 03 20 57 12 46. www.auxmoules.com.* A multitude of mussels *(moules)* and a few other Flemish specialities await customers in this 1930s style brasserie located in a lively pedestrian street.

⊜⊜ **Estaminet du Rijsel** – *25 r. de Gand. 03 20 15 01 59. Closed Sun–Mon.* This *estaminet* is located in a street crowded with restaurants. The appealing Flemish décor features photos, posters and advertisements.

⊜⊜ **Le Passe-Porc** – *155 r. de Solférino. 03 20 42 83 93. Reservations required.* The tiled floor, wall seats and enamelled plaques on the walls act as the backdrop for a remarkable collection of pigs.

⊜⊜ **La Tête de l'Art** – *10 r. de l'Arc. 03 20 54 68 89. www.latetedelart-lille.com. Closed Sun & evenings except Fri–Sat. Reservations required.* A charming, lively restaurant is hidden behind a pink façade.

⊜⊜⊜ **La Cave aux Fioles** – *39 r. de Gand. 03 20 55 18 43. www.lacaveauxfioles.com. Closed Sun & Public Holidays – Reservations required.* The interior is unexpectedly warm and pleasant:

brick, wood, beams and paintings by local artists.

⊜⊜🍱🍱 **L'Huitrière** XXX – *3 r. des Chats Bossus. 03 20 55 43 41. www. huitriere.fr. Closed Public Holidays.* A former fish-mongers, the restaurant has stayed true to its heritage, serving spectacularly fresh fish and seafood in three resplendent dining rooms.

NORMANDY
Rouen

⊜⊜ **Les Maraîchers** – *37 pl. du Vieux-Marché. 02 35 71 57 73. www.les-maraichers.fr.* A restaurant with Parisian bistro airs in a half-timbered house. Wall seats, a bar, tables set close to one another, old advertising plaques, hat and jug collections – nothing's missing! Improvised cuisine. Norman-style second dining room on the ground floor.

⊜⊜ **Pascaline** – *5 r. de la Poterne. 02 35 89 67 44. www.pascaline.fr. Reservations recommended.* Located next to the courthouse, this restaurant with a bistro façade is very nice. Brasserie décor with handsome wood counters, long seats and yellow walls.

⊜⊜🍱🍱 **Le Beffroy** – *15 r. Beffroy. 02 35 71 55 27. Closed Sun eve and Tue. Reservations required.* This 16C Norman half-timbered house offers the choice between three pretty dining rooms, all equally inviting. A fine address for savouring plentiful fare prepared with quality ingredients.

⊜⊜🍱🍱 **La Couronne** XXX – *31 pl. du Vieux-Marché. 02 35 71 40 90. www.lacouronne.com.fr.* The décor of this 14C house on the market place is simply superb. beams, carved woodwork, hearths and frescoes.

Caen

⊜⊜ **Le Bouchon du Vaugueux** X 😊 – *12 r. du Graindorge. 02 31 44 26 26. Closed Sun–Mon.* This tavern (*bouchon*) is situated near the château and old Caen. Crowded tables add to the friendly ambience.

⊜⊜🍱 **L'Insolite** – *16 r. du Vaugueux. 02 31 43 83 87. www. restaurantlinsolite.com. Closed Sun–Mon except Jul–Aug, public holidays. Reservations recommded.* Take time to discover this half-timbered 16C house with its unusual décor combining rustic frescoes, mirrors and dried flowers. Fish and seafood dishes on the menu.

⊜⊜🍱 **P'tit B** – *15 r. Vaugueux. 02 31 93 50 76.* Charming 17C house with a rustic interior artfully modernised, including a superb fireplace. Relaxed atmosphere, a view of the kitchen, and seasonal dishes.

Bayeux

⊜⊜🍱 **Hostellerie St-Martin** XX – *6 pl. Edmond Paillaud, Creully. 02 31 80 10 11. Closed 1–14 Jan.* Today it's a restaurant, but in the past the large vaulted rooms dating from the 16C housed the village market. Exposed stone, a fireplace, sculptures and a view of the wine cellar make up the curious décor. Classic cuisine. A few bedrooms.

⊜⊜ **Le Petit Bistrot** – *2 r. du Bienvenu. 02 31 51 85 40. Closed Sun, Wed, Mon (low season).* An inventive cuisine prepared by a keen chef is the main attraction of this small establishment facing the cathedral. Original dishes inspired by Mediterranean cuisine are served in a Provençal-style décor with an ochre colour scheme, watercolours and drawings.

RESTAURANTS

🍽️🍴 **Le Pommier** X – *38–40 r. des Cuisiniers. 02 31 21 52 10. www. restaurantlepommier.com. Closed 14 Dec–18 Jan, Sun (Nov–Mar).* No place could be more centrally located, near the cathedral, its inviting apple-green façade announcing its rich Norman cuisine: smoked ham, *tripes à la mode de Caen*, cream sauces and, of course, apples. There are also vegetarian dishes. The vaulted dining-room with stone walls adds charming authenticity.

🍴🍽️ **La Rapière** XX – *53 r. St-Jean. 02 31 21 05 45. Closed mid-Dec–mid-Jan, Wed & Thu.* A 15C house situated in old Bayeux. A lovely, rustic interior and tasty food using local produce.

Coutances

🍴🍽️ **Pré Salé** – *Restaurant belonging to the Hôtel Mercure – 2km/1.2mi S of Mont-St-Michel via D 976. 02 33 60 14 18. www.hotel mercure-montsaintmichel.com.* Located along the River Couesnon at the start of the dike, the Hôtel Mercure welcomes you into its bright dining room.

🍴🍽️ **La Sirène** – *located inside the walls. 02 33 60 08 60.* This crêperie was an inn for many years. The frosted-glass windows, their panes separated by metal mullions, confirm the genuine flavour of the place.

CHATEAUX OF THE LOIRE
Angers

🍴 **La Ferme** – *2 pl. Freppel, Angers. 02 41 87 09 90. Closed Sun eve and Wed. Reservations required.* A well-known restaurant near the cathedral, where you can enjoy traditional local cooking in a simple setting. The terrace is one of the nicest in town.

🍴🍽️ **Provence Caffé** XX – *9 pl. du Ralliement, Angers. 02 41 87 44 15. Closed Sun and Mon. Reservations required.* This popular restaurant next to the Hôtel St-Julien is often full both at lunchtime and in the evenings. The patron is from the south of France and the menu reflects this, with its Mediterranean flavours. The dining room has a Provençal atmosphere too. Carefully prepared cuisine at moderate prices.

🍴🍽️ **Le Relais** XX – *9 r. de la Gare, Angers. 02 41 88 42 51. Closed Sun and Mon.* The woodwork and the murals in this charming tavern recall the vineyard and the harvest. The traditional cooking is satisfying and simple, at affordable prices.

Le Mans

🍴🍽️ **Le Fontainebleau** – *12 pl. St-Pierre. 02 43 14 25 74. Closed Tue.* A rustic atmosphere with walls dating from 1720, this restaurant in Old Mans offers modern cuisine according to the season. Faultless table settings and friendly welcome.

🍴🍽️ **Le Grenier à sel** XX – *26 pl. de l'Eperon. 02 43 23 26 30. www. restaurant-le-grenier-a-sel.fr. Closed Sun-Mon.* Right in the town centre, this former salt store now houses a restaurant serving modern cuisine. Menu changes daily.

🍴🍽️ **Mercure Batignolles** – *r. Pointe. 02 43 72 27 20. Closed Mon lunch.* Establishment housing modern, practical and well-kept rooms; those to the rear are quieter. Garden with crazy golf. Dining room decorated with photographs recalling the legendary Le Mans 24-hr race. Traditional repertory.

Tours

🍽 **Le Vieux Mûrier** – *11 pl. Plumereau – 02 47 61 04 77. www.levieuxmurier.fr. Closed Sun, Mon.* This is one of the oldest cafés in place Plumereau and it has that extra hint of character that is so often missing from modern establishments.

🍽 **Bistrot de la Tranchée** 😊 ✕ – *103 ave Tranchée. 02 47 41 09 08. Closed Sun and Mon.* Dark wood panelling, bottles of wine, comfortable wall sofas and old-fashioned pizza ovens make up the décor of this pleasant bistro. Enjoy a good selection of small dishes typical to this type of restaurant. Definitely worth a visit.

🍽🍽 **Cap Sud** – *88 r. Colbert. 02 47 05 24 81. Closed Sun and Mon. http://capsudrestaurant.fr.* This little restaurant has a Mediterranean atmosphere, both in its warm décor and up-to-date cuisine. Short, well-selected wine list.

🍽🍽 **Léonard de Vinci** – *19 r. de la Monnaie. 02 47 61 07 88. www.leonard-de-vinci.info. Closed Sun eve and Mon. Reservations required in eve.* A taste of Tuscany in the heart of the Touraine. This Italian restaurant's claim to fame is that it doesn't serve pizzas! A chance to discover different Italian dishes, with a décor that highlights models of Leonardo da Vinci's inventions.

🍽🍽🍽🍽 **La Roche Le Roy** ✿ ✕✕✕ – *55 rte de St-Avertin. 02 47 27 22 00. www.rocheleroy.com. Closed Sun and Mon.* The restaurant in this Touraine manor house will be much appreciated by gourmets. Sample the cooking, which varies with the seasons, in the intimate dining room or the pretty enclosed courtyard in summer.

ALSACE LORRAINE CHAMPAGNE
Metz

🍽🍽 **La Gargouille** – *29 pl. de Chambre. 03 87 36 65 77. www.lagargouille.com. Closed Mon lunch, Tue eve and Wed.* Don't be fooled by the ordinary façade of this restaurant located down from the cathedral: behind it lies a sumptuous interior with velvet-covered seats, cosy little booths and 1900-style décor typical of the Nancy School, all making for a warm ambience. The food is exceedingly refined: carpaccio de fois gras au sel de Guérande, or joue de bœuf sauce vigneronne.

🍽🍽 **La Robe des Champs** – *14 en Nouvelle rue. 03 87 36 32 19.* You can't miss the yellow façade and Provençal-style terrace of this pleasant bistro in a pedestrian town-centre street. Potatoes, as the name infers ("in its jacket"), take pride of place in this friendly, unpretentious establishment.

🍽🍽 **Restaurant du Fort** – *Allée du Fort – 57070 St-Julien-lès-Metz, 8km/5mi NE of Metz, Bouzonville direction on D3, then a minor road. 03 87 75 71 16. Closed Sun eve and Wed. Booking advisable at weekends.* At the end of a forest track you will be amazed to discover this 1870 fort, evidence of the Moselle's turbulent history. Part of it has been restored to create a restaurant offering Lorraine cuisine.

🍽🍽 **Restaurant du Pont-St-Marcel** – *1 r. du Pont-St-Marcel. 03 87 30 12 29. www.port-saint-marcel.com.* A 17C restaurant not far from St Étienne's cathedral, standing on piles beside a branch of the Moselle. Inside, an amusing contemporary fresco depicts a 17C fairground scene, complete with

RESTAURANTS

acrobats and theatre. The staff wear costumes to serve the local cuisine.

⊖⊜🥤 **L'Écluse** – *45 pl. de la Chambre. 03 87 75 42 38. Closed Sat noon and Sun and Mon eves.* Refined modern style, with art on display, and well-prepared contemporary dishes.

⊖⊜🥤🍽 **Maire** – *1 r. du Pont-des-Morts. 03 87 32 43 12. www. restaurant-maire.com. Closed Wed lunch and Tue.* There is a superb view of the Moselle from this town-centre restaurant. Enjoy the chef's carefully prepared dishes, whether in the salmon-pink dining room with its pale wood furniture or on the terrace.

Nancy

⊖⊜ **Grand Café Foy** – *1 pl. Stanislas. 03 83 32 15 97. www.grand-cafe-foy-restaurant.fr. Closed Sun eve, Tue eve and Wed.* Climb the lovely stone staircase to reach this first-floor restaurant above the café-brasserie of the same name in place Stanislas.

⊖⊜ **Les Pissenlits** ✕ – *25 bis r. des Ponts. 03 83 37 43 97. www.les-pissenlits.com. Closed Sun and Mon.* There's always a crowd in this bistro near the market. The atmosphere is relaxed, the cuisine innovative and diverse.

⊖⊜ **Le V Four** ✕ – *10 r. St-Michel. 03 83 32 49 48. www.levfour.fr. Closed Sat lunch, Sun eve and Mon.* It may be small, but this restaurant in the heart of the old city is popular among the locals.

⊖⊜🥤 **Le Gastrolâtre** – *1 pl. Vaudémont. 03 83 35 51 94. Closed Mon lunch, Thu eve and Sun.* This popular bistro just behind place Stanislas is run with a master's hand by a media boss. Its mouth-watering menu and characterful

cuisine combine local flavours with those from the south of France.

⊖⊜🥤 **Grenier à Sel** – *28 r. Gustave-Simon. 03 83 32 31 98. Closed Sun and Mon.* This restaurant is in a little-frequented street on the first floor of one of the oldest houses in town. In the large country-style dining room you can enjoy food with a modern flair.

Strasbourg

⊖ **Pommes de Terre et Cie** – *4 r. de l'Écurie. 03 88 22 36 82. www.pommes-de-terre-cie.com. Booking advisable.* If you want a change from *choucroute*, this friendly restaurant specialises in jacket potatoes accompanied by meat, fish or cheese. Local produce.

⊖ **Flam's** – *29 r. des Frères. 03 88 36 36 90. www.flams.fr. Booking advisable at weekends.* This half-timbered house very close to the cathedral houses a restaurant specialising in *flammekueches*. 15C painted ceiling.

⊖⊜ **Pfifferbriader** – *6 pl. du Marché-aux-Cochons-de-Lait. 03 88 24 46 56. www.winstublepfiff. com. Closed Sun.* Feel at home in this low-beamed dining room, with windows decorated with wine-making scenes. Tasty regional dishes including *käseknefples*, *choucroute* and *bäeckehoffe* are served along with classic French cuisine. Good choice of regional wines.

🍲⊖⊜ **Le Pigeon** – *23 r. des Tonneliers. 03 88 23 31 30.* This typical *winstub* owes its name to two pigeons sculpted on the façade of one of the oldest houses in Strasbourg. Traditional Alsatian cooking.

La Taverne du Sommelier – *Ruelle de la Bruche (Krutenau distict). 03 88 24 14 10. Booking essential.* The type of little restaurant it's always a pleasure to discover. The décor is perfect to set off the intimate atmosphere. The menu follows the seasons, while the wine list features wines from the Languedoc and the Rhône Valley.

Petit Ours – *3 r. de l'Écurie (quartier des Tonneliers). 03 88 32 13 21. www.resto-petitours.com. Booking advisable.* Great little restaurant decorated with Tuscan-inspired colours. Light floods through the bay windows of one room, and the cellar is also very pleasant. Each dish (mostly fish) is characterised by a particular herb or spice.

Au Renard Prêchant – *34 r. de Zürich. 03 88 35 62 87. www.renard-prechant.com. Closed lunchtime on Sat, Sun and public holidays.* A 16C chapel in a pedestrianised street, which takes its name from the murals decorating its walls telling the story of the preaching fox. Rustic dining room, pretty terrace in summer, and reasonable fixed-price lunches.

L'Ami Schutz ※ **–** *1 Ponts Couverts. 03 88 32 76 98. www.ami-schutz.com. Closed Christmas Holidays.* Between the Meanders of the Ill, typical cosy *winstub* with wood panelling (the smaller dining room has greater charm). Terrace beneath the lime trees.

Au Pont du Corbeau ※ **–** *21 quai St-Nicolas. 03 88 35 60 68. Closed Sun lunch and Sat except Dec.* A renowned restaurant on the banks of the Ill, next to the Alsatian Folk Art Museum. Regionally inspired menu that focuses on local specialities.

La Vignette ※ **–** *29 rue Mélanie at La Robertsau. 03 88 31 38 10. http://lavignette-strasbourg-robertsau.com.* An earthenware stove and old photos of the neighbourhood adorn the dining room of this café-restaurant. Appetising, market-inspired cuisine.

Ancienne Douane – *6 r. de la Douane. 03 88 15 78 78. www.anciennedouane.fr.* This building, on the banks of the River Ill, dating from 1358 has had a variety of uses but is now a charming restaurant in the centre of the old city.

Tire Bouchon – *5 rue des Tailleurs de Pierre1 Ponts Couverts. 03 88 22 16 32. www.letirebouchon.fr.* Charming restaurant located near the cathedral in a typical narrow Alsatian street, with an extensive wine cellar and offering traditional cuisine.

Aux Armes de Strasbourg – *9 pl. Gutenberg. 03 88 32 85 62.* An oasis of peace in the famous place Gutenberg in the old town.

L'Épicerie – *6 r. de Vieux Seigle. 03 88 32 52 41. www.lepicerie-strasbourg.com. Closed 22 Dec–7 Jan, holidays.* Hearty tartines served with French songs and accordion music. Nostalgic atmosphere with a 1960s ambience.

S'Burjerstuewel - Chez Yvonne – *10 r. Sanglier. 03 88 32 84 15. www.chez-yvonne.net. Closed Christmas holidays.* This *winstub* is one of the city's institutions, evidenced by the photos and dedications of its famous guests. Regional cuisine.

Le Clou ※ **–** *3 r. du Chaudron. 03 88 32 11 67. www.le-clou.com. Closed Sun and holidays.* This small wine bar in a little street

RESTAURANTS

near the cathedral is eternally popular, with its typical décor, friendly atmosphere and good Alsace cooking.

⊖⊖🍴 **Fleur de Sel** – *22 quai des Batelliers. 03 88 36 01 54.* Opened in 2005 on the south bank of the Ill across the Pont Ste Madeleine. Traditional Alsatian and French cuisine.

⊖⊖🍴🍴 **Buerehiesel** ✕✕✕ ✿ – *In the Parc de l'Orangerie. 03 88 45 56 65. www.buerehiesel.fr. Closed 2 Aug–24 Aug, 30 Dec–21 Jan, Sun and Mon.* Famous chef Antine Westermann has handed over to his son Eric in the kitchens, but this remains one of Alsace's gastronomic temples. The setting is a beautiful half-timbered farmhouse.

Colmar

⊖ **Le Caveau St-Pierre** – *24 r. de la Herse (Little Venice). 03 89 41 99 33. www.lecaveausaintpierre-colmar. com. Closed Sun eve & Mon. Booking advisable.* A pretty wooden footbridge across the Lauch leads to this 17C house, which offers a little slice of paradise with its rustic, local-style décor and a terrace over the water. Local cuisine.

⊖ **La Maison Rouge** – *9 r. des Écoles. 03 89 23 53 22. http://maison-rouge.net.* The somewhat ordinary façade hides a delightful rustic interior. Regional and home-made cooking take pride of place.

⊖ **Schwendi Bier-U-Wistub** – *23–25 Grand'Rue. 03 89 23 66 26.* You will instantly warm to this charming winstub with its ideal location in the heart of old Colmar. The principally wooden décor and the cooking, which is good quality and served in generous portions, are a tribute

to Alsace. Huge terrace to be enjoyed in summer.

⊖ **Winstub La Krutenau** – *1 r. de la Poissonnerie. 03 89 41 18 80. Closed Sun and Mon out of season.* At this *winstub* beside the River Lauch you can go boating in Little Venice and eat a *flammekueche* on the flower-decked terrace beside the canal in summer. A fun way, with no obligations, to learn about this lovely part of Colmar – recommended.

⊖⊖ **Caveau Chez Bacchus** – *2 Grand'Rue, Katzenthal, 5km/3mi NW of Colmar, Kaysersberg direction, then D10. 03 89 27 32 25. Closed at varying times; call in advance.* There's a friendly atmosphere in this wine bar dating from 1789 in a wine-making village. Massive exposed beams and helpings of Alsatian cuisine to match – guaranteed to satisfy the healthiest of appetites. Automated puppets will entertain the children with a lively show.

⊖⊖ **Winstub Brenner** ✕ – *1 r. de Turenne. 03 89 41 42 33. www.wistub-brenner.fr. Open daily noon-4pm, 7-10pm.* The terrace by the Lauch in Little Venice is very popular on fine days. Not surprising, as the setting is ideal and the food, though simple, is served in generous portions.

Riquewihr

⊖ **Auberge St-Alexis** – *68240 St-Alexis 6km/4mi W of Riquewihr on minor road and path. 03 89 73 90 38. Closed Fri.* It's worth venturing into the forest along a dirt track to this former 17C hermitage.

⊖⊖🍴 **Le Sarment d'Or** ✕✕ – *4 r. du Cerf. 03 89 86 02 86. www.riquewihr-sarment-dor. com. Closed Sun eve, Tue lunch* and Mon. Pale wood panelling, copper light fittings, fireplace and huge beams create a lovely warm atmosphere in this restaurant. The cooking is traditional and uses seasonal ingredients.

Reims

⊜⊜ **Brasserie Le Boulingrin** ✕ – 48 r. Mars. 03 26 40 96 22. www.boulingrin.fr. Closed Sun. This Art Deco-style restaurant dating from 1925 has become an institution in Reims life. The owner is much in evidence, overseeing the operations and creating a congenial atmosphere. The menu is inventive and the prices reasonable.

⊜⊜ **Café du Palais** – 14 pl. Myron-Herrick. 03 26 47 52 54. www.cafedupalais.fr. Closed Mon and Sun. This lively café near the cathedral was founded in 1930. With its original glass roof and a warm red décor, it serves generous portions of salad and other daily dishes, which are much appreciated, as are the home-made pastries. You can also enjoy a reasonably priced glass of champagne.

⊜⊜ **Da Nello** – 39 r. Cérès. 03 26 47 33 25. A Mediterranean welcome awaits you at this Italian restaurant where the tables look onto the kitchen and the pizzas are baked in the oven in the centre of the room. Fresh pasta, grilled dishes and daily specials according to what the market has to offer… and all served with an authentic Italian accent.

⊜⊜ **La Table Anna** – 6 r. Gambetta. 03 26 89 12 12. www.latableanna.fr. Closed Mon. Champagne takes pride of place in the window of this establishment next door to the

music conservatory. Some of the paintings adorning the walls are the work of the owner. Traditional dishes are renewed with the seasons.

⊜⊜ **La Vigneraie** ✕✕✕ – 14 r. de Thillois. 03 26 88 67 27. www.vigneraie.com. A celebrated gastronomic halt in the centre of Reims, La Vigneraie boasts a fantastic collection of carafes. Tasty classical menu and fine wine list. Excellent value for money; all is calm, luxurious elegance and courtesy, just steps from the cathedral.

⊜⊜⊜ **Au Petit Comptoir** ✕✕ – 17 r. de Mars. 03 26 40 58 58. www.au-petit-comptoir.fr. Closed Sun, Mon. This imposing restaurant with its wooden terrace is right behind the town hall. Inside the black-and-white décor and studied lighting lend a cosy atmosphere. Traditional cooking and spit-roast dishes.

Troyes

⊜⊜ **Aux Crieurs de Vin** – 4–6 pl. Jean-Jaurès. 03 25 40 01 01. www.auxcrieursdevin.com. Closed Sun and Mon. Wine connoisseurs will appreciate this establishment, which is part wine and spirits shop, part atmospheric pre-1940s-style bistro.

⊜⊜ **Bistro DuPont** ✕ – 5 pl. Charles-de-Gaulle, 10150 Pont-Ste-Marie, 3km/1.8mi NE of Troyes on N 77. 03 25 80 90 99. http://bistro tdupont.com. Closed Sun eve, Mon, and Thur eve. Flowers and smiles from the staff provide a fine welcome. In a simple but carefully planned setting, the cheap and cheerful dishes suit the style of the bistro.

⊜⊜⊜ **Le Bistroquet** – *10 r. Louis Ulbach. 03 25 73 65 65. www.bistroquet-troyes.fr. Closed Sun July-9 Sept.* This restaurant is situated in the centre of the pedestrianised part of Troyes, and is reminiscent of a Parisian brasserie. The large dining room is attractively lit by a decorated glass ceiling, and has leather seats, indoor plants and a lively atmosphere.

BURGUNDY
Dijon
Restaurants
⊜ **Le Chabrot** – *36 r. Monge. 03 80 30 69 61.* If you're after traditional tastes and a laid-back ambience, this bistro is right up your street.

⊜ **La Comédie** – *3 pl. du Théâtre. 03 80 67 11 62. www.la-comedie. com.* This bistro appeals to those seeking traditional flavours and atmosphere.

⊜ **Le Dôme** – *16 bis, r. Quentin. 03 80 30 58 92.* This modern restaurant deals in traditional and contemporary cooking, with a good showing of Burgundian specialities.

⊜ **L'Émile Brochettes** – *16 pl. Émile-Zola. 03 80 49 81 04.* This quirky cavern-style restaurant looking onto lovely place Émile Zola celebrates the kebab in all of its savoury and sweet forms.

⊜ **La Mère Folle** –*102 r. Berbisey. 03 80 50 19 76. www.lamerefolle.fr.* This small, town-centre restaurant offers regional specialities. Convivial atmosphere, good service and 1930s-style décor.

⊜⊜ **Le Bistrot des Halles** ✗ – *10 r. Bannelier. 03 80 49 94 15. Closed Sun and Mon.* A typical bistro a stone's throw from the covered market.

⊜⊜ **Le Bento** – *29 r. de la Chaudron-nerie. 03 80 67 11 50. Sun noon–6pm.* Japanese food fans should try this place – the chef invents new sushi, sashimi and maki dishes every day.

⊜⊜ **La Dame d'Aquitaine** ✗✗✗ – *23 pl. Bossuet. 03 80 30 45 65. www.ladamedaquitaine.fr. Closed Mon lunch and Sun. Closed for lunch in summer.* In the town centre, a paved courtyard and a long flight of steps descend to a superb 13C vaulted dining hall.

⊜⊜ **Le DZ'Envies** ✗ – *12 r. Odebert. 03 80 50 09 26. www. dzenvies.com.* This contemporary gastronomic bistro on the market square reworks French cuisine with Japanese and North African touches.

Cafes
Comptoir des Colonies – *12 pl. François-Rude. 03 80 30 28 22. Open Mon–Sat 8am–7.30pm.* Colonial-style tea shop, with a large sunny terrace.

Maison Millière – *10 r. de la Chouette. 03 80 30 99 99. www.maison-milliere.fr. Open Tue–Sun 10am–7pm, Fri & Sat eve.* Pleasant tearoom in a former 15C fabric shop.

La Causerie des Mondes – *16 r. Vauban. 03 80 49 96 59. www.lacauseriedesmondes.fr. Open 11am–7pm. Closed sun & Mon, and last 2 weeks of Aug.* Asian-themed décor and mood music make for an exotic take on the tearoom.

Mulot et Petitjean – *13 pl. Bossuet. 03 80 30 07 10. www.mulotpetit jean.fr. Open Mon 2–7pm, Tue–Sat 9am–noon, 2–7pm.* This Dijon institution, founded in 1796, specialises in gingerbread.

Besançon

☕ **Le Cavalier Rouge** – *3 r. Mégevand. 03 81 83 41 02. www. cavalierrouge.com. Closed Sun.* A trendy urban atmosphere and speedy service.

☕ **Au Petit Polonais** – *81 r. des Granges. 03 81 81 23 67. Open lunch Tue–Sun; evenings Thu–Sat. Closed Mon.* A simple, unpretentious setting for traditional local cuisine. Warm, congenial atmosphere.

☕ **La Femme du Boulanger** – *8 r. Morand. 03 81 82 09 56. Closed Sun.* This friendly tea room and baker's café offers sandwiches made with Poilâne bread, salads and a dish of the day served both lunchtimes and evenings.

☕ **Miam** – *8 r. Morand. 03 81 82 09 56. Closed Sun.* A very chic, designer restaurant which will whisk your palate far away from the banks of the Doubs River.

☕☕ **La Source** ✕ – *4 r. des Sources, 25170 Champvans-les-Moulins. 8km/5mi NW of Besançon. 03 81 59 90 57. www.lasource-besancon.com. Closed Wed eve except Jun–Aug, Sun eve and Mon.* Big bay windows bathe the main room on the mezzanine with light. Regional and traditional food is served.

ALPS RHÔNE VALLEY
Lyon

☕ **Le Vieux Lyon** – *44 r. St-Jean. 04 78 42 48 89. Closed Sun evening.* Local epicureans are all familiar with this tavern, in operation since 1947, where good humour and hospitality reign.

☕☕ **Restaurant de Fourvière** – *9 pl. de Fourvière. 04 78 25 21 15. www.latassee.fr.* Perfectly situated, this restaurant enjoys a superb panorama.

☕☕ **Lolo Quoi** – *42 r. Mercière. 04 72 77 60 90. www.loloquoi.com.* In this pedestrian street, those in the know go to Lolo.

☕☕ **Brunet** – *23 r. Claudia. 04 78 37 44 31. www.bouchon lyonnaisbrunet.fr. Closed Sun–Mon and Tue lunch. Reserve ahead.* An authentic Lyon *bouchon* (tavern), with elbow-to-elbow tables, and tasty little dishes enhanced by an enticing selection of wines by the carafe.

☕☕ **Le Mercière** – *56 r. Mercière. 04 78 37 67 35. www.le-merciere.com. Reserve ahead.* Located in a passageway giving onto one of the most popular restaurant streets in town, this old house serves traditional cuisine.

☕☕ **La Table d'Hippolyte** – *22 r. Hippolyte-Flandrin. 04 78 27 75 59. Closed Sat lunch, Sun–Mon.* The ideal setting for a candlelit supper.

☕☕ **Maison Villemanzy** ✕ – *25 montée St-Sébastien. 04 72 98 21 21. www.maison-villemanzy.com. Closed Sun, and Mon lunch.* Perched on the slopes of Croix Rousse, this restaurant offers a superb terrace view over the city.

☕☕ **Le St-Florent** – *106 cours Gambetta. 04 78 72 32 68. www.lesaintflorent.com. Closed Sun and Mon.* The place to head for to appreciate an authentic *poulet-de-Bresse.*

☕☕ **L'Orangerie de Sébastien** – *Domaine de Lacroix-Laval, 69280 Marcy-l'Étoile. 04 78 87 45 95. www.orangeriedesebastien.fr. Closed Sun evening, Mon and Tue.* The orangery is part of a 17C château, and serves dishes of the day on a beautiful terrace.

RESTAURANTS

BORDEAUX

Chez Mémère – *11 r. de la Devise. 05 56 81 88 20.* Under the vaulted ceiling of this 16C workshop, discover the flavour and ambience of a fine meal Chez Mémère (at 'granny's house').

Lou Magret – *62 r. St-Rémi. 05 56 44 77 94. Closed Sun and public holidays.* If overwhelmed by the choice of restaurants in this street, try this pleasant establishment whose speciality is canard de Chalosse, duck served grilled or with a delicious sauce.

La Table du Pain – *6 pl. du Parlement. 05 56 81 01 00.* A wide selection of sandwiches, toasts and salads is offered at this restaurant with stone walls, old shelves and waxed pine furnishings.

Le Bistro du Musée – *37 pl. Pey-Berland. 05 56 52 99 69. www.lebistrodumusee.com. Closed Sun.* This bistro with a pretty green wood entrance makes a promising impression from the start. Southwest cuisine and a fine Bordeaux wine menu.

La Rochelle
Restaurants

André ✕ – *5 r. St Jean du Pérot. 05 46 41 28 24. www.barandre.com.* A visit to La Rochelle is not complete without a meal at André! On the old docks, facing the Tour de la Chaîne, this enormous restaurant comprises a dozen bistro-style dining rooms where customers sit elbow to elbow to feast on seafood.

Le Boute-en-Train – *7 r. des Bonnes-Femmes. 05 46 41 73 74. Closed Sun, Mon.* Near the markets, this charming restaurant serves a variety of quiches and food fresh from the marketplace.

À Côté de chez Fred – *32–34 r. St-Nicolas. Closed Sun, Mon. 05 46 41 65 76. Reservations recommended.* This little restaurant gets its provisions from its neighbour and sister… the fishmonger.

Le Mistral *Quai Simenon, in the Le Gabut district. 05 46 41 24 42. http://restaurant-lemistral.fr. Closed Sun.* This wood-clad house is located a stone's throw from the tourist office.

Le Petit Rochelais – *25 r. St-Jean-du-Pérot. Closed Sun. 05 46 41 28 43.* An inviting atmosphere complements the traditional French cuisine.

Bars & Cafes

Café de la Paix – *54 r. Chaudrier. 05 46 41 39 79.* Behind its carved wood façade, this big café was a hospital in 1709, a theatre during the Revolution and since 1900 a café popular with visiting artists such as Colette.

Cave de la Guignette – *8 r. St-Nicolas. 05 46 41 05 75.* Try the house speciality, *Guignette*, an aperitif made of wine and fruit.

Biarritz
Restaurants

La Goélette – *4 r. du Port-Vieux. 05 59 24 84 65.* Take a break from shopping and treat yourself to a meal in this pleasant restaurant. Cuisine with an accent on fish and salads.

Le Clos Basque – *12 r. Louis-Barthou. 05 59 24 24 96. Closed a fortnight in Feb and Jun, Sun eve (Sept–Jun), Mon.* Excellent local cuisine and a warm, friendly atmosphere mean that there's rarely a spare table in this popular restaurant.

⊜⊜ **La Pizzeria des Arceaux** –
20 av. Edouard VII. 05 59 24 11 47.
www.la-pizzeria-des-arceaux.com.
Closed Mon, Tue lunch. This lively
pizzeria just a stone's throw from
the city hall is particularly popular
with a young, trendy crowd.

⊜⊜⊜⊜ **Chez Albert** ✕ – *r. du*
Port Vieux. 05 59 24 43 84. www.
chezalbert.fr. Closed Wed (Sept–Jun).
Situated close to the church of
Saint Eugénie, this busy fish and
seafood restaurant affords fine
views over the fishing port.

⊜⊜⊜⊜ **Plaisir des Mets** –
5 r. Centre. 05 59 24 34 66. Closed
Tue eve, Wed–Thu. This attractive
small restaurant is situated near
the market hall, just a short stroll
from the sea. The modern cuisine
highlights seasonal and regional
produce. Light, modern décor.

Bars & Cafes

L'Impérial (Hôtel du Palais) –
1 av. de l'Impératrice. 05 59 41 64 00.
www.hotel-du-palais.com. " La Villa
Eugénie", the scene of Napoleon
III's love affair with the Empress
Eugénie, became the majestic
Hôtel du Palais in 1893. Enjoy a
glass of champagne and savour the
atmosphere in the hotel's elegant
bar, the Impérial, where a pianist
makes the ambience complete
from 7.30–11pm every evening.

Le Caveau – *4 r. Gambetta. 05 59 24*
16 17. http://lecaveau-biarritz.com.
One of the trendiest bar-
discotheques in the region, Le
Caveau is popular with locals and
visitors, as well as the inevitable
stars on holiday. *The* place to be
seen in Biarritz.

La Santa Maria – *esplanade du*
Port-Vieux. 05 59 24 53 11. The
splendid view of the Rocher de la
Vierge and the Port Vieux beach is

one of the attractions of this little
bar perched on a rock. A terrace,
a few stools and a bar counter
in a cave make this a pleasant,
unpretentious spot where you can
sample tapas while listening to the
little orchestra.

Périgueux

⊜ **Au Bien Bon** – *15 r. des Places.*
05 53 09 69 91. Closed Sat lunch,
Sun, Mon and public holidays. The
menu here is firmly influenced by
seasonal local products.

⊜ **Au Temps de Vivre** – *10 r. St-*
Silain. 05 53 09 87 18. Closed eves
(except summer 7–9.30pm), Sun and
Mon. Reservations recommended.
Tucked away in a pleasant street in
the old town, this restaurant serves
daily specials, plus savoury and
sweet pies.

⊜⊜ **Le Clos Saint-Front** ✕✕ –
5 r. de la Vertu. 05 53 46 78 58.
www.leclossaintfront.com. Open
daily Jun-Sept, rest of year Tue-Sun
lunch. This old house, with its
exposed beams, fireplace and
Louis XVI furniture, is now home
to an elegant restaurant which is
resolutely devoted to Périgourdine
cuisine with an inventive twist.

⊜⊜⊜ **Hercule Poireau** ✕✕ – *2 r.*
de la Nation. 05 53 08 90 76. Closed
Sat–Sun. In a vaulted 16C cellar,
this place is popular with locals,
who come here for the varied
menu, which includes several
healthy options.

LANGUEDOC ROUSSILLON
Toulouse

⊜ **La Cave des Blanchers** – *29 r.*
des Blanchers, Toulouse. 05 61 22 47
47. Closed Tue. An attractive spot,
situated among other restaurants
on a street that is very popular

in the evenings. Regional cuisine blending characteristic sweet and sour flavours.

La Faim des Haricots – *3 r. du Puit Vert, Toulouse. 05 61 22 49 25. www.lafaimdesharicots.fr. Closed Sun.* A mere stone's throw from the Capitole, this vegetarian restaurant gives diners a choice of varied, plentiful fixed-price menus at painless prices.

Jean Chiche – *3 r. St-Pantaléon, Toulouse. 05 61 21 80 80.* This pleasant pâtisserie and tearoom is close to the Capitole. The menu offers a choice of around a dozen light meals, plus cakes and ice creams.

Bon Vivre – *15 bis, pl. Wilson, Toulouse. 05 61 23 07 17. www.lebonvivre.com.* With its terrace giving onto Place Wilson and an attractive interior decorated with photos of Gers (where the proprietor was born), this is an appealing spot with a solid traditional menu.

Le Châteaubriand – *42 r. Pargaminières, Toulouse. 05 61 21 50 58. Closed Sun.* The atmosphere in this little restaurant in old Toulouse is particularly pleasant. Cosy interior with a parquet floor, red-brick walls, a huge mirror and house plants.

Grand Café de l'Opéra – *1 pl. du Capitole, Toulouse. 05 61 21 37 03. www.brasserieopera.com. Closed Sun.* The brasserie of the Grand Hôtel de l'Opéra is the essential place to see and be seen.

Le Mangevins – *46 r. Pharaon, Toulouse. 05 61 52 79 16. Closed Sun.* In this local tavern where salted foie gras and beef are sold by weight, the bawdy, fun atmosphere is enhanced by ribald songs. There is no menu, but a set meal for hearty appetites.

La Régalade – *16 r. Gambetta, Toulouse. 05 61 23 20 11. Closed Sat– Sun.* Located between the Capitole and the Garonne, this small restaurant's pink brick façade leads to a pleasant interior of exposed beams, modern art, wood furniture and bistro chairs.

Brasserie "Beaux Arts" – *1 quai Daurade, Toulouse. 05 61 21 12 12. www.brasserielesbeauxarts. com.* The atmosphere of a 1930s brasserie with bistro-style chairs, wall seats, retro lighting, wood panelling and mirrors.

Le Colombier – *14 r. Bayard, Toulouse. 05 61 62 40 05. www.restaurant-lecolombier. com. Closed public hols and Sun.* Opened in 1874, this is an essential stopping point for culinary pilgrims in search of authentic cassoulet.

La Madeleine de Proust – *11 r. Riquet, Toulouse. 05 61 63 80 88. www.madeleinedeproust.com. Closed Sun.* Childhood memories inspire the original, carefully designed décor of this restaurant featuring waxed tables, antique toys, an old school desk and a time-worn cupboard.

L'Envers du Décor – *22 r. des Blanchers, Toulouse. 05 61 23 85 33. www.enversdudecor.info. Closed Sun; Mon–Tue for lunch.* Cuisine of the southwest with some exotic touches is served in this restaurant in a busy street not far from the Garonne.

En Marge ⊛ ✗✗ – *8 r. Marge, Toulouse. 05 61 53 07 24. www.restaurantenmarge.com.* Excellent French cuisine located in the old district. Chef Frank Renimel produces a new menu every fortnight.

7 Place St-Sernin ✗✗ –
*7 pl. St-Sernin, Toulouse. 05 62 30
05 30. www.7placesaintsernin.com.
Closed Sat lunch, Sun.* This pretty
19C house typical of Toulouse
stands opposite the basilica. Bright
red and yellow Catalan colours,
contemporary furniture and a
display of paintings from a local art
gallery garnish the dining room.
Contemporary cuisine.

Le Chapon Fin – *3 Pl. des
Récollets, Rodez. 05 63 95 07 54.
www.hotelchaponfin.fr. Closed
Mon between Nov and Easter.* This
establishment on the market
square pampers its customers. The
Lutosa restaurant in contemporary
pastels serves classic cuisine.

Chez Simone – *r. du Musée,
St-Bertrand-de-Cominges. 05 61
94 91 05. Closed Toussaint and
Christmas school holidays, and
evenings off-season.* A couple of
streets from the cathedral, Simone
offers simple family fare

Carcassonne

Le Bar à Vins – *6 r. du Plo. 04
68 47 38 38.* In the heart of the
medieval Cité, this wine bar's
shady garden has a view of the
St-Nazaire basilica.

La Tête de l'Art – *37 bis, r.
Trivalle. 04 68 47 36 36. Closed Sun in
winter. Reservations recommended
at weekends.* This restaurant,
specialising in pork dishes, also
exhibits works of modern painting
and sculpture.

**Auberge de Dame
Carcas** – *3 pl. du Château. 04 68 71
23 23. www.damecarcas.com.* This
popular establishment in the Cité
has a generous menu.

La Marquière – *13 r. St-Jean.
04 68 71 52 00. www.lamarquiere.
com. Closed Wed and Thu.*

Roughcast building near northern
ramparts. Serves traditional cuisine.

Comte Roger ✗✗ –
*14 r. St-Louis. 04 68 11 93 40.
www.comteroger.com. Closed
Sun and Mon.* A stroll through
La Cité may well lead you to this
sheltered spot.

PROVENCE
Marseille

Le Salon Provençal – *pl.
Benjamin Chappe, 13190 Allauch,
15km/9mi NE. 04 91 68 39 92.
www.salon-provencal.fr. Closed
Thu.* An adorable small place in
old Allauch. Amiable tea parlour,
terrace and three small rooms
where you can eat in peace.

Axis ✗ – *8 r. Ste-Victoire,
Castellane. 04 91 57 14 70.
www.restaurant-axis.com. Closed Sat
lunch, Sun, Mon eve.* The seasonal,
contemporary-style cuisine makes
this establishment worth a detour.
Modern décor, with views of the
chefs in action.

Le Café des Épices ✗ –
*4 r. Lacydon, Vieux Port. 04 91 91
22 69. Reservations advised.* This
tiny restaurant seats just 20, but
the esplanade terrace and its
olive grove in the background
are delightful.

Le Charité Café – *2 r. de la
Charité, Colbert. 04 91 91 08 41.*
Very pleasant brasserie. Salads,
sandwiches, desserts and drinks,
etc. to eat in or take away.

Charles Livon ✗ – *89 bd
Ch. Livon. 04 91 52 22 41. www.
charleslivon.fr. Closed Tue and
Wed.* Opposite the Palais du Pharo,
this restaurant has a minimalist
décor adorned with orchids.
Reinterpreted regional cuisine;
fine selection of Provence and
Rhône wines.

RESTAURANTS

Chez Madie Les Galinettes – 138 quai du Port, Vieux Port. 04 91 90 40 87. Closed Sat lunch in Jul, Sun. This Provençal restaurant with terrace gives onto the old port.

Cyprien ✗✗ – 56 ave de Toulon, La Timone. 04 91 25 50 00. www.restaurant-cyprien.com. Closed Mon eve, Sat lunch, Sun, public holidays. This restaurant near the place Castellane offers classic, tasty cuisine and a décor to match. Interior adorned with floral touches and paintings.

Miramar ✗✗✗ – 12 quai du Port. Vieux Port. 04 91 91 10 40. www.lemiramar.com. This restaurant, serving bouillabaisse and other fish specialities on the Vieux Port, has a 1960s style with varnished wood and red chairs.

La Part des Anges – 33 r. Sainte. Vieux Port. 04 91 33 55 70. www.lapartdesanges.com. This wine bar is fairly lively in the evening. Taste wine by the glass or bottle or take away. Cold cuts, cheese, etc. to accompany the wine. Rustic décor.

Le Resto Provençal – 64 cours Julien, Cours-Julien. 04 91 48 85 12. Closed Sun, Mon, Wed eve (except Mon and Wed in Aug), every afternoon in Aug. A cosy place with Provençal specialities including sea bream soup and fig tart.

Une Table, au Sud ✗✗✗ ✿ – 2 quai du Port (1st floor). Vieux Port. 04 91 90 63 53. Closed Sun–Mon. This colourful restaurant delights both the eye and the taste buds, thanks to its inventive cuisine with delicious southern accents, as well as views of the forts and hilltop basilica.

La Virgule – 27 r. de la Loge. Vieux Port. 04 91 90 91 11. Closed Sun-Mon. Culinary surprises await you at this restaurant with black, white and steel décor.

Les Arcenaulx – 25 cours d'Estienne-d'Orves. Vieux Port. 04 91 59 80 30. www.les-arcenaulx.com. Closed Sun (Sun & Mon in Jul & Aug). Dine surrounded by books that cover the walls of this restaurant: it's combined with a bookshop and publishers, located in the original warehouses of the 17C Arsenal des Galères.

Bateau-Restaurant Le Marseillois – quai du Port-Marine, just by the Town Hall. Vieux Port. 04 91 90 72 52. www.lemarseillois.com. Closed Sun–Mon, Feb. A 19C building opposite the mairie. Provençal cuisine, particularly seafood.

Les Buvards – 34 Grand'Rue. Vieux Port. 04 91 90 69 98. Friendly bistro with tasty, affordable cuisine and a decent wine list. Great place to meet in the evenings.

Chez Fonfon ✗✗ – 140 Vallon-des-Auffes. 04 91 52 14 38. www.chez-fonfon.com. Closed Mon lunch, Sun. The dining room of this renowned restaurant dominates the Vallon des Auffes harbour. Every morning fresh fish and seafood are brought in by "pointus", the local fishing boats.

L'Épuisette ✗✗✗ ✿ – quartier du Vallon des Auffes. 04 91 52 17 82. www.l-epuisette.fr. Closed Sun–Mon. Set near the rocks in the picturesque Auffes Valley, this restaurant takes you on a pleasant culinary voyage in a light, warm and refined atmosphere. Attentive staff.

Le Moment ✗✗ – 5 pl. Sadi Carnot, Colbert. 04 91 52 47 49. www.lemoment-marseille.com. Run by chef Christian Ernst, this new trendy restaurant near the old port offers a contemporary dining room, sitting rooms upstairs, workshops, wine library and takeaway dishes.

Arles

⊜⊖ **Le Criquet** – *21 r. Porte-de-Laure. 04 90 96 80 51. Closed Wed.* Go for the charming dining room with its beams and exposed stonework rather than the terrace, in this little restaurant near the amphitheatre.

⊖⊖⊜ **Jardin de Manon** – *14 ave des Alyscamps. 04 90 93 38 68. Closed public holidays.* Situated just outside the city centre, near the Roman Alyscamps necropolis, this place's interior courtyard terrace, full of trees and flowers, will appeal to lovers of alfresco dining. There are two dining rooms, and the local cooking, which uses seasonal market produce, offers good value for money.

⊖⊖⊜ **Lou Calèu** – *27 r. Porte-de-Laure. 04 90 49 71 77. www. restaurant-lou-caleu-arles.com. Closed Sun, Mon.* A real classic: fresh salads, *taureau* stew, lamb with rosemary. All Arles' delights are at your fingertips. An excellent wine list. The place for gourmets.

Nîmes

⊖⊖ **Bistrot des Arènes** – *11 r. Bigot. 04 66 21 40 18. Closed Aug, Sat lunch and Sun.* Lyon specialities in a delightful setting crammed with objects including Lyonnais Guignol puppets.

⊖⊖⊜ **Le Bouchon et L'Assiette** – *5 bis, r. Sauve. 04 66 62 02 93. Closed Tue, Wed.* A carefully chosen décor, warm welcome, and tasty seasonal cooking.

⊖⊖⊜ **Le Chapon Fin** – *3 pl. du Château-Fadaise. 04 66 67 34 73.*

www.chaponfin-restaurant-nimes. com. Closed Sat, Sun. Quirky bistro with feria and film posters.

⊖⊖⊜⊜ **Aux Plaisirs des Halles** ✗✗ 🅰 – *4 r. l ittré. 04 66 36 01 02. www.auxplaisirsdeshalles. com. Closed Sun, Mon.* Behind a discreet façade is an elegant room with armchairs draped in fabric, a pretty patio terrace, and good food and wine.

Avignon

⊖ **Ginette et Marcel** – *25 pl. des Corps Saints. 04 90 85 58 70. Closed sat, Sun.* More a bistro/cafteria than a restaurant, you can grab a decent sandwich or salad here.

⊖⊖ **Entrée des Artistes** – *1 pl. des Carmes. 04 90 82 46 90. Closed Sat–Sun.* The dining room of this restaurant is decorated in the style of a Parisian bistro, with old posters and movie memorabilia. Tables are placed close together and the cooking is traditional.

⊖⊖ **L'Ami Voyage… en compagnie** – *5 r. Prevot. 04 90 87 41 51.* French cuisine is served at this cute place set in an old library. An air of elegance reigns here.

⊖⊖ **Le Jardin de la Tour** – *9 r. de la Tour. 04 90 85 66 50. www.jardindelatour.fr. Closed Sun–Mon.* Situated near the ramparts, this restaurant has a lovely garden. Provençal cuisine.

⊖⊖ **L'Isle Sonnante** – *7 r. Racine. 04 90 82 56 01. Closed lunch in Aug, Sun, Mon.* This restaurant near the town hall is proud of its Rabelaisian name. Cosy interior combines rustic style with warm tones.

⊖⊖ **Piedoie** – *26 r. 3-Faucons* ✗✗. *04 90 85 17 32. Closed last week Aug, last week Nov, Feb school holidays, Mon off season, Wed.* Beams, parquet flooring and white

195

walls hung with contemporary paintings for the décor and creative cuisine based on market produce. A family atmosphere.

⊜⊜🍴 **Christian Étienne** ☓☓☓ ✿ – *10 r. Mons. 04 90 86 16 50. www.christian-etienne.fr. Closed Sun and Mon.* Historically charged setting in 13C and 14C buildings adjoining the Palais des Papes. Here the chef produces fine cuisine that pays tribute to the Provence of his birth.

⊜⊜🍴 **Le Grand Café** – *La Manutention, r. des Escaliers Ste Anne. 04 90 86 86 77. www.legrandcafe-avignon.fr. Closed Sun and Mon.* Backing onto the buttresses of the Palais des Papes, these old barracks have become an essential part of local life.

⊜⊜🍴 **Le Moutardier du Pape** ☓☓ – *15 pl. du Palais-des-Papes. 04 90 85 34 76. www.restaurant-moutardier.fr.* This 18C building, listed in France's National Heritage, makes an exceptional setting for a simple, fresh meal.

⊜⊜🍴🍴 **L'Essentiel** ☓☓ – *2 r. Petite-Fusterie. 04 90 85 87 12. www.restaurantlessentiel.com. Closed Wed & Sun.* This restaurant focuses on the "essential", delighting guests with its generous cuisine, full of sunny French and Italian flavours. Modern décor.

⊜⊜🍴🍴 **La Mirande** ☓☓☓ – *4 pl. Amirande. 04 90 14 20 20. www.la-mirande.fr. Closed Tue–Wed.* An 18C Provençal décor, antiques, ornaments and a profusion of refined detail set the stunning scene here.

CÔTE DAZUR
Nice

⊜ **La Tapenade** – *6 r. Ste-Réparate. 04 93 80 65 63. Closed Mon.* Curious décor re-creating a typical street from the south of France, with its shutters, terracotta flower pots and strings of garlic.

⊜🍴 **Lou Balico** – *20/22 ave St-Jean-Baptiste. 04 93 85 93 71. www.loubalico.com. Closed lunch in Jul–Aug.* Three generations of the same family have been serving classic Niçois dishes in this cosy dining room.

⊜🍴 **L'Escalinada** – *22 r. Pairolière. 04 93 62 11 71. www.escalinada.fr.* Nestling in the old quarter, this charming restaurant offers attractively presented regional cuisine.

⊜🍴 **Le Pain Quotidien** – *3 r. St-François-de-Paul (Cours Saleya). 04 93 62 94 32. Closed Tue.* This country-style restaurant specialising in brunch has long wooden tables where guests sit side by side, an original formula conducive to a friendly, convivial atmosphere. .

⊜🍴 **La Table d'Alziari** – *4 r. François-Zanin. 04 93 80 34 03. Closed Sun–Mon.* Unpretentious family restaurant set up in a small alley of the old district. Typical dishes from Nice and the Provence area.

⊜⊜🍴 **Grand Café de Turin** – *5 pl. Garibaldi. 04 93 62 29 52. www.cafedeturin.fr. Open every day from 8am to 10pm.* This brasserie, which is over 200 years old, has become an institution in Nice.

Monaco

😊🍴🍽 **Polpetta** – *2 r. Paradis. 00 377 93 50 67 84. Closed Sat lunch & Tue.* A small Italian restaurant offering three different settings in which to enjoy a tasty tagliatelle alla carbonara or vitello al funghi: the verandah giving onto the street, the rustic-style dining hall or the cosy, intimate room at the back.

😊🍽 **La Maison du Caviar** 🍴🍴 – *1 ave St-Charles. 00 377 93 30 80 06. Closed Sat lunch and Sun.* This prestigious house has been serving choice caviar to Monaco residents for the past 50 years. In an unusual setting made up of bottle racks and wooden panelling, you can also purchase salmon, foie gras or bœuf strogonoff. Definitely worth a visit.

😊🍴🍽 **Vistamar** – *Hôtel Hermitage, Square Beaumarchais. 00 377 98 06 98 98. www.hotel hermitagemontecarlo.com. Closed for lunch Jul–Aug.* An elegant restaurant specialising in fresh seafood, with one of the best panoramic views of the Principality from its top-floor terrace.

😊🍴🍽 **Zebra Square** – *Grimaldi Forum, 10 ave Princesse Grâce. 00 377 99 99 25 50. Closed 3 weeks in Feb.* This stylish restaurant has the same sleek décor as its Parisian namesake, featuring modern fusion cuisine and panoramic views over the sea from the terrace. At night the bar is packed with a young and trendy crowd.

Cannes

😊 **Le Côte d'Azur** – *3 r. Jean-Daumas. 04 93 38 60 02. Closed evenings and Sun.* Modest restaurant with a friendly ambience and cosy setting with period furnishings. The traditional cooking attracts a great many locals.

😊🍽 **Aux Bons Enfants** 🍴 😊 – *80 r. Meynadier. Closed 1 Dec–2 Jan.* Simplicity, generosity and congeniality are the hallmarks of this informal establishment where there's no telephone and customers are required to pay in cash. A true locals' hangout since 1935, with tasty Mediterranean dishes.

😊🍽 **Le Comptoir des Vins** – *13 bd de la République. 04 93 68 13 26. www.lecomptoirdesvins-cannes. com. Closed a fortnight in Feb and a fortnight in Sept; all Sun.* This handsomely stocked wine boutique leads to a colourful dining area where light snacks can be served, washed down with a glass of wine.

😊🍽 **Le Caveau 30** 🍴 – *45 r. Félix-Faure. 04 93 39 06 33. www.lecaveau30.com.* Large restaurant comprising two dining rooms done up in the style of a 1930s brasserie. The terrace overlooks a shaded square popular among *boules* players. Fish and seafood are the specialities of the house.

😊🍽 **Fred l'écailler** – *7 pl. de l'Étang. 04 93 43 15 85. http:// fredlecailler.com.* A large neon sign marks the entrance to this rustic-style restaurant whose walls are draped with fishing nets. The tiny square affords a glimpse of village life with its bustling activity and daily games of *pétanque*. Fine selection of freshly caught fish and seafood.

😊🍽 **Au Poisson Grillé** – *8 quai St-Pierre, Vieux Port. 04 93 39 44 68. www.poisson-grille.com.* Appropriately located in the old port, this fish restaurant was

RESTAURANTS

opened back in 1949. It serves grilled fish alongside many other Mediterranean dishes, in a warm setting of varnished wood evoking the interior of a luxury cabin. Attentive service at affordable prices.

St Tropez

⊖⊜ **Leï Salins** – *rte des Salins. 04 94 97 04 40. http://leisalins.chez. com.* Open-air beach restaurant offering a tasty bill of fare consisting of salads and grilled, freshly caught fish. Charming seaside location coupled with attractive surroundings.

⊖⊜⊜ **Leï Mouscardins** – *1 r. Portalet. 04 94 97 29 00. www.alpazurhotels.com. Closed Wed off-season.* Tucked away behind the harbour, near Tour du Portalet, this restaurant pays homage to Mediterranean tradition. It has a faithful following of food lovers, lured by its creative and lovingly prepared cuisine, presented to you in two dining rooms opening out onto St-Tropez Bay.

⊖⊜⊜ **Régis Restaurant** – *19 r. de la Citadelle. 04 94 97 15 53.* Pasta in all shapes and sizes, cooked in various ways, as well as sushi and wok stir-fries, attract a regular clientele to this restaurant located on a steep, narrow street in St-Tropez.

⊖⊜⊜ **La Table du Marché** – *21 bis r. Allard. 04 94 97 02 58. www.christophe-leroy.com/ restaurants/table-du-marche-st-tropez.html.* Gourmets will love this temple of gastronomy located near Place des Lices, open all day. In addition to the restaurant offering traditional French cuisine, La Table du Marché is also known for its home made pastries that can be purchased on the premises.

Route Napoleon

⊖⊜ **Nounou** ✗✗ – *On the beach at Golfe-Juan. 04 93 63 71 73. www.nounou.fr. Closed Nov–Mar.* Regional cuisine and seafood specialities.

HOTELS

MICHELIN GUIDE

We've selected a few restaurants from the Michelin red guide. Look for red entries in the listings and the following comfort ratings:

🏠 | 🏡 | 🏨 | 🏨 | 🏨

WHERE TO STAY

	Provinces	Cities
🛏	<40€	<60€
🛏🛏	40–65€	60–90€
🛏🛏🛏	65–100€	90–130€
🛏🛏🛏🛏	>100€	>130

PARIS

🛏🛏🛏 **Louvre Ste-Anne** – *32 r. Ste-Anne, 75001.* 🚇*Pyramides. 01 40 20 02 35. www.louvre-ste-anne.fr. 20rms.* This hotel has small but well-equipped rooms.

🛏🛏🛏 **Etats-Unis Opéra** – *16 r. d'Antin, 75002.* 🚇*Opéra. 01 42 65 05 05. www.hotel-paris-opera.com. 45rms.* Nestled by a quiet street, this hotel in a 1930s building offers modern, comfortable rooms.

🛏🛏🛏 **Hôtel des Archives** 🏨 – *87 r. des Archives, 75003.* 🚇*Temple. 01 44 78 08 00. www.hoteldes archives.com. 19rms.* Charming hotel near the National Archives, with small yet prettily decorated, comfortable rooms.

🛏🛏🛏 **Beaubourg** 🏨 – *11 r. S. Le Franc, 75004.* 🚇*Rambuteau. 01 42 74 34 24. www.hotelbeaubourg.com. 28rms.* Nestled in a tiny street behind the Georges-Pompidou Centre.

🛏🛏 **Familia** – *11 r. des Ecoles, 75005.* 🚇*Cardinal Lemoine. 01 43 54 55 27. www.familiahotel.com. 30rms.* Notre-Dame and the Collège des Bernardins provide the backdrop for rustic rooms adorned with sepia frescoes.

🛏🛏🛏 **Elysées Mermoz** – *30 r. J. Mermoz, 75008.* 🚇*Franklin D. Roosevelt. 01 42 25 75 30. www. hotel-elyseesmermoz.com. 22rms.* This cosy hotel has rooms in sunny colours or shades of grey. Varnished wood panelling and blue stone in the bathrooms as well as a cane-furnished lounge.

🛏🛏 **Nord et Est** – *49 r. Malte, 75011.* 🚇*Oberkampf. 01 47 00 71 70. www.paris-hotel-nordest.com. 45rms.* The warm family atmosphere and reasonable prices draw regulars to this hotel near Place de la République.

🛏🛏 **Delambre** – *35 r. Delambre, 75014.* 🚇*Edgar Quinet. 01 43 20 66 31. www.delambre-paris-hotel.com. 30rms.* French poet André Breton stayed in this hotel located in a quiet street close to Montparnasse railway station.

🛏🛏 **Aberotel** 🏨 – *24 r. Blomet, 75015.* 🚇*Volontaires. 01 40 61 70 50. www.aberotel.com. 28rms.* A popular hotel with stylish rooms and an inner courtyard for summer breakfasts. It has a pleasant lounge adorned with paintings of playing cards.

🛏🛏🛏 **Le Hameau de Passy** – *48 r. Passy, 75016.* 🚇*La Muette. 01 42 88 47 55. www.hameaudepassy.com. 32rms.* A private lane leads to this hamlet with a charming inner courtyard overrun with greenery.

🍽 🛏🛏🛏 **7 Eiffel** – *17 bis r. Amélie, 75007.* 🚇*La Tour Maubourg. 01 45 55 10 01. www.hotel-7eiffel-paris.com. 32 rooms and junior suites.* Sleek contemporary design reigns in this elegant Left-Bank hotel. A rooftop summer terrace complete with bee hives affords great city views.

Versailles

🛏️🍽️ **Ibis** – *4 ave Gén. de Gaulle. 01 39 53 03 30. www.ibishotel.com. 85rms. €8.* Near the château and town hall, offering the chain's latest standards of comfort. Poppy red rooms, which are functional and attractive.

🛏️🍽️ **Mercure** – *19 r. Ph. de Dangeau. 01 39 50 44 10. www.mercure.com. 60rms. €12.* In a quiet area, an establishment with particularly practical rooms. Well-furnished lobby giving on to a pleasant breakfast room.

🛏️🍽️🍽️ **Novotel Château de Versailles** 🏰 – *4 bd St-Antoine, 78152 Le Chesnay. 01 39 54 96 96. www.novotel.com. 105rms. €14. Restaurant*🛏️🍽️. Hotel at the entrance to the town, on the place de la Loi. Functional rooms lead off an atrium made into a lounge (numerous green plants). Restaurant with modern, bistro-style interior and traditional menu.

🛏️🍽️🍽️ **Hôtel Le Versailles** – *7 r. Ste-Anne. 01 39 50 64 65. www.hotel-le-versailles.fr. 46rms. €14.* This hotel is situated in a quiet side street not far from the château. The Art Deco-style rooms are spacious, bright and elegant. Cosy bar-lounge and terrace where breakfast is served in summer.

🛏️🍽️🍽️ **Résidence du Berry** 🏰 – *14 r. d'Anjou. 01 39 49 07 07. www.hotel-berry.com. 38rms. €14.* Located in the Saint-Louis quarter, this 18C edifice has been entirely restored by Les Bâtiments de France. Comfort and top-quality materials await you in rooms with time-worn beams overhead. In summer breakfast is taken on a veranda that opens onto the patio.

Fontainebleau

🛏️🍽️ **Hôtel de la Chancellerie** – *1 r. de la Chancellerie. 01 64 22 21 70. www.hotel-chancellerie.com. 25rms. €6.* This small hotel in the heart of the city is located in the former buildings of the chancellery. The small rooms are bright and practical.

🛏️🍽️🍽️ **Hôtel Victoria** – *112–122 r. de France. 01 60 74 90 00. www.hotel victoria.com. 37rms. €8.* This 19C building is a pleasant, relaxing place to stay only five minutes on foot from the Château and the centre of town. Most of the rooms on its three floors have been redecorated in shades of yellow and blue; five of them have a marble fireplace.

Chartres

🛏️🍽️ **Chambre d'hôte La Ferme du Château** – *Levesville, Bailleau-l'Évêque. 7km/4.3mi NW of Chartres via N 154 and D 134. 02 37 22 97 02. Closed 25 Dec, 1 Jan. 3rms.* This elegant Beauce farm offers comfortable rooms.

🛏️🍽️🍽️ **Le Grand Monarque** – *22 pl. des Épars. 02 37 18 15 15. www.bw-grand-monarque.com. 55rms. €15. Le Georges restaurant*🛏️🍽️🍽️. A 16C coaching inn at the heart of the city. The comfortable rooms have a personal touch; some are embellished with cheerfully flowered patterns and canopies while others are more sober.

Compiègne

🛏️🍽️ **Auberge de la Vieille Ferme** – *58 r. de la République, Meux. 03 44 41 58 54. www.auberge-lemeux. com. 14rms. 9.50€. Restaurant*🛏️🍽️. This old farmhouse built of Oise Valley brick offers rooms that are simple but well-kept and practical. The restaurant sports exposed beams, rustic furniture, a tile floor and gleaming copperware. The menu offers traditional and regional cuisine.

⊖⊖⊟ **Hôtel des Beaux Arts** – *33 cours Guynemer. 03 44 92 26 26. www.compiegne-hotel.com. 50rms. 12€.* Located along the Oise waterfront, here's a contemporary hotel whose modern, well-soundproofed rooms have been furnished in teak or laminated wood. Some are larger and have a kitchenette.

Lille

⊖ **Chez B&B** – *78 r. Caumartin. 03 61 50 16 42. www.chezbandb.com. Closed 15 Jul–15 Aug. 3rms.* The comfortable rooms are nicely furnished; two with sloping ceilings. Cosy sitting room.

⊖⊖ **Hôtel Flandre Angleterre** – *13 pl. de la Gare. 03 20 06 04 12. www.hotel-flandreangleterre-lille. com. 44rms. €8.* Situated opposite the train station and near the pedestrian streets, this family-run hotel presents modern rooms that are comfortable and cosy.

⊖⊖⊟ **Hôtel Brueghel** – *3–5 parvis St-Maurice. 03 20 06 06 69. www.hotel-brueghel.com. 65rms. €9.50.* This Flemish-style house is conveniently located in the pedestrian part of town quite near the train station.

⊖⊖⊟⊟ **L'Hermitage Gantois** – *224 r. Paris. 03 20 85 30 30. www.hotelhermitagegantois. com. 69rms. €19. L'Estaminet Restaurant⊖⊖⊟⊟.* Comfort, history and design in one. Delightful personalised rooms in a 14C hospice and listed building.

Rouen

⊖⊖ **Hôtel des Carmes** – *33 pl. des Carmes. 02 35 71 92 31. www. hoteldescarmes.com. 12 rooms. €8.* Situated in the town centre, not far from the cathedral, this hotel is an appealing halt. The delightfully decorated reception area hints of Bohemia, and the clutter-free bedrooms are charming and well fitted out.

⊖⊖ **Hôtel Versan** – *3 r. Jean-Lecanuet. 02 35 07 77 07. www. rouen-hotel-versan.com. 34 rooms. €9.* A practical address on a busy boulevard not far from the town hall. The rooms are all similar, functional and well equipped.

⊖⊖⊟⊟ **Hôtel Dandy** – *93 r. Cauchoise. 02 35 07 32 00. www.hotel-dandy-rouen.federal-hotel.com. Closed 26 Dec–2 Jan. 18 rooms. €11.* Situated in a pedestrian street downtown, close to place du Vieux-Marché, this little hotel decorated with care has a certain charm. The rooms, rather too cluttered for some tastes, are quite cosy. Breakfast served in a pretty little room.

Caen

⊖ **Hôtel St-Étienne** – *2 r. de l'Académie. 02 31 86 35 82. www. hotel-saint-etienne.com. 11rms. €7.* This house, going back to the Revolution, is located in a quiet district close to the Abbaye-aux-Hommes. Note the fine wooden staircase with its beautiful woodwork and the smart bedrooms, some of them with fireplaces.

⊖⊖ **Hôtel Bernières** – *50 r. de Bernières. 02 31 86 01 26. www. hotelbernieres.com. 17rms. €6.* Don't miss the discreet entrance

HOTELS

of this hotel, with its convivial welcome, charming breakfast room and drawing room and delightful bedrooms.

⊖⊜🛏 **Le Bristol** – *31 r. du 11-Novembre. 02 31 84 59 76. www.hotelbristolcaen.com. 24rms. €9.* Those who prefer to be at a distance from the bustle of the centre will appreciate this hotel just a minute from the Orne and the racetrack.

Bayeux

⊖⊜ **La Ferme des Châtaigniers** – *Vienne-en-Bessin, 7.5km/4.6mi E of Bayeux via D 126. 02 31 92 54 70. 3rms.* Set apart from the farmhouse, this converted farm building contains simple, yet pleasant, comfortable rooms. Guests have the use of a fitted kitchen. Peace and quiet is guaranteed in this house set in the fields.

⊖⊜ **La Ferme de Fumichon** – *Vaux-sur-Aure, 3km/1.8mi N of Bayeux via D 104. 02 31 21 78 51. www.fermedefumichon.com. 4rms.* Once part of Longues-sur-Mer Abbey, this fortified 17C farm, with its square courtyard and characteristic porch, is today a dairy and cider-making farm. The attic rooms are plain but pleasant.

⊖⊜ **Hôtel Reine Mathilde** – *23 r. Larcher. 02 31 92 08 13. www.hotel-reinemathilde.com. Closed 15 Nov–15 Feb. 16rms. €7.50.* If you wish to stay in the old town, this small family hotel is conveniently situated a stone's throw from the cathedral and the famous tapestry. Exposed beams and light-wood furniture. Plain rooms, some of them with sloping ceilings.

⊖⊜🛏 **Chambre d'hôte Le Moulin de Hard** – *Area called "Le Moulin de Hard", 14400 Subles, 6km/3.7mi SW of Bayeux. 02 31 21 37 17. 3 rooms.* 🍴. Large rooms in a restored 18C watermill near a small river with a beautiful garden.

⊖⊜🛏 **Chambre d'hôte Manoir de Crépon** – *Anne-Marie Poisson, Crépon, 14km/8.7mi NE of Bayeux via D 12. 02 31 22 21 27. www.manoirdecrepon.com. Closed 10 Jan–10 Feb. 4rms.* This 17C and 18C house is typical of the area, with its oxblood-coloured roughcast. You will like the stone floors and fireplaces, the vast, tastefully furnished bedrooms and the authentic atmosphere of the former kitchen converted into a breakfast room.

⊖⊜🛏 **Hotel Le Bayeux** – *9 r. Tardif. 02 31 92 70 08. www.hotelle bayeux.com. 30rms. WiFi. €9.50.* Functional and well-kept facilities in a modern style, hidden in a quiet side street.

Coutances

⊖ **Amaryllis Bed and Breakfast** – *Le Bas-Pays, Beauvoir. 02 33 58 46 79. 5rms. €6.* This recently built stone house was designed as a B&B. The impeccably clean rooms feature well-equipped bathrooms and a furnished terrace.

⊖ **La Tour Brette** – *8 r. Couesnon, Pontorson. 02 33 60 10 69. www. fraysse.phpnet.org. Closed 14–22 Mar, 1–20 Dec, Wed except Jul–Aug. 10rms. €7.* This small, centrally located hotel is named after the tower that used to protect Normandy from the Duchy of Brittany's assaults. The rooms are not very large but they've been recently renovated. Restaurant in a simple setting with a long, traditional menu.

⊕⊟ Hôtel de Bretagne –
*r. Couesnon, Pontorson. 02 33 60
10 55. www.hotelrestaurantde
bretagne.fr. Closed 20 Jan–5 Feb.
12rms. €7. Regional-style house.*
Admire the lovely 18C wood panels
and the grey-marble fireplace
in the first room. Cosy, typically
British bar and spacious, pleasantly
furnished rooms.

⊕⊟ Chambre d'hôte Bergerie –
*La Poultière, Roz-sur-Couesnon.
02 99 80 29 68. www.la-bergerie-
mont-saint-michel.com. 5rms.*
Located in the former sheepfold,
the rooms are comfortable
and benefit from the peaceful
atmosphere of the small hamlet.
The kitchen set aside for guests
is very much appreciated. A self-
catering cottage is also available.

**⊕⊟ Chambre d'hôte Mme
Gillet** – *3 Le Val-St-Revert, Roz-
sur-Couesnon. 02 99 80 27 85.
3rms.* This family house overlooks
the bay and offers a beautiful
view of Mont-St-Michel and the
surrounding countryside.

⊕⊟⊟ Les Vieilles Digues – *rte du
Mont-St-Michel, Beauvoir. 02 33 58
55 30. www.bnb-normandy.com.
Closed Dec, Jan. 7rms.* This pretty
stone house boasts spacious
rooms thoughtfully furnished with
handsome pieces.

CHATEAUX OF
THE LOIRE
Angers

**⊕ Chambre d'hôte La Ferme
Chauvet** – *72430 Chantenay-
Villedieu. 3km/2mi E of village. 02
43 95 77 57. 5rms. ⌂.* All modern
comforts at a reasonable price;
working farm.

⊕ Chambre d'hôte Le Fresne –
*72300 Solesmes. 02 43 95 92 55.
www.lefresne.com. 3rms. ⌂.*

Discover the delights of a working
farm; rooms are in an annex.

**⊕ Chambre d'hôte Mme
Bordeau** – *Le Monet . 72190
Coulaines. 5km/3mi N of Le Mans.
02 43 89 45 56. 2rms. ⌂.* A chance
to stay in the countryside, but
not too far from town. This typical
regional house has been restored
but has retained its original
character.

**⊕ Chambre d'hôte Le Petit
Pont** – *3 r. du Petit-Pont . 72230
Moncé-en- Belin. 11km/6.8mi S of Le
Mans on D 147 towards Arnage, then
D 307. 02 43 42 03 32. 5rms. Evening
meal ⊕⊟.* The rooms are simply
decorated and well equipped.
The property is situated on a
working farm.

⊕ Chambre d'hôte La Truffière –
*72430 Asnières-sue-Vègre. 2km/1mi
NE of Asnières-sue-Vègre. 02 43 95
12 16. 3rms. ⌂.* On a working farm;
regional cuisine.

**⊕⊟ Chambre d'hôte Grand
Talon** – *3 rte des Chapelles.
49800 Andard, 11km/6.8mi E of
Angers on N 147 (towards Saumur)
then D 113. 02 41 80 42 85. 3rms.*
This elegant 18C house just outside
Angers, decked out with leafy
vines of Virginia creeper, is a haven
of peace. You can picnic in the
park, or relax in the lovely square
courtyard. The rooms are pretty
and the owners extend a very
warm welcome.

⊕⊟ Hôtel Cavier – *La Croix-
Cadeau – 49240 Avrillé, 8km/5mi NW
of Angers on N 162. 02 41 42 30 45.
www.hotelrestaurantlecavier.com.
43rms. €10.* The sails of this 18C
windmill still turn! Inside its old
stone walls is the dining room, near
the original machinery. Modern
bedrooms in a recent wing. Terrace
next to the outdoor pool.

☎☎ **Hôtel du Mail** 🏛 – *8 r. des Ursules, Angers. 02 41 25 05 25. www.hotel-du-mail.com. 26rms. €10.* The thick walls of this former Ursuline convent in a peaceful street prevent the noise from the nearby town centre from penetrating. The fairly spacious rooms have a personal touch and are under the sloping roof on the top floor.

☎☎ **Le Progrès** – *26 r. Denis-Papin, Angers. 02 41 88 10 14. www.hotelleprogres.com. Closed 7–15 Aug, 24 Dec–3 Jan. 41rms. €9.* Conveniently located near the train station, this is a friendly place with modern, well-lit and practical rooms. Before setting out to tour the château, enjoy your coffee in the breakfast room, with its décor inspired by the bright colours of Provence.

Tours

☎☎ **Chambre d'hôte Le Moulin Hodoux** – *37230 Luynes, 14km/8.7mi W of Tours on N 152 and minor road. 02 47 55 76 27. www.moulin-hodoux.com. 5rms.* In a peaceful country setting not far from Tours, near the castle at Luynes, this 18–19C watermill provides comfortable, well-equipped rooms. In the lovely garden there are tables, chairs and a barbecue, as well as a swimming pool.

☎☎ **Hôtel du Cygne** – *6 r. du Cygne. 02 47 66 66 41. www.hotel-cygne-tours.com. Closed Christmas. 16rms. €7.* One of Tours' oldest hotels (18C). Rooms have been renovated, but their character has been preserved. In winter, a fine 16C fireplace warms the little lounge. There is a pleasant family atmosphere.

☎☎ **Hôtel du Relais St-Éloi** – *8 r. Giraudeau. 02 47 38 18 19. www.au-relais-st-eloi.com. 56rms. €8.50.* Recent building with small, practical rooms. Some, with a mezzanine, are particularly suitable for families. No-frills décor and regular maintenance. Modern dining room, but traditional culinary repertoire.

☎☎ **Central Hôtel** – *21 r. Berthelot. 02 47 05 46 44. 37 rooms. €14.* A quiet, comfortable hotel in the old part of Tours, near the busy pedestrian-only districts. The staff are reserved but pleasant. There is a small, peaceful garden behind the hotel and you can eat breakfast on the terrace.

ALSACE LORRAINE CHAMPAGNE

Metz

☎ **Chambre d'hôte Bigare** – *23 r. Principale – 57530 Ars-Laquenexy, 9km/5.6mi E of Metz, Château-Salins direction then D 999. 03 87 38 13 88. 2rms.* If the bustle of city life doesn't suit you, a short journey will bring you to this friendly local village house. Simple rooms and reasonable prices.

☎☎ **Hôtel de la Cathédrale** – *25 pl. de la Chambre. 03 87 75 00 02. www.hotelcathedrale-metz.fr. 20rms. €11.* A charming hotel situated in a lovely 17C house, completely restored. The attractive rooms have cast-iron or cane beds, old parquet flooring and furniture, some of which is oriental. Most rooms face the cathedral, just opposite.

Nancy

☎☎ **Portes d'Or** – *21 r. Stanislas. 03 83 35 42 34. www.hotel-lesportes dor.com. 20 rooms. €6–9.* The main advantage of this hotel is its

proximity to place Stanislas.
The pastel-coloured rooms are
not very large but have modern
furniture and are reasonably well
equipped.

⊖⊜🛏 **Maison d'hôte Myon** –
*7 r. Mably. 03 83 46 56 56.
www.maisondemyon.com. 5 rooms.*
An entirely restored 18C hotel
transformed into a *maison d'hôte*
in the heart of Nancy near the
Place Stanislas.

⊖⊜🛏 **Hôtel Crystal** – *5 r. Chanzy.
03 83 17 54 00. 58 rooms. €12.* This
hotel near the station is a good
place to stay in Nancy. Its modern,
spacious rooms have been nicely
arranged and decorated and
feel welcoming.

Strasbourg

⊖⊜ **Couvent du Franciscain** –
*18 r. du Fg-de-Pierre. 03 88 32 93 93.
www.hotel-franciscain.com. Closed
last week Jul, 1st week Aug. 43rms.
€9.50.* At the end of a cul-de-sac
you will find these two joined
buildings. We recommend the
rooms in the new wing. A good
option within walking distance of
the old city.

⊖⊜ **Hôtel Pax** – *24 r. du Fg-
National 03 88 32 14 54. www.pax
hotel.com. Closed 23 Dec– 4 Jan.
106rms. €9. Restaurant ⊖⊜.*
A family hotel in a busy street on
the edge of the city's old district. Its
plain rooms are well kept, and its
restaurant serves regional dishes.

⊖⊜ **EtC Hôtel** – *7 r. de la Chaine.
03 88 32 66 60. www.etc-hotel.com.
35rms. €8.50.* Situated in a peaceful
area beside the cathedral and
la Petite France in the heart of
the old city.

⊖⊜ **Aux Trois Roses** – *7 r. Zürich.
03 88 36 56 95. www.hotel3roses-
strasbourg.com. 32rms. €8.90.*

Cosy duvets and pine furniture
add to the welcoming feel of the
quiet guest rooms in this elegant
building on the banks of the Ill.
Fitness area with sauna and
jacuzzi.

⊖⊜ **Hôtel de l'Ill** – *8 r. des
Bateliers. 03 88 36 20 01. www.hotel-
ill.com. 27rms. €7.90.* Renovated
hotel with family atmosphere.
The rooms of differing sizes are
impeccably clean, while the old-
fashioned breakfast room has a
cuckoo clock.

⊖⊜ **Le Kléber** 🛏 – *29 pl. Kléber.
03 88 32 09 53. http://hotel-kleber.
com. 30rms. €8.50.* "Meringue",
"Strawberry" and "Cinnamon" are
just a few of the names of the
rooms in this comfortable hotel.
Contemporary, colourful décor
with a sweet-and-savoury theme.

⊖⊜🛏 **Des Princes** – *33 r. Geiler.
03 88 61 55 19. www.hotel-princes.
com. Closed 25 Jul–25 Aug, Jan 2-10.
43rms. €13.* A welcoming hotel in a
quiet residential neighbourhood.
Guest rooms with classic
furnishings and large bathrooms.
Breakfast served to a backdrop
of bucolic frescoes.

⊖⊜🛏 **Hôtel Cardinal de
Rohan** – *17 r. Maroquin. 03 88 32
85 11. www.hotel-rohan.com.
36rms. €14.* Named after the
nearby Palais de Rohan, this little
hotel is on a pedestrian street
near the cathedral. Its quiet,
pleasant rooms are furnished in
Louis XV, Louis XVI or rustic style;
those on the south side have air
conditioning.

⊖⊜🛏 **Gutenberg** – *31 r. des
Serruriers. 03 88 32 17 15. www.
hotel-gutenberg.com. 42rms. €11.*
This building, dating back to 1745,
is now a hotel with an eclectic
mix of spacious guest rooms.

HOTELS

Colmar

⊖ **Chambre d'hôte Les Framboises** – *128 r. des Trois-Épis, 68230 Katzenthal, 5km/3mi NW of Colmar, Kaysersberg direction then D10. 03 89 27 48 85. 4rms.* Head for the open countryside and this village among the vines. The proprietor distils his own *marc* (grape brandy) from Gewürztraminer and provides accommodation in wood-panelled attic rooms. Don't miss the puppet show in the mornings!

⊖ **Colbert** – *2 r. des Trois-Épis. 03 89 41 31 05. www.hotel-colbert.net. 50rms. €6.* This functional hotel near the station provides a comfortable place to stay. The rooms are well equipped with new bedding, effective soundproofing and air conditioning, and some have a balcony. Bar and disco for those in search of nightlife.

⊖⊜ **Hôtel Au Moulin** – *Rte d'Herrlisheim – 68127 Ste-Croix-en-Plaine, 10km/6.2mi S of Colmar on A35 and D1. 03 89 49 31 20. www.aumoulin.net. Closed 5 Nov–31 Mar. 14rms. €9–10.* This old mill deep in the country is perfect for those seeking peace and quiet. Its spacious rooms are all the same but nicely arranged. A small museum of old local objects has been created in a neighbouring building.

⊖⊜ **Hôtel Turenne** – *10 rte de Bâle. 03 89 21 58 58. www.turenne.com. 83rms. €8.50.* On the edge of the old town, this hotel occupies a pleasing building with a pink and yellow façade. Its rooms have been nicely renovated and are well soundproofed. A few small but neat and reasonably priced single rooms are available.

⊖⊜⊜ **Hôtel le Colombier** – *7 r. de Turenne. 03 89 23 96 00.*

www.hotel-le-colombier.fr. 24rms. €12.50. This lovely 15C house in old Colmar combines old stone and contemporary décor by retaining elements from its past, such as the superb Renaissance staircase. Contemporary furniture, modern paintings and carefully arranged rooms.

Riquewihr

⊖ **Chambre d'hôte Gérard Schmitt** – *3 chemin des Vignes. 03 89 47 89 72. Closed Jan–Mar. 2rms.* A house with a garden in the higher part of the village, on the edge of a vineyard. The wood-panelled rooms have sloping ceilings. High standard of cleanliness and reasonable prices.

⊖⊜⊜ **Hôtel L'Oriel** – *3 r. des Écuries-Seigneuriales. 03 89 49 03 13. www.hotel-oriel.com. 22rms. €12.50.* This 16C hotel is easily recognised by its wrought-iron sign. The lack of straight lines in the building, combined with simple décor and old Alsatian furniture and exposed beams, creates a romantic atmosphere.

Reims

⊖ **Ardenn Hôtel** – *6 r. Caqué. 03 26 47 42 38. www.ardennhotel.fr. Closed Dec–early Jan. 14rms. €5.50.* This hotel, behind an attractive brick façade in a quiet little town-centre street, has tastefully decorated rooms and smiling service.

⊖⊜ **Crystal** – *86 pl. Drouet-d'Erlon. 03 26 88 44 44. www.hotel-crystal.fr. 31rms. €9.* A haven of greenery right in the centre of town is the main attraction of this 1920s house. The renovated bedrooms all have excellent bedding. Breakfast is served in a delightful flowered courtyard garden in summer.

ⓔⓢ **Hôtel La Cathédrale** –
20 r. Libergier. 03 26 47 28 46. 14rms.
€7. This smart, welcoming hotel
stands in a street leading to the
cathedral and has small, bright and
cheerful rooms with comfortable
beds, while the breakfast room is
decorated with old engravings.
ⓔⓢ **Hôtel Continental** – *93 pl.*
Drouet-d'Erlon. 03 26 40 39 35.
www.grandhotelcontinental.com.
Closed 21 Dec–7 Jan. 61rms. €14.
The attractive façade of this central
hotel adorns one of the city's
liveliest squares. The rooms, in
varying styles, are reached by a
splendid staircase. Elegant Belle
Epoque sitting rooms.
ⓔⓢ **Grand Hôtel du Nord** –
75 pl. Drouet-d'Erlon. 03 26 47 39 03.
www.hotel-nord-reims.com. Closed
Christmas period. 50rms. €9.
Recently renovated rooms with all
mod-cons in a 1920s building set
in a pedestrians-only square. The
rooms facing the back are quieter.
Many restaurants nearby.
ⓔⓢⓢ **Hôtel Porte Mars** ⚶ –
2 pl. de la République. 03 26 40 28 35.
www.hotelportemars.com. 24rms.
€12.50. Drink tea in the cosy
sitting room, or enjoy a drink in
the sophisticated bar. A delicious
breakfast is served in the attractive
glass-roofed dining room
decorated with photographs and
old mirrors. The comfortable, well
sound-proofed rooms all have a
personal touch.

Troyes
ⓔ **Les Comtes de Champagne** –
56 r. de la Monnaie. 03 25 73 11 70.
www.comtesdechampagne.com.
29rms. €9. It is said that the four
12C houses which make up this
hotel used to belong to the counts
of Champagne who minted their

coins here. Renovated rooms;
those with kitchen facilities could
be ideal for families.
ⓔ **Motel Savinien** – *87 r. Fontaine,*
at Ste-Savinien, 3km/1.8mi W of
city centre. 03 25 79 24 90.
www.motelsavinien.com. Closed
Sun and Mon. 49rms. €10. This
conveniently placed motel by
the ring road on the west of the
city centre is a large, quiet, well-
maintained 1970s building. Rooms
are practical, regularly updated.
Traditional cuisine on the terrace.

BURGUNDY
Dijon
ⓔⓢ**B & B Hôtels** – *5 r. du Château.*
03 892 707 506. www.hotel-bb.com.
55rms. €6.10. If you don't mind the
rather formulaic character of chain
hotels, you'll have a happy stay in
this town-centre hotel.
ⓔⓢ **Hostellerie le Sauvage** –
64 r. Monge. 03 80 41 31 21.
www.hotellesauvage.com. 22rms.
€7. This 15C coaching inn has a
prime spot, just a ten-minute walk
from the Ducal Palace and in the
middle of a lively quarter with a
great café and restaurant scene.
ⓔⓢ **Hôtel Montigny** ⚶ – *8 r.*
Montigny. 03 80 30 96 86. www.
hotelmontigny.com. WiFi. 28rms.
€7.50. Efficiently run hotel near the
town centre with secure parking.
ⓔⓢ **Hôtel Victor Hugo** – *23 r.*
Fleurs. 03 80 43 63 45. www.hotel
victorhugo-dijon.com. WiFi. 23rms.
€6. A friendly place with bright,
smartly decorated and well-kept
rooms.
ⓔⓢⓢ **Hôtel Wilson** ⚶ –
1 r. de Longvic. 03 80 66 82 50.
www.wilson-hotel.com. WiFi. 27rms.
€12. This former post house has
retained its traditional charm
and charisma.

HOTELS

⊝🍴🛏 **Hôtel Du Nord** – *pl. Darcy. 03 80 50 80 50. www.hotel-nord.fr. Closed 17 Dec–2 Jan. 27rms. €12.* Right on the bustle of Dijon's central shopping square.

Bescançon

⊝🍴 **Hôtel Siatel Chateaufarine** – *8 r. Moncey. 03 81 81 34 56. www. hotel-du-nord-besancon.com. 44rms. €7.* Situated in the historic quarter, this hotel dating from the 19C is a perfect base for venturing out into the old town.

⊝🍴 **Hôtel Foch** – *7 bis av. Foch. 03 81 80 30 41. www.hotel-foch-besancon.com. 27rms. €7.50.* The rather severe façade of this large building on the corner reveals a well-run hotel.

⊝🍴 **Citotel Granvelle** – *13 r. Lecourbe. 03 81 81 33 92. www.hotel-granvelle.fr. 30rms. WiFi. €8.* This stone building has an ideal location just a few steps from the historic town centre.

⊝🍴 **Hôtel Siatel** – *3 Chemin des Founottes. 03 81 80 41 41. www.hotelsiatel.com.* 🅿 *40rms. WiFi. €7.* A functional hotel close to a busy main road, but the identical rooms are well sound-proofed. The dining room offers buffets, traditional meals and grills.

⊝🍴🛏 **Mercure Parc Micaud** – *3 av. Ed.-Droz. 03 81 40 34 34. www.mercure.com.* 🅿 *91rms. €15.* Opposite the Doubs River, close to the old town where Victor Hugo was born in 1802. Rooms suit the demands of a business clientele; there is a decent bar and the modern-styled restaurant has a view to the gardens of the casino.

ALPS RHÔNE VALLEY
Lyon

⊝🍴 **Hôtel St-Paul** – *6 r. Lainerie. 04 78 28 13 29. www.hotelsaintpaul.eu. 20 rms. 7€.* A small Renaissance hotel at the centre of Vieux-Lyon.

⊝🍴🛏 **Maisons d'Hôtes du Greillon** – *12 montée du Greillont. 06 08 22 26 33. www.legreillon.com. 5rms.* Away from the noise of the city, this 18C house has a terrace and garden, unique for hotels in the centre of the city.

⊝🍴🛏 **Hotel des Artistes** ♨ – *8 r. G-André. 04 78 42 04 88. www.hotel-des-artistes.fr. 45rms. €12.* The proximity of the theatre, and the fact that many artists have stayed at the hotel, have influenced its decoration.

⊝ **Hôtel B&B** – *93 cours Gambetta. 08 92 707 534. www.hotel-bb.com. 114 rms. €6.10.* A chain hotel offering a central location, with spacious and comfortable rooms and king-size beds.

⊝🍴🛏 **Hôtel Ariana** – *163 cours Émile-Zola, 69100 Villeurbanne. 04 78 85 32 33. www.ariana-hotel.fr. 102 rms. €13.* This is a practical address for those who wish to stay amid the 1930s high-rises of Villeurbanne.

BORDEAUX & DORDOGNE
Bordeaux

⊝ **Hôtel Acanthe** – *12 r. St-Rémi. 05 56 81 66 58. www.acanthe-hotel-bordeaux.com. 20rms. €7.50.* A central location and very reasonable prices are strong points of this recently renovated hotel. The bright rooms are big enough and well sound-proofed.

⊝ **Hôtel Notre-Dame** – *36 r. Notre-Dame. 05 56 52 88 24. www. hotelnotredame.free.fr. 21rms. €7.*

An unpretentious little family hotel in an 18C house just behind the Quai des Chartrons. Rooms small but well kept.

⊝ **Hôtel de l'Opéra** – *35 r. de l'Esprit-des-Lois. 05 56 81 41 27. www.hotel-bordeaux-centre.com. 27rms. €8.* Near the Grand Théâtre et the Allées de Tourny, here's a modest little family hotel.

⊝⊝ **Hôtel Continental** 🏨 – *10 r. Montesquieu. 05 56 52 66 00. www.hotel-le-continental.com. 50rms.* In the old city, here's a venerable 18C mansion with a fine staircase in the hall.

⊝⊝ **Hôtel de la Presse** – *6–8 r. de la Porte-Dijeaux. 05 56 48 53 88. www.hoteldelapresse.com. 27rms. €12.* In the pedestrian shopping quarter of the old city, this is a nice little hotel despite the rather difficult access by car.

La Rochelle

⊝⊝⊝⊝ **Hôtel les Brises** 🏨 – *chemin digue Richelieu (av. P.-Vinçent). 05 46 43 89 37. www.hotellesbrises.com. 48rms. €12.* This 1960s hotel is well situated and has lovely views.

⊝⊝⊝⊝ **Hôtel Champlain** 🏨 – *30 r. Rambaud. 05 46 41 23 99. www.hotelchamplain.com. 36rms. €12.* On a busy street near the historic district, this 16C convent features a discreet, pleasant garden – a marvellous place to unwind after a busy day in town.

⊝⊝⊝⊝ **Hôtel de la Monnaie** 🏨 – *3 r. de la Monnaie. 05 46 50 65 65. 35rms. www.hotel-monnaie.com. €13.* Right behind the Tour de la Lanterne, this splendid 17C mansion, where coins used to be made, is an agreeable address.

Biarritz

🛁 ⊝⊝ **Hôtel Atalaye** – *6 r. des Goëlands, Plateau de l'Atalaye. 05 59 24 06 76. www.hotelatalaye.com. €6.50. 24rms. Closed 15 Nov–18 Dec.* This imposing villa owes its name to the superb Atalaye plateau overlooking the Atlantic Ocean. The rooms with a sea view are especially attractive. Free parking nearby (Oct–mid-Jun).

⊝⊝ **Hôtel Gardenia** – *19 av. Carnot. 05 59 24 10 46. www.hotel-gardenia.com. 19rms. €7.10. Closed Dec–Feb.* This central hotel with a pink façade has all the charm of a private home. Its quiet, attractive rooms are regularly redecorated.

⊝⊝⊝ **Hôtel Maïtagaria** 🏨 – *34 av. Carnot. 05 59 24 26 65. www.hotel-maitagaria.com. 16rms. €9.50.* A warm, friendly reception in this little hotel near the garden, just 500m/550yd from the beach. The rooms, of varying sizes, are bright and functional. Small, flower-filled garden at the back.

⊝⊝⊝ **Le Petit Hôtel** – *11 r. Gardères. 05 59 24 87 00. www.petithotel-biarritz.com. 12rms. €6. Closed fortnight in Nov and Feb.* This appealing hotel is ideally located for exploring the town or spending time on the beach. Its soundproofed rooms have been renovated in tones of blue or yellow; all have internet access.

⊝⊝⊝⊝ **Brit Hotel Marbella** 🏨 – *11 r. du Port Vieux. 05 59 24 04 06. www.hotel-marbella.fr. 29rms. €10. Restaurant*⊝⊝⊝. A five-minute walk from the beaches and la Rocher de la Vierge in the old harbour district, this hotel offers bright rooms with a sea view, and air conditioning. The hotel restaurant serves Basque and Spanish cuisine within a rustic ambience.

Périgueux

⊖⊜ **Comfort Hôtel Régina** – *14 r. Denis-Papin (opposite the railway station). 05 53 08 40 44. 41rms.* It is easy to spot this hotel, thanks to its yellow façade. The rooms are small, functional and colourful.

⊖⊜ **Hôtel-Restaurant L'Écluse** – *at Antonne-et-Trigonant, 10km/ 6.2mi NE of Périgueux. 05 53 06 00 04. www.ecluse-perigord.com. 43rms.* The River Isle flows gently past the hotel's small waterfront. Rooms on the main façade have balconies which overlook the river.

LANGUEDOC ROUSSILLON
Toulouse

⊖⊜ **Hôtel le Capitole** – *10 r. Rivals, Toulouse. 05 61 23 21 28. www.capitole-hotel.com. 33rms. €8.* Situated very near to the Place du Capitole, this old mansion has a brick façade that has recently been redone. Some of the spacious bedrooms are sparkling new, and half are air-conditioned. A bonus: breakfast is served until noon.

⊖⊜ **Hôtel Castellane** – *17 r. Castellane, Toulouse. 05 61 62 18 82. www.castellanehotel.com. 53rms. €8.50.* This small hotel close to the Capitole is slightly set back from the main thoroughfare. The simple, practical rooms are housed in three different buildings.

⊖⊜ **Hôtel de France** – *5 r. d'Austerlitz, Toulouse. 05 61 21 88 24. www.hotel-france-toulouse.com. 64rms. €8.* In business since 1910, this attractive hotel is situated a few steps from Place Wilson. The rooms are of various sizes; though not luxurious, they are shipshape and affordable. Some of the largest come with a balcony.

⊖⊜ **Hôtel Ours Blanc** – *25 pl. Victor-Hugo, Toulouse. 05 61 23 14 55. www.hotel-oursblanc.com. 38rms. €7.* Situated opposite the marché Victor-Hugo, this hotel has simple yet comfortable rooms (recently renovated) which are air-conditioned and soundproofed; bright breakfast room with some attractive pictures embellishing its walls.

⊖⊜⊜ **Hôtel Mermoz** – *50 r. Matabiau, Toulouse. 05 61 63 04 04. www.hotel-mermoz.com. 52rms. €15.* The inner flower garden of this hotel near the city centre provides a haven of calm. Many decorative touches, notably portraits of pilots, bring aviation's early years to mind.

⊖⊜⊜⊜ **Citiz Hôtel** 🏨 – *18 Allées Jean Jaurès, Toulouse. 05 61 11 18 18. www.citizhotel.com. 56rms. €10.* Only two minutes from Place Wilson, this renovated hotel is a marvel of contemporary design, and, considering its central location, very peaceful. Complimentary parking in adjacent underground car park; excellent buffet breakfasts.

Carcassonnne

⊖ **Camping Le Martinet Rouge** – *11390 Brousses-et-Villaret. 04 68 26 51 98. Reservations advised for Jul–Aug. 35 places.* In a fabulous setting in the Montagne Noire. Swimming pool.

⊖⊜ **Hôtel Espace Cité** – *132 r. Trivalle – 04 68 25 24 24. www. inter-hotel-carcassonne.fr. 48rms. €8.50.* Modern hotel at the foot of the citadel, with bright and functional rooms.

⊖⊜ **Hôtel Montmorency** – *2 r. Camille-St-Saens. 04 68 11 96 70. www.hotelduchateau-carcassonne. com. 20rms. €12.* Close to La Cité.

Very smart rooms, well furnished, but simple.

⊝🍽 **Chambre d'hôte L'Olivette** – *r. Pierre-Duhem, 11160 Cabrespine. 04 68 26 19 25. 3rms.* Charming simplicity; located not far from the gouffre de Cabrespine.

⊝🍽 **Auberge du Château** – *Château de Cavanac, 11570 Cavanac 04 68 79 61 04. www.chateau-de-cavanac.fr. Closed Jan–Feb and 2 wks in Nov. 24rms. €12. Restaurant ⊝🍽.* Beautiful rooms with view over vineyard; fine restaurant serving own wines.

⊝🍽 **Chambre d'hôte La Maison sur la Colline** – *Lieu-dit Ste-Croix. 04 68 47 57 94. Closed 1 Dec–15 Feb. Reservation recommended in summer. 5rms.* This restored farm has a spectacular hillside view of the Cité from its garden.

⊝🍽🏠 **Hôtel la Bergerie** – *Allée Pech-Marie, 11600 Aragon. 04 68 26 10 65. www.labergeriearagon. com. 8rms. €10. Restaurant. ⊝🍽🏠.* In a lovely village; rooms have views over vineyard.

🛁 ⊝🍽🏠 **Hôtel le Donjon and les Remparts** – *2 r. du Comte-Roger. 04 68 11 23 00. www.hotel-donjon.fr. 62rms.* This hotel with old stonework and renovated décor, is in a 15C orphanage.

PROVENCE
Marseille

⊝🍽 **Hôtel Benidorm** – *734 chemin du Littoral (Estaque), 12km/7.4mi NW. 04 91 46 12 91. www.hotelbenidormlestaque.org. 26rms. €6.* The only hotel in Estaque, the building is white and rooms are simple and practical.

⊝🍽 **Hôtel Relax** – *4 r. Corneille, Vieux Port. 04 91 33 15 87. www.hotelrelax.fr. 21rms. €7.* Situated near Marseille's shopping area and a 2min walk from Vieux Port, the location is ideal. Rooms are neatly laid out with homely furnishings.

⊝🍽 **Hotel Le Richelieu** – *52 Corniche Kennedy. 04 91 31 01 92. www.lerichelieu-marseille.com. 17rms. €8.* Charming hotel near the Catalans beach.

⊝🍽 **Hôtel Edmond Rostand** – *31 r. du Dragon, Castellane. 04 91 37 74 95. www.hoteledmond rostand.com. 15rms. €9.50.* Clean, simple contemporary rooms with comfortable beds. Very reasonable price.

⊝🍽 **Hôtel Vertigo** – *42 r. des Petites Maries, Vieux Port. 04 91 91 07 11. www.hotelvertigo.fr.* Situated in the historic Belsunce neighbourhood, this place offers varying accommodation types from hostel-style sharing to twin or double rooms. Very nicely renovated.

⊝🍽🏠 **Hôtel Azur** – *24 cour Franklin Roosevelt, Réformés. 04 91 42 74 38. www.azur-hotel.fr. 18rms. €8. Restaurant⊝🍽.* Very near the Canabière, this hotel is in typical Provençal style. Rooms are spread across four floors; some give onto the garden, where you can take breakfast. Friendly staff.

⊝🍽🏠 **Chambre d'hôte Villa Marie-Jeanne** – *4 r. Chicot, Cinq Avenue Long Champs. 04 91 85 51 31. 3rms. €12.* A 19C building in a residential quarter of the city. Traditional, elegant Provençal touch, old-fashioned furniture with modern amenities.

⊝🍽🏠 **Hôtel Le Corbusier** – *280 bd Michelet. 04 91 16 78 00. www.hotellecorbusier.com. 21rms. €9. Restaurant⊝🍽. Closed 1 week in Jan.* This unique hotel is located on three floors of Le Corbusier's Cité Radieuse, a short bus ride from the centre of town. Rooms all have original minimalist features and accessories and there's a 360-degree view from the roof. Great location for football fans as it's a 10min walk from the Stade Vélodrome.

⊝⊝🍴 **Chambre d'hote Villa Monticelli** – *96 r. du Cdt-Rolland, Rond-Point du Prado. 04 91 22 15 20. www.villamonticelli.com. 5rms.* 🍴. This Art Deco building near the centre has an unusual, colourful interior. Modest, comfortable rooms.

⊝⊝🍴 **Hôtel les Cigales** – *rte Enco-de-Botte, 13190 Allauch, 15km/9.3mi NE. 04 91 68 17 07. www.hotel-lescigales.fr. 6rms, 1 suite. €8.50.* A recent building between Marseille and Allauch, rooms are tranquil and families welcome. Garden with pool.

⊝⊝🍴🍴 **Hôtel Hermès** – *25 r. Bonneterie, Vieux Port. 04 96 11 63 63. www.hotelmarseille.com/hermes. 28rms. €9.* Unpretentious, centrally located hotel with small, well-kept rooms; those on the fifth floor have a terrace overlooking the quayside. Panoramic rooftop sundeck.

⊝⊝🍴🍴 **Hôtel Le Ryad** – *16 r. Sénac de Meilhan, Vieux Port. 04 91 47 74 54. www.leryad.fr. 9rms. €12.* The Moroccan-inspired beautiful, stylish rooms are very inviting. Visit the colourful tea room in the afternoon or the hotel's little restaurant.

⊝⊝🍴🍴 **New Hôtel Vieux Port** 🏠 – *3 bis, r. Reine-Elisabeth, Vieux Port. 04 91 99 23 23. www.new-hotel.com/vieuxport. 42rms. €11.* Well located in the centre of Marseille by the Vieux Port, this hotel's rooms are pretty and decorated in exotic themes: Pondichery, Rising sun, Arabian

Nights, Vera Cruz or Tropical Africa. An invitation to relax and unwind!

⊝⊝🍴 **Radisson SAS Hotel** – *38 quai de Rive Neuve, Vieux Port. 04 88 92 19 50. www.radissonblu.com. 189rms. €12. Restaurant* ⊝🍴🍴. Right by Vieux Port, this plush establishment, between Fort St-Nicolas and Théâtre de la Criée, is furnished beautifully. Immaculate, bright rooms.

Arles

⊝🍴 **Hôtel Muette** 🏠 – *15 r. des Suisses. 04 90 96 15 39. www.hotel-muette.com. Closed Feb. 18rms. 8€.* A beautiful building (originally 15C and 17C) in the heart of historic Arles. Solid stone walls in authentic Provençal rooms guarantees they are soundproof.

⊝🍴 **Hôtel du Musée** – *11 r. du Grand-Prieuré. 04 90 93 88 88. www.hoteldumusee.com.fr. Closed Jan. 28rms. €8.* Facing the Musée Réattu, this hotel was built in the 17C. It's a charming labyrinth of green pathways through intimate courtyards, with tranquil rooms.

⊝🍴 **Le Relais de Poste** – *2 r. Molière. 04 90 52 05 76. www.hotel relaisdeposte.fr.16rms. €7.* This centrally based hotel was once the 18C postal relay. The restaurant evokes its era, with beams and frescoes.

🍴⊝🍴 **Hôtel d'Arlatan** 🏠 – *26 r. Sauvage. 04 90 93 56 66. www.hotel-arlatan.fr. 41rms. €9-15.* Fall under the spell of this old mansion dating from the 15C, a stone's throw from place du Forum. Admire the underground Roman fragments through the glass floor of the bar and the drawing room. Rooms furnished with antiques and pretty fabrics.

ᗲᗝᗱᗳ **Hôtel Mireille** – *Rive droite, Trinquetaille. 04 90 93 70 74. www.hotel-mireille.com. 34rms. €13.* Dive into the swimming pool at this peaceful hotel outside the city centre. Good size, colourful rooms with Provençal furniture.

ᗲᗝᗱᗳ **Hôtel Calendal** – *5 r. Porte-de-Laure. 04 90 96 11 89. www.lecalendal.com. 38rms. €12.* This hotel has all the stylishness of Provençal interiors with its colourful façade, pretty inner shaded garden and cosy sitting room. Blue and yellow make up the colour scheme of furniture, fabrics and ceramics.

Nîmes

ᗲᗝ–ᗲᗝᗱ **Hôtel Côté Patio** – *31 r. de Beaucaire. 04 66 67 60 17. www.hotel-cote-patio.com. 17rms. €10.* Charming hotel with a lively feel to it. Very near old Nîmes and the Arènes. Advance reservations around Feria.

ᗲᗝᗱ **Hôtel l'Orangerie** 🏚🏚 – *755 r. de la Tour-de-l'Évêque. 04 66 84 50 57. www.orangerie.fr. 37rms. €9. Restaurant*ᗲᗝ. A new building with the air of an old *mas*, 1km/0.6mi from the town centre. Spacious and individual bedrooms; some have terraces, some jacuzzis. Provençal theme throughout.

ᗲᗝᗱ **Chambre d'hôte La Mazade** – *12 r. de la Mazade, 30730 St-Mamert-du-Gard, 14km/9.3mi W via D 999 and D 1. 04 66 81 17 56. www.bbfrance.com/couston.html. 4rms, 1 gîte.* Modern equipment combines with antique furniture in the well fitted-out, bright rooms of this B&B in a quiet, rural location.

ᗲᗝᗱ **Hôtel Royal** – *3 bd Alphonse Daudet. 04 66 58 28 27. www.royalhotel-nimes.com. 22rms.* Stylish boutique hotel next to the Carré d'Art. Original features and fittings complement minimalist colour and design. Loved by bullfighting superstars, there's an excellent tapas bar, La Bodeguita, downstairs. Can get lively and noisy at weekends.

ᗲᗝᗱᗳ **New Hôtel La Baume** 🏚🏚 – *21 r. Nationale. 04 66 76 28 42. www.new-hotel.com. 34rms. €12.* This 17C mansion successfully blends contemporary and antique styles. An interior stone staircase leads to the simple bedrooms, a few of which have pretty, French-style painted ceilings.

Avignon

ᗲᗝ **La Ferme** – *110 chemin des Bois, Île de la Barthelasse, 5km/3mi N. 04 90 82 57 53. www.hotel-laferme-avignon.com. 20rms. €10. Closed Mon lunch, Wed lunch.* Country-style dining room with beams, fireplace and old stone can be found at this haven of peace.

ᗲᗝ–ᗲᗝᗱ **Bagatelle** – *25 allées Antoine Pinay, Île de la Barthelasse. 4 90 86 30 39. www.campingbagatelle.com. 10rms for 2–4 people at the hotel, 230 placements at the campsite.* Large campground with a separate hotel. Great setting on an island near Pont St-Bénezet.

ᗲᗝ–ᗲᗝᗱ **Boquier** – *6 r. du Portail Boquier. 04 90 82 34 43. www.hotel-boquier.com. 12rms. €8.* Each room is individually and tastefully decorated.

ᗲᗝ–ᗲᗝᗱ **Hôtel Bristol** – *44 cours J.-Jaurès. 04 90 16 48 48. www.bristol-hotel-avignon.com. 11rms. €12. Closed 15 Dec–14 Jan.* Situated on the main avenue of the walled city. Spacious and sensibly

HOTELS

213

functional rooms, most overlook the inside courtyards.

⊖⊜⊜ **Chambre d'hôte Villa Agapè** – *13 r. Agricol. 04 90 85 21 92. 3rms. Closed 1–15 May, Jul, Feb.* It's easy to forget the town-centre location of this attractive villa, with its verdant terrace and swimming pool.

⊖⊜⊜ **Colbert** – *7 r. Agricol Perdiguier. 04 90 86 20 20. www.avignon-hotel-colbert.com. Closed Nov–Feb. 15rms. €12.* Simplicity and family home atmosphere in this discreet hotel. Bedrooms are decorated with Provençal colours, antiques and billboards.

⊖⊜⊜ **Hôtel de Blauvac** – *11 r. de la Bancasse. 04 90 86 34 11. www.hotel-blauvac.com. 16rms. €8.* The former home of the Marquis de Tonduly, Lord of Blauvac, in the 17C, is one of the best value-for-money hotels in town.

⊖⊜⊜ **Mignon** – *12 r. Joseph Vernet. 04 90 82 17 30. www.hotel-mignon.com. 16rms.* A small hotel in the heart of Avignon's historic centre. All rooms are soundproofed.

⊖⊜⊜⊜ **Banasterie** – *11 r. de la Banasterie. 04 32 76 30 78. www.labanasterie.com. 5rms.* A Virgin with Child adorns the listed façade of this 16C edifice. A cosy, romantic interior.

⊖⊜⊜⊜ **Hôtel Cloître St-Louis** 🏛 – *20 r. Portail Boquier. 04 90 27 55 55. www.cloitre-saint-louis.com. 77rms. €14. Restaurant*⊖⊜⊜⊜. Situated in 16C cloisters, part of this hotel was designed by Jean Nouvel. The building uses a variety of materials including glass, steel and stone.

⊖⊜⊜⊜ **Hôtel du Palais des Papes** – *1 r. Gérard Philipe. 4 90 86 04 13. www.hotel-avignon.com. 27rms. €8.* Beautiful rooms and beautiful views at this luxurious, reasonably priced hotel in the old centre.

⊖⊜⊜⊜ **Maison d'hôte Lumani** – *37 r. du Rempart St-Lazare. 04 90 82 94 11. www.avignon-lumani.com. 5rms.* Artists are particularly welcome in this fine 19C manor house, which has an attractive courtyard shaded by a couple of hundred-year-old plane trees.

CÔTE D'AZUR
Nice

⊖⊜ **Clair Hotel** – *23 bd Carnot, Impasse Terra Amata. 04 93 89 69 89. 10rms. €8.* This converted schoolhouse near the archaeological museum has rooms all on one floor (in the old classrooms) and a Mediterranean garden terrace where breakfast is served in the summer.

⊖⊜ **Star Hôtel** – *14 r. Biscarra. 04 93 85 19 03. www.hotel-star.com. Closed 18 Nov–25 Dec. 20rms. €7.50.* Small hotel away from the bustling town centre offering simple accommodations, some with a balcony. Close to the Nice-Étoile shopping centre.

⊖⊜⊜⊜ **La Pérouse** – *11 quai Rauba-Capéu. 04 93 62 34 63. www.hotel-la-perouse.com. 58rms. €21.* A prime seaside location overlooking the Baie des Anges from the foot of the Château hill, this cosy Provençal-style hotel features a heated swimming pool and grill restaurant set within a garden against the rocky hill.

Monaco

⊜⊜⊜ **Hôtel de France** – *6 r. de la Turbie. 00 377 93 30 24 64. www. monte-carlo.mc/france. 27rms. €10.* Charming, soundproofed rooms decorated in Provençal hues, and a modern breakfast lounge enhanced with metal and wood furniture.

⊜⊜⊜⊜ **Columbus Hôtel** – *23 ave des Papalins. 00 377 92 05 92 22. www.columbushotels.com. 181rms. €25.* Clean, contemporary lines and a soothing palette are combined with cosy fabrics and warm wood furnishings. A lounge bar and Italian-style brasserie with terrace seating attract fashionable locals. Access to a private pool; the heliport is just a block away.

⊜⊜⊜⊜ **Metropole** 🏛🏛🏛 – *4 ave de la Madone. 00 377 93 15 15 15. www.metropole.com. 141rms. €37.* This 1886 hotel got a complete face-lift by the hot Parisian designer Jacques Garcia, with luxurious fabrics and timeless style. The outdoor pool and solarium have views overlooking the rooftops of the Place du Casino. The restaurant is managed by leading French chef Joël Robuchon.

Cannes

⊜⊜ **Hôtel Alnea** – *20 r. Jean de Riouffe. 04 93 68 77 77. www. hotel-alnea.com. Closed 3 weeks in Dec. 14rms. €7.50.* A family-run establishment with simple well-kept and colourful rooms. Located just a couple of minutes from La Croisette in the heart of Cannes.

⊜⊜ **Hôtel Appia** – *6 r. Marceau. 04 93 06 59 59. www.appia-hotel. com. Closed 21 Nov–28 Dec, 5–14 Jan. 32rms. €7.50.* Practicality takes precedence over comfort in this downtown hotel where the well-kept, smallish rooms are both

air-conditioned and soundproofed. Pristine bathrooms.

⊜⊜⊜ **Villa l'Églantier** – *14 r. Campestra. 04 93 68 22 43. 3rms.* Impressive white villa dating from 1920, surrounded by palm trees and other exotic species, dominating the city of Cannes. The large, peaceful rooms are all extended by a terrace or a balcony.

St Tropez

⊜⊜ **Bello Visto** – *pl. deï Barri, Gassin, 8km/5mi SW of St-Tropez. 04 94 56 17 30. Closed Jan and Nov. 9 rms. €8.* There's truth in the name of this small family-run out-of-town hotel and restaurant at the top of Gassin village. Most rooms, like the terrace, profit from a "beautiful vista" over the Massif des Maures and the gulf of St-Tropez. Dining room with Provençal cuisine.

🐾 ⊜⊜⊜ **Hôtel Lou Cagnard** – *ave Paul-Roussel. 04 94 97 04 24. www.hotel-lou-cagnard.com. Closed 1 Nov–26 Dec. 19 rooms. €11.* Enjoy breakfast in the shade of a mulberry tree in the tiny garden of this pretty Provençal house, just off Place des Lices. At night you'll be lulled to sleep by the chirping of cicadas. Modest prices, for St-Tropez.

⊜⊜⊜ **Hôtel de La Ponche** – *3 r. des Remparts. 04 94 97 02 53. www.laponche.com. Closed 2 Nov–3 Apr. 18rms. €20.* The rooms of this cosy hotel occupy four village houses formerly belonging to fishermen; the blue one was a favourite of actress Romy Schneider's. The rooftop terraces nestle between the citadel and the bell tower, and the warm, bright hues, combined with considerate service, make the Hôtel Ponche an absolute must.

HOTELS

FRANCE

INDEX

xwordinfo.com

INDEX